Unfinished Utopia

Unfinished Utopia

Nowa Huta, Stalinism, and Polish Society, 1949–56

Katherine Lebow

CORNELL UNIVERSITY PRESS   *Ithaca and London*

First published 2013 by Cornell University Press
First printing, Cornell Paperbacks, 2016

Library of Congress Cataloging-in-Publication Data

Lebow, Katherine, 1970– author.
    Unfinished utopia : Nowa Huta, Stalinism, and Polish society, 1949–56 / Katherine Lebow.
        pages cm
    Includes bibliographical references and index.
    ISBN 978-0-8014-5124-9 (cloth : alk. paper)
    ISBN 978-1-5017-0438-3 (pbk. : alk. paper)
    1. Nowa Huta (Kraków, Poland)—History—20th century. 2. Nowa Huta (Kraków, Poland)—Social life and customs—20th century. 3. Communism and culture—Poland—Kraków—History. 4. Work-life balance—Poland—Kraków—History—20th century. I. Title.
    DK4727.N69L43   2013
    943.8'62—dc23   2012048678

Cornell University Press strives to use environmentally responsible suppliers and materials to the fullest extent possible in the publishing of its books. Such materials include vegetable-based, low-VOC inks and acid-free papers that are recycled, totally chlorine-free, or partly composed of nonwood fibers. For further information, visit our website at www.cornellpress.cornell.edu.

For Andrew, Naomi, and Jacob

Contents

Acknowledgments

A book so long in the making incurs many debts, and it is a long-awaited pleasure to acknowledge some of them here.

Financial support for research was provided by the American Council of Learned Societies, Fulbright-IIE, the European University Institute, New-castle University, and the University of Virginia. Earlier versions of chapters appeared in David Crowley and Susan E. Reid, eds., *Pleasures in Socialism: Leisure and Luxury in the Eastern Bloc* (Evanston: Northwestern University Press, 2010), and *Contemporary European History* 10, no. 2 (2001): 199–219. I thank Northwestern and Cambridge University Press for permitting me to use them here.

More like a fairy godfather and godmother than a *Doktorvater und -Mutter*, István Deák and Victoria de Grazia at Columbia University have watched over me for years, providing input and advice when most needed. I am extremely grateful for everything they have done. At Columbia, Anna Frajlich-Zając taught me Polish as only a poet could. Fran Rosenfeld commented extensively on an early draft, while the "Deák" cohort formed the nucleus of what has turned out to be a collegial, lively, and ever-expanding intellectual community of East Central Europeanists, inspired by the humanistic scholarship of our legendary mentor. Its members, broadly understood, have contributed to this project in many ways.

During my research in Poland I benefited enormously from Jacek Purchla's generous offer of mentorship. Others who shared their expertise on Nowa Huta and Polish history included Adam Bartosz, Jędrzej Chumiński, Dorota Gut, Dariusz Jarosz, Henryk Kazimierski, Jacek Kochanowicz, Monika Kozubek, and Maciej Miezian; I am also very grateful to my interviewees for their time and willingness to share their stories. I was helped by many staff members of the Archive of Modern Records, the Archive of the City of Kraków, the Institute of National Memory, and the Jagiellonian University Library;

special thanks are due Szczepan Świątek and the late Sławomir Radoń of the National Archive in Kraków. Meanwhile, it is a pleasure to acknowledge the hospitality and friendship of the Geisler family, Dmitrij Glinka and Irena Glinka-Wierzbicka, Monika Murzyn-Kupisz, and Annamaria Orla-Bukowska, among others.

Throughout the long haul of revisions, the input and encouragement of the "ladies" (Małgorzata Fidelis, Irina Gigova, Emily Greble, and Andrea Orzoff) was a lifeline. I am thankful for their careful comments and dependable presence in cyberspace, as well as for Gosia and Emily's practical and intellectual support outside the framework of our monthly exchanges. Małgorzata Mazurek, meanwhile, has been another generous and valued friend and interlocutor. David Crowley, Dagmara Jajeśniak-Quast, Basia Nowak, Bernadeta Stano, Keely Stauter-Halsted, Alison Stenning, and Marcin Zaremba have provided feedback, suggestions, sources, and other acts of kindness along the way. Padraic Kenney's insights into Polish and East Central European Communism have been essential to this book; I am also grateful to the anonymous reviewers of my manuscript for their helpful comments. Finally, I would like to thank the many local writers, researchers, bloggers, artists, activists, curators, volunteers, and enthusiasts who have contributed to an upsurge in interest in Nowa Huta's past in recent years, and whose efforts have enriched this book immeasurably.

I held down three different jobs while writing this, and I was lucky to have good colleagues and supportive supervisors at each. My colleagues at the College of Charleston provided a welcoming environment at my first job. At the University of Virginia, Alon Confino, Chuck McCurdy, Duane Osheim, and Jeff Rossman supported both me and this project, while Margarita Nafpaktitis and Elizabeth Thompson offered helpful feedback on early drafts. Special mention goes to UVA's wonderful libraries, and librarians, particularly George Crafts. At Newcastle University, Joan Allen, Tim Kirk, Diana Paton, and Susan-Mary Grant softened the blows of austerity and made me laugh at department meetings. I extend thanks to all my colleagues at the School of Historical Studies for their collegiality and professionalism.

Working with John Ackerman at Cornell University Press has been a consistent pleasure, and I am very grateful to him for taking on this project and seeing it through with care and attention. Thanks are also due to Karen Laun and Mary Petrusewicz for their excellent work on production and copyediting, respectively. Paweł Jagło at the Historical Museum of Kraków helpfully hunted down scans of many of the illustrations, while Tadeusz Binek, Marek Sigmund and Marta Sigmund-Kozak, and Arkadiusz Sitarski graciously allowed me to reproduce their family photographs in this book.

Many friends should be thanked here, but I will have to mention just a few. First and foremost, Edinburgh's gray days became much brighter in the company of Ola Helwak and Grzegorz Kudła, who also provided a second home for our children at crucial moments. Ilona Barratto, Gabriela Langowska, and Małgosia Szoblik helped keep me on my toes (linguistically and otherwise), and Christina Ball and Dana Rosen have always been there when most needed.

My family has been a constant source of encouragement and support. Jane Dickler Lebow, Ned Lebow, Carol Bohmer, and Chris and Dia Lawrence provided endless hours of babysitting and countless other, intangible forms of assistance. Jane Lebow also performed heroically in her role of first-line copyeditor; I thank her for this labor of love, and for everything else. I would also like to express gratitude and affection for the brilliant people of Congregation Beth Israel Preschool, Scuola Materna "Nathan Cassuto," Busy Bees Nursery, and Uni-Tots Nursery, and for Ia Mshchedlishvili and Vanessa Coles, without whose care this book simply would not have been possible.

I would like to make special mention of two people who I think would have enjoyed each other's company, had they ever had the chance to meet. The first is my beloved grandmother Ruth Dickler. If readers find a fraction of her wide-ranging curiosity and skill as a *raconteur* reflected here, I will be glad. The second is Mark Pittaway. Mark invited me to present on Nowa Huta at my first major conference and supported this project in many ways, large and small, over the years. Mark was as generous as he was brilliant, and as I discovered after his death in 2010, scores of my colleagues felt the same loyalty and admiration for him that I did. His influence is present throughout this book.

Finally, none of this would have been imaginable without Andrew Lawrence's daily presence as a partner, kibbitzer, reader, hand-holder, editor, punner, and father. Naomi and Jacob: admittedly, it's not as exciting as Harry Potter or as funny as Asterix, but I hope, nonetheless, you will be proud of this book, and of your most loving mama.

Abbreviations

CUP   Central Bureau of Planning (*Centralny Urząd Planowania*)

CZPH   Central Management for the Steel Industry (*Centralny Zarząd Przemysłu Hutniczego*)

DRN   District National Council of Nowa Huta (*Dzielnicowa Rada Narodowa Nowa Huta*)

HiL   Lenin Steelworks (*Huta im. Lenina*)

IBM   Housing Institute (*Instytut Budownictwa Miezkaniowego*)

LK   Women's League (*Liga Kobiet*)

MKR   Inter-Union Workers' Club (*Międzyzwiązkowy Klub Robotników*)

MO   Citizens' Militia (*Milicja Obywatelska*)

PKPG   National Commission for Economic Planning (*Państwowa Komisja Planowania Gospodarczego*)

PKWN   Polish Committee of National Liberation (*Polski Komitet Wyzwolenia Narodowego*)

PO "SP"   Universal Organization "Service for Poland" (*Powszechna Organizacja "Służba Polsce"*)

PPR   Polish Workers' Party (*Polska Partia Robotnicza*)

PPS   Polish Socialist Party (*Polska Partia Socjalistyczna*)

PSL   Polish Populist Party (*Polskie Stronnictwo Ludowe*)

PZPR   Polish United Workers' Party (*Polska Zjednoczona Partia Robotnicza*)

RTRP   Provisional Government of the Republic of Poland (*Rząd Tymczasowej Rzeczpospolitej Polskiej*)

SD   Democratic Party (*Stronnictwo Demokratyczne*)

SL   Populist Party (*Stronnictwo Ludowe*)

TRJN   Provisional Government of National Unity (*Tymczasowy Rząd Jedności Narodowej*)

ZBMNH   Associated Firms for the Urban Construction of Nowa Huta (*Zjednoczenie Budownictwa Miejskiego Nowa Huta*)

ZMP   Union of Polish Youth (*Związek Młodzieży Polskiej*)

ZPBHiL   Associated Industries for the Construction of the Lenin Steelworks
(*Zjednoczenie Przemysłowe Budowy Huty im. Lenina*)
ZPBNH   Associated Industries for the Construction of Nowa Huta (*Zjednoczenie Przemysłowe Budowy Nowej Huty*)
ZPiT   Ensemble for Song and Dance of the Lenin Steelworks (*Zespół Pieśni i Tańca HiL*)

For abbreviations in citations, see bibliography.

Unfinished Utopia

Introduction

In August 1980, Polish film director Andrzej Wajda stood before the gates of the Lenin Shipyard in Gdańsk. Wajda, a two-time Cannes prizewinner, had come to show his support for the shipyard's striking workers. The strikes that had begun there had spread across the Baltic coast region and then the country, ultimately giving rise to the independent trade union Solidarity—the first in the Soviet bloc, an oasis of freedom in the desert of late communism. Celebrities like Wajda joined foreign delegations and thousands of ordinary Poles providing food, clothes, medical care, and logistical support for the occupying workers; the shipyard gates became a meeting place and a public forum, an open-air theater and a religious sanctuary. Solidarity's supporters would remember that summer as something like a miracle: in adviser Jacek Kuroń's words, "I thought it was impossible, it was impossible, and"—he commented later—"I still think it was impossible."[1]

Beside the shipyard gates brightly festooned with flowers and religious pictures, Wajda gave an interview to the independent *Solidarity Strike Bulletin*. In it, the interviewer began by praising Wajda's 1977 film, *Man of Marble*, calling it "one of the best films about the situation of workers today." He then asked the director how he understood "the origin of the strike leaders—how do you view these men and the reasons behind their activity?" Wajda responded:

> I think that what is happening here is in a line of continuity with the past. I would like to make a sequel to the film [realized in 1981 as *Man of Iron*], because I see that what we need most is a feeling of our continuity. Nothing starts from square one: everything has roots in another time and place. We did not just begin on Monday to be honest people; there were also honest people before.

What is more, Wajda added, "Even if they suffered defeats, or at least did not know success, it would not be good if we started again from scratch."[2]

Wajda's reference to "honest people," no doubt, would have reminded many *Strike Bulletin* readers of the hero of *Man of Marble*—an initially naïve and hapless worker caught up in the turbulence of Poland's Stalinist era (ca. 1948–56).[3] In the film, Mateusz Birkut, a semiliterate peasant from a dirt-poor village, seeks work in what was then dubbed the "great building site of socialism": the new steelworks and "socialist city" of Nowa Huta. In Nowa Huta (literally, "new steelworks" or "new foundry"), Birkut becomes a bricklayer, takes night classes, and is smitten by visions of the bright new world he believes Nowa Huta will become. Party agitators feed his imagination with descriptions of how the inchoate and muddy construction site would look in a few years: Nowa Huta would be a beautiful city of airy, many-roomed apartments for workers' families; it would have wide, tree-lined avenues flanked by state-subsidized theaters, libraries, and cinemas; and there would be sports pavilions, parks, hospitals, and schools, free and open to all. Just as important, Nowa Huta's great Lenin Steelworks would provide skills, training, and stable, well-paying jobs for thousands like him, young men and women from unproductive, land-starved villages across Poland. This industrial colossus would be larger and more powerful than anything yet seen in Poland—indeed, it would be the most modern in Europe. Nowa Huta would be a city of labor and progress, inhabited by "new men" full of faith in socialism and the future. Nowa Huta would generate not only steel, but hope for Poland following the immeasurable destruction of World War II.

While *Man of Marble* was a work of fiction, Nowa Huta was not; nor, this book argues, were the visions of urban utopia and social justice that it engendered. It is these visions, and their contested nature, that I explore in the following account of how Nowa Huta was conjured from the rye fields and orchards outside Kraków, focusing on the period from 1949 (when building first began) to 1956—roughly, the years in which the Stalinist system of rule flourished and fell in Poland. I do so primarily by seeking out voices of Nowa Huta's builders and first inhabitants and juxtaposing these against both the official and unofficial transcripts of the party state, thereby revealing a social and cultural landscape that is at once strangely exotic and surprisingly familiar. Like new towns built in Western Europe after World War II, Nowa Huta represented a promise of freedom, choice, and mobility to its inhabitants, embodying Poland's transition from postfeudalism to modernity.[4] However, unlike new towns in the West, Nowa Huta was also a highly charged symbol of national rebirth and social revolution—a symbol deriving its power not only from Soviet Communist ideology, but also from memories of Poland's past dependency on, and recent destruction by, foreign enemies, not least, the Soviet Union itself. To understand the outcomes of Stalinist attempts to transform Poland's social, cultural, and political landscape, we must confront these legacies and their complex interplay.[5]

Wajda's decision to locate Birkut's story in Nowa Huta was apt, as no other place was more closely associated in the Polish mind with Stalinist efforts to transform the country's economy, culture, and society. Nowa Huta was one member of a family of "socialist cities" built across the Soviet bloc after World War II, in imitation of new cities like Komsomolsk or Magnitogorsk built in Stalin's industrialization drive of the 1930s.[6] Stalinstadt in East Germany, Sztálinváros in Hungary, or Dimitrovgrad in Bulgaria all served not only as implicit homage to Soviet civilization, but also, as historian Anders Åman puts it, as "glimpses of tomorrow's reality"—a foretaste of what socialism would offer when fully achieved. From architecture, design, and layout, to methods used in their construction, the new towns were to be nothing less than socialism made concrete in brick and mortar.[7]

Nowa Huta, however, was the largest and most ambitious of all the socialist cities of the "People's Democracies," dwarfing all others in size and national political significance. The town's massive Lenin Steelworks, built for an initial output of 1.5 million tons, was the signature investment of the Six-Year Plan, aimed at Poland's transformation from a backward, agrarian country into a modern, industrialized nation. Containing some 500 "objects," or individual productive units, and an internal rail network 150 kilometers long, the steelworks was itself the size of a small city. To house its workers and their families, the accompanying settlement was projected for a population of 100,000; this number ultimately grew to some 250,000 persons on a terrain of 76.5 square kilometers.[8] (By contrast, British new towns like Stevenage or Harlow, built in the same period, were initially planned for populations of about 60,000).[9]

Nowa Huta's proportions in the sphere of propaganda were equally epic. Feature films depicted the heroic drama of building socialism in Nowa Huta "faster, better, cheaper"; renowned composer Witold Lutosławski penned mass songs in the new town's honor. Nowa Huta became a site of "obligatory literary pilgrimage" for a generation of young Polish writers—Ryszard Kapuściński, Tadeusz Konwicki, Sławomir Mrożek, Wisława Szymborska— some of whose first widely published works sang its praises.[10] International visitors included Nikita Khrushchev, Charles de Gaulle, Indira Gandhi, Haile Selassie, and Kwame Nkrumah. Fidel Castro, on his trip to Kraków, allegedly showed little interest in touring the historic Wawel Castle, instead demanding to be taken to the new city without delay.[11] As Åman notes, the semantic association between the words "Nowa Huta" and "socialism" was so close that the eight letters of its name, blown up to monumental proportions, could be carried in parades and political demonstrations without any further exposition. They spoke for themselves.[12]

More than two decades since the collapse of communism in Eastern Europe, history has taken a jaundiced view of the promise symbolized by those letters. It is not just that state socialism's promised shortcut to modernity led to consumer shortages, environmental degradation, technological obsolescence, and labor exploitation. Our age is generally skeptical of utopian impulses, associating them with large, state-led projects of social and economic engineering that have not only broadly failed to achieve the wondrous benefits promised, but, all too often, have also been accompanied by coercion and violence. James C. Scott has dubbed such top-down efforts to impose man-made, "rational" order on the messy unpredictability of human life "authoritarian high modernism": a feature of state actors (and their allies) across the ideological spectrum, it has motivated, he argues, much of the last century's pervasive violence against locally diverse cultures and ways of life.[13]

New towns are among those "schemes to improve the human condition," in Scott's words, that are often seen as typifying the modern state's coercive tendencies. Henri Lefebvre, writing as France was about to embark on a major program of new town construction in the 1970s, contrasted the medieval French village of Navarrenx to the postwar new town of Mourenx; he likened the former to a seashell, secreted over the centuries by its inhabitants, and the latter to a "propaganda leaflet." Despite his hopes that the new town could ultimately become a site of resistance, Lefebvre could not help seeing Mourenx as the essence of authoritarian modernity, of that "abstraction which rides roughshod over everyday life."[14] Citing examples from the outsized, windswept experiment of Brazil's capital, Brasília, to the high-rise "filing cabinets for people" of the Gorbals in Glasgow, other critics have not only argued that new towns fail to meet their inhabitants' needs, but have also seen them as vehicles of repression and social control.[15] As Lefebvre sadly concluded, "The text of the [new] town is totally legible, as impoverished as it is clear, despite the architects' efforts to vary the lines. Surprise? Possibilities? From this place, which should have been the home of all that is possible, they have vanished without trace."[16]

This book shows, however, that Nowa Huta came closer to Lefebvre's hopes for meaningful experimentation than he might have imagined: its history is full of surprise, possibility, and, ultimately, resistance. Far from being a gray and regimented landscape, Nowa Huta in the 1950s was colorful and anarchic, a place where the formerly disenfranchised hastened to assert their leading role in "building socialism"—but rarely in ways that authorities had anticipated.

Increasingly, moreover, Nowa Huta became a flashpoint of overt struggle and dissent: In October 1956, steelworkers and students joined in nationwide protests marking the end of Stalinism. In 1960, residents rioted for days in "struggle for the cross," demanding the right to build a church. In the 1980s, Nowa Huta emerged as Solidarity's stronghold in southern Poland; striking one week after Gdańsk, the Lenin Steelworks boasted the largest workplace chapter of Solidarity in the country, with a membership rate of 97 percent. When Solidarity was banned and martial law imposed in 1981, Nowa Huta's underground activists were among the most militant and organized; throughout the decade, young people fought ongoing battles with riot police in some of the country's largest street protests. Finally, a strike at the steelworks played a precipitating role in the negotiated transition to democracy in 1989.[17] In post-Communist Poland, Nowa Huta's turbulent history has often been portrayed as the ultimate proof of Communist hubris: those who settled in the new town, according to this view, sent a clear message to authorities that they would not consent to being turned into "new men."[18] This book, however, will explore another possibility: that it was precisely the encounter with Stalinist ideology and practice in the late 1940s to mid-1950s—including the attempt to create a new, better, and more egalitarian civilization—that generated such fertile ground for solidaristic protest in subsequent years.

Following Wajda's dictum that "nothing starts from scratch," the book begins at the beginning, focusing on the first phase of Nowa Huta's growth, from 1949 to 1956. The first date marks the beginning of construction on the new town, a year after Poland's formal adoption of a Soviet-style system of government and forced industrialization policy; the second reflects upheavals within the Polish Communist party, supported by Khrushchev's drive toward de-Stalinization, that marked the definitive end of the Stalinist "moment" in Poland. During this period, the Stalinist drive to "build socialism" effected far-reaching transformations of society, culture, economics, and everyday life across Poland, and indeed, East Central Europe. Nowa Huta was just one sign of the extraordinary demographic transformations taking place in Poland between 1939 and 1960, when traditional urban elites, decimated by World War II, were replaced by an influx of rural migrants to the cities and, later, to the new industrial centers created by Stalinist forced industrialization. The result was a veritable social revolution, begun in wartime and extended and consolidated during the Stalinist period.[19] These changes were deeply destabilizing, but they also generated new possibilities: as Stephen Kotkin writes of the Soviet new town of Magnitogorsk, they created new "fields for action" for ordinary citizens whose participation was needed to build Stalinism's brave new world.[20]

The book thus explores how a diverse sample of Nowa Huta's planners, builders, workers, and inhabitants pursued their individual and collective aspirations within the new town's spaces—engineers and architects; "worker heroes" and youth-league activists; and unruly housewives, jitterbugging teenagers, trowel-wielding Gypsies, trysting couples, drunken bachelors, and other figures from the margins of Poland's postwar history.[21] It pays special attention, moreover, to connections between the industrial workplace and the home, work and leisure, and public and private. I find that it was precisely where Stalinism most disrupted the conventional geographies of everyday life that Nowa Huta's occupants were able to carve out spaces of (relative) freedom from the surveillance of party, activists, and police—helping to explain why, in some people's reminiscences of life in the new town in these early days, this most Stalinist of cities seemed a place where one felt, somehow, "free."[22]

My approach draws liberally on other historians' ongoing engagement with questions of power and everyday life in the so-called People's Democracies, and, in particular, on their efforts to replace cold-war paradigms with more nuanced models for understanding the dynamics of state–society relations in postwar East Central Europe. The dominant totalitarian model of much previous scholarship attributed communist power to social atomization, achieved through the application of coercion and violence.[23] The opening of archives in East Central Europe in 1989, however, demonstrated that terror had been a "necessary but insufficient condition" for the establishment and maintenance of communist regimes, and that while it might explain "*how* Communists ruled," it could "not explain *why* they ruled as they did."[24] New research on East Central Europe under communist rule revealed that even coercion had had its limits as an effective strategy of social control; that societies were never passive, even at the height of state repression and violence; that power structures comprised groups and individuals with competing agendas; and that communist leaders, in order to achieve their goals, often sought popular participation and acquiescence, accommodating, in turn, to a variety of pressures from below.[25]

The story told here illustrates each of these points and broadly confirms recent trends in East Central European historiography. On the other hand, it focuses on a period—namely, Stalinism—that is still largely a "black box,"[26] inadequately researched and conceptualized in emerging narratives of the recent past. For some, as for sociologist Alain Touraine, Stalinism was "only a brief, black episode," a kind of "frozen" time during which the ordinary flow of Polish history temporarily ceased.[27] Others view Stalinism in East Central Europe as a somehow watered-down version of Soviet Stalinism, a (seemingly oxymoronic) "milder" form of totalitarianism. Krystyna Kersten and Jerzy Eisler, for instance, describe the Stalinist period as a "totalitarian dress rehearsal" (for an opening-night performance that, presumably, never came) with all of the hallmarks of totalitarianism: a swollen security apparatus, the "militarization of public life," "a constant search for internal and external enemies," "state intervention in all areas of public life," the "impulse to create a 'new socialist man,'" the "replacement of information by propaganda and agitation," the "conduct of the economy according to ideological and political dogmas," and so on.[28] But such definitions are problematic—not least because each of the criteria these scholars list can also be found in the periods preceding and following Stalinism. (For example, as Kersten points out elsewhere, as measured by the sheer number of victims, terror was greater in Poland in 1944–48 than during "full-fledged Stalinism.")[29] And yet the idea that Stalinism may have differed from other phases of communism merely by degree, rather than in kind, is unsatisfying.

What was distinctive about Stalinism, in fact, was ideology. It is widely asserted that, in the post-Stalinist (or post-totalitarian) era, ideology no longer held sway over East Europeans' hearts and minds—or even, largely, over those of Communists themselves.[30] To say that ideology mattered during the Stalinist period is not to the same as claiming that great numbers of Poles and other East Europeans unquestioningly accepted the orthodox party line; it does, however, mean that ideology was a force to be reckoned with. Following Jochen Hellbeck, I am interested less in exploring ideology in Nowa Huta as a set of dogmas imposed from above (which it was, of course, too) than in observing "the workings of ideology and, indeed, its very generation, in localized, individual acts of appropriation and self-becoming."[31] Participation in Nowa Huta's construction "made" ideology, just as much as ideology "made" Nowa Huta; in one sense, the central narrative of this book is how "individual acts of appropriation and self-becoming" both converged and collided with the Stalinist idea of creating new men. But the lived, everyday ideology of building socialism in Nowa Huta was an unstable mix. Drawing both on the Stalinist rhetoric of social revolution, collective effort, and productive citizenship, and on other available traditions—peasant moral economies, Polish noble patriotism, intellectual legacies—participants in this story struggled to find a meaningful shared language to describe the realities they faced. This book takes such efforts seriously, placing them in the context of other, longer-term projects by Poles and others to define the nature of justice, freedom, and community.

Just as building Nowa Huta was a chaotic enterprise, so, necessarily, was researching it. From among a wide range of primary sources, I draw especially on the reports, minutes, and memoranda of bodies responsible for governing, controlling, and mobilizing Nowa Huta's population: the party, secret police, city government, trade unions, youth organizations, and women's organizations (mainly, though not exclusively, at the local level). Like any other set of sources, those generated by the organs of "People's Democracy" in Eastern Europe present their own opportunities and challenges.[32] Most of my research year was spent poring over cardboard folders stuffed to overflowing with documents (often misspelled, third-generation carbon copies) in no particular chronological or thematic order; it soon became clear that Nowa Huta's governing apparatus in the late 1940s to mid-1950s, although absurdly top-heavy, was overwhelmed by large flows of information from "the terrain." (No doubt this influenced my perception of Nowa Huta as space particularly resistant to effective social control!) Ultimately, however, these turned out to be rich, if uneven, sources. Although the party-state's totalitarian ambitions led to the accumulation of much information useless both for it and for me, occasionally its granular gaze focused on vivid details that jumped off pages otherwise awash in Stalinist gray. In my reading of these documents, then, I paid special attention to places where their authors broke the script of Stalinist master narratives or where a polyphony of views and voices emerged.

A second important set of sources for this book were personal narratives by those who witnessed and participated in the historical events it describes: oral histories and interviews, written memoirs, and autobiographies by Nowa Huta's builders, planners, and early inhabitants. Needless to say, all ego documents must be read with due attention to context and purpose, and in this case we need to be especially sensitive to the role that autobiographical narrative played in communist discourse. As Gina Herrmann notes, "Communists thought, spoke, and wrote about themselves constantly," and they did so in certain characteristic ways, relying on a set of key tropes and storylines.[33] The presence of such generic forms can be seen in many of the narratives cited here. At the same time, many also show the influence of strong pre-war Polish autobiographical traditions (for example, in memoirs' treatment of rural poverty).[34] On the whole, the memoirs are too multivalent and, often, contradictory to be read as the product of a single hegemonic discourse. Nowohucian stories are typically those of personal realization and the overcoming of hardship, but these often serve as vehicles of a fundamental ambivalence. As will be clear later in these pages, one autobiographer could maintain a position of ironic skepticism toward Stalinist propaganda as a whole, yet recall his sincere enthusiasm for labor competition; another could describe his heartfelt devotion to party doctrine, yet consistently undermine party claims by piling up damning details about everyday life in Nowa Huta.[35] What interests me is how, within the constraints and unfreedoms of Stalinism, individuals creatively used the materials at hand to shape meaningful stories of their own experience; for Nowa Huta's pioneers, those stories are limned with an uneasy awareness of both the costs and benefits of life in the new town. In this sense, they can be seen as reflecting the more general ambivalence of many Poles toward the legacies of the period 1944–89.

The book's first chapter explores the unstable interplay of visions, plans, and realities in Nowa Huta across several critical junctures in Polish history. Contrary to popular images of Nowa Huta as a Soviet initiative imposed on Poland from without, the reality is more complex. Nowa Huta evolved most immediately from plans developed by Polish military and economic experts prior to World War II, but also reflected more deeply rooted traditions of Polish economic, political, and urbanist thought. Nowa Huta's general plan, as finalized in 1951, thus represented the interplay of these older, indigenous visions with those of party officials and Soviet advisers. The city that was ultimately built, however, reflected still other, unanticipated factors: as this chapter will show, much that was built in Nowa Huta was unplanned, and much that was planned remained unbuilt. Political and economic changes after Stalin's death in 1953, especially, forced far-reaching alterations to the new town at the levels of vision, plan, and reality.

Exploring another set of visions and realities, chapter 2 deals with those who came to build, work, and live in Nowa Huta from 1949 to 1956. The majority were under the age of thirty and rural in origin, part of a vast migratory wave that would transform the Polish working class in the two decades or so after World War II. Considering both the push of the Polish countryside and the pull of what migrants imagined Nowa Huta to be, it asks what happened when imagination and reality collided under the impact of Stalinist industrialization in the 1950s. About one third of those who passed through the new town in its first half-decade remained to work in its factories and live in apartments they had sometimes built with their own hands. In later years, Nowa Huta would provide the stability that many Europeans sought in the postwar decades of normalization. But in the town's first half-decade, the city's attraction was something else: chaotic, unfinished, at times anarchic, Nowa Huta was, as one scholar puts it, a "synonym of the 'wider world,' of something completely different from the landscape of their birthplace, of another life."[36] The chapter thus presents "becoming Nowohucian" as a process of self-invention—a willed act, for many of its pioneers, of becoming modern, urban citizens of their self-built "small fatherland" (*mała ojczyzna*).

In Nowa Huta, as one activist wrote, "everything [was] agitation, a momentous kind of politics," and thus chapter 3 addresses agitation and mobilization in Nowa Huta—particularly, the almost relentless labor competition campaigns urging workers to build socialism "faster, better, cheaper." The chapter addresses a seeming paradox: Labor competition elicited genuine enthusiasm among certain workers in Nowa Huta—especially new workers (that is, those from a peasant background) and youth. At the same time, party activists struggled—to little avail—to mold local labor heroes or "model workers" to fit the party's image of model socialist citizens. The chapter suggests, therefore, that enthusiastic participation in Stalinist mobilization campaigns had both complex roots and unanticipated consequences. The visions of collective effort and shared reward evoked by labor competition, in particular, reinforced popular understandings of a moral community of labor in Nowa Huta. This moral community, moreover, would increasingly be understood as excluding party bosses and their allies.

Chapter 4 revisits the question of Stalinism's emancipatory promises through the lenses of gender and ethnicity: it reframes the question, did communism liberate women?, by juxtaposing women's experiences with those of the Roma (Gypsy) minority. According to the propaganda surrounding Nowa Huta, Stalinist industrialization offered to "productivize" and emancipate both groups, extending special guardianship and care over women and Roma workers in the new town. Women in Nowa Huta were trained as bricklayers and steelworkers to prove that they could work as well as men at the production site; Roma recruited from highland villages, offered brand-new apartments in Nowa Huta, were supposed to throw over their allegedly wandering way of life and become just like so-called civilized Poles. Many women and Roma did, in fact, embrace the opportunities for jobs and housing in Nowa Huta, provoking challenges from coworkers, neighbors, activists, and officials often indifferent or hostile to the regime's formal commitments to equality. But however contradictory and limited Stalinism's effort to reshape gender and ethnicity, the period after Stalin's death in 1953 brought about a marked deterioration on both fronts—rolling back women's opportunities in the workplace and substituting coercive police surveillance for paternalism in its policies toward the Roma.

Meanwhile, a moral panic about reportedly high levels of prostitution and infanticide in Nowa Huta fed growing reformist critiques at the national level, a theme explored further in the discussion in chapter 5 of culture and leisure in the new town. Stalinists shared the Polish intelligentsia's historic interest in the cultural enlightenment of the masses, a task deemed all the more urgent in Nowa Huta because of the uneducated peasant origins of so many inhabitants. But inadequate funding for cultural institutions, on the one hand, and a pervasive tendency among young workers to prefer jazz, jitterbugging, and drinking to high cultural pursuits—symbolized by the countercultural figures of so-called hooligans and bikini boys—led to increasingly stinging critiques of Nowa Huta's cultural experiment. This came to a head with Adam Ważyk's scandalous 1955 "Poem for Adults," depicting Nowa Huta's human byproduct as a depraved mass beset by social dislocation, sexual promiscuity, and alcoholism. But while de-Stalinization became an argument for reasserting traditional hierarchies of cultural value, rising demands for jazz, American-style fashion, and greater sexual and personal autonomy represented a generational challenge that would increasingly link Nowa Huta's youth to their age cohort on both sides of the Iron Curtain.

Chapter 6, finally, explores Nowa Huta's odyssey from the turbulent month of October 1956 through the collapse of communism in 1989. The generation that made the new town one of the most militant centers of the Solidarity movement in the 1980s was made up of sons and daughters of Nowa Huta's builders who had learned their lessons from their parents' past. A selective memory of Stalinism, I argue, provided Nowohucians with a usable set of tools for struggle and dissent, while Nowa Huta's distinctive industrial and urban geography proved particularly conducive to organization and protest. The chapter thus argues that primordialist explanations of Polish protest fail to grasp the reasons behind the exceptional strength and intensity of resistance in Nowa Huta, which must consider the encounter with Stalinism as a formative experience. This perspective illuminates, among other things, the central role in Solidarity played by the Catholic church, which mirrored and built on an ideology of construction and popular ownership inherited from the town's founding years.

While the implosion of communism brought many changes for Poland's "first socialist city," there have also been surprising continuities across the rupture of 1989, a theme taken up in the conclusion of the book. In 2009 Nowa Huta celebrated its sixtieth anniversary with a postmodern blend of hip-hop and socialist realism, industrial sound and symphonies. Despite such creative attempts at cultural synthesis, the meaning of Nowa Huta's urban landscape is still contested. While Nowa Huta remains an unwelcome reminder of the communist past for some, it also has a growing core of fans and enthusiasts. Comprising both long-time locals and a new wave of settlers, they are intrigued by the possibilities suggested by Nowa Huta's unfinished utopia. For many current inhabitants, Wajda's warning against amnesia seems to remain a good guide to an uncertain future: "Even if they suffered defeats, or at least did not know success, it would not be good if we started again from scratch."

1

Unplanned City

In 1948, as now, the city of Kraków occupied a special place in the Polish imagination. Kraków, Poland's capital until 1569, had grown up at the foot of the ancient Wawel Castle, which, along with the delicate twin steeples of St. Mary's Cathedral, dominated the city's skyline. It was here that Poland's monarchs had been crowned and its greatest heroes buried; through the dark years of Polish statelessness (1795–1918), the Wawel had served as a towering reminder of Poland's past (and, it was hoped, future) glories. Polish children grew up fed on stories of Kraków's dragon and the clever boy who slew him; of the bugler, high in St. Mary's tower, shot through the throat by a Tatar archer; of Queen Wanda, who threw herself into the Vistula River rather than marry a German prince. Life in Kraków had traditionally been dominated by merchants, scholars, and churchmen: its intellectual traditions went back to the Middle Ages with the founding of the Jagiellonian University, Copernicus's alma mater. Little had changed in modern times. Kraków remained relatively untouched by industrialization, and by the turn of the twentieth century, the liberal atmosphere of late-Habsburg rule had made Kraków a bubbling center of Polish cultural, artistic, and student life.

During World War II, Kraków was among the few Polish cities to escape major war damage. The contrast with Warsaw's smoking ruins could hardly have been greater: the atmosphere prevailing in Kraków during the immediate postwar years struck visitors as unique, not only in Poland but also, perhaps, anywhere on the war-ravaged continent. "Uppercrust life in Krakow has achieved a normality which gives the city a cultural activity and gaiety found nowhere else in the European war zone," wrote American journalist Irving Brant. The city became Poland's "salon," a magnet for artists and intellectuals from all over the country, with new journals and magazines appearing on the scene as early as 1945.[1] The city's independent cosmopolitanism, however, did not sit well with Poland's new, Communist-dominated government, and tensions quickly flared between the Polish Workers' Party (PPR) and local elites. They came to a head with the national referendum of June 30, 1946, in which Poles were urged by government propaganda to vote "three times yes." Kraków did not oblige, returning results unfavorable to what the regime saw as a general referendum on its rule.[2] This elicited a barrage of official invective against Kraków's "bastion of reaction," proposals for the forced resettlement of the city's "palace dwellers" and "unnecessary people," and a series of ominous show trials from August to September 1947.[3]

None of this, however, matched the bombshell that was about to explode on the city and its inhabitants. In February 1949, references began appearing in the press about an enormous new steelworks to be built outside Kraków, some 10 kilometers to the east of the medieval city center. Soon, reports described how a new city for a hundred thousand inhabitants (Kraków's population at the time was just three hundred thousand) would be built alongside the steelworks to house its workers and their families. It was said that the new town's proximity to the older city would provide a much-needed antidote to Kraków's "unhealthy" atmosphere, grafting fresh, proletarian branches onto Kraków's "rotten wood." Premier Józef Cyrankiewicz, for instance, proclaimed in July that the new town would bring "winds of change" to the city, "driving out the remains of a musty atmosphere and giving the city a socialist imprint."[4] The new town was to be called Nowa Huta—"new foundry" or "new steelworks."

For many inhabitants of "old" Kraków, Nowa Huta was (and is) an unwelcome imposition, an act of political violence to their city's historic makeup and character. Ultimately, Nowa Huta became a sprawling, unwieldy suburb; although it was annexed to Kraków in 1953, many from the older city always considered it foreign and other. In this view, the only "winds of change" Nowa Huta brought were polluting emissions from the steelworks' smokestacks, blamed by Krakovians for eating away at the city's old stones and destroying its air quality.[5] Given the official rhetoric that accompanied Nowa Huta's construction, moreover, it seems inevitable that the new town would be perceived not just as a physical assault but also as a spiritual and ideological one. As one Solidarity leader from Nowa Huta later explained, "the aims of the Marxist ideologues were directed at neutralizing conservative Kraków. The neutralizing agent was to be Nowa Huta."[6]

To be sure, the propaganda of the day embedded Nowa Huta in a triumphalist rhetoric of class warfare and socialist supremacy. Nowa Huta was to be Poland's "first socialist city": following in the footsteps of Soviet new towns like Komsomolsk or Magnitogorsk, it would represent a new kind of civilization, peopled by "new men" forged in the town's purpose-built, socialist spaces. This was the Nowa Huta the nation saw and heard about in a constant flow of films, newsreels, newspaper features, speeches, stories, novels, poems, and songs—the "great building site of socialism," the heroic proof of socialism's superiority over capitalism, evidence of the peace-loving Soviet Union's "friendship" for its Polish neighbor. This propaganda was inescapable—not least, in Nowa Huta itself. This chapter, however, probes the limits of such propaganda (and the ideology behind it) by asking how those involved in the new town's planning and construction perceived their participation in what was officially called "building socialism" in Nowa Huta. As we shall see, they attached a very different set of meanings to Nowa Huta, alongside—or even against—the official version trumpeted in the public sphere.

While subsequent chapters will focus on the workers who built and settled in Nowa Huta, here I shall concentrate on the so-called professional intelligentsia—planners, architects, engineers—who perhaps more than anyone else were responsible for turning the propaganda about Nowa Huta into concrete reality. Overwhelmingly members of the hereditary Polish intelligentsia, many had fought against both the Nazis and the Soviets in World War II and felt distance from, if not hostility toward, the country's new rulers after 1944. And yet they were more often than not enthusiastic—even passionate—about seeing the construction of Poland's "first socialist city" through to reality. Their experiences can provide insights into how large numbers of non- and even anti-Communist Poles were able to accommodate to the "new reality" of the Stalinist system (lasting roughly 1948–1956). Such Poles chose to work within and alongside a system that they regarded as foreign and even illegitimate in order to realize their own complex agendas.

In the case of Nowa Huta, particular traditions and models rooted in the Polish past were key in shaping how professionals understood the meaning of the new steelworks and model city they were tasked with building. The first part of the chapter will explore some of these legacies, focusing on the period of partition (1772–1918) and the Second Republic (1918–39). Such professionals can be seen as heirs to a pragmatic tradition of Polish nationalism dating back to the second half of the nineteenth century, one that linked Polish national revival to overcoming economic and social underdevelopment. For them, as for many who shared these traditions of thought, the near total breakdown of World War II also offered hopes of finally realizing this program of social and economic transformation. As journalist Edmund Osmańczyk put it in a popular series of articles in 1946, Poles may have lost the war, but with a coordinated effort of "brains and brawn," they could still "win the peace." To do so, however, each and every Polish patriot, and especially those with "brains" (i.e., skills and scientific know-how), had to roll up his sleeves and get to work.[7] A few years later, Nowa Huta offered a golden opportunity to put this principle into action: as one engineer who was transferred to the

Lenin Steelworks in 1954 put it, "I resolved to give myself entirely over to my work—to the steelworks—to the fatherland."[8]

Needless to say, Communist power and policy limited the pathways such patriotic efforts could take. In the case of Nowa Huta, there were dramatic differences, for instance, between the plans that Polish economists initially conceived and those that ultimately took shape under pressure from Soviet "advisers" or Warsaw Party officials. This raises the larger question of how visions and plans are translated into reality during the planning process in any political system. As Anne Mosher points out in her study of the nineteenth-century steel town Vandergrift, Pennsylvania, there can be many a slip between cup and lip: "urban visions are seldom smoothly and inexorably translated into urban design and then into urban landscape," even when "shepherded along by politically or economically powerful" sponsors.[9] Planning, in other words, is a far from robust process and is subject to a host of forces that can easily derail the realization of planners' visions. Nowa Huta proves that Mosher's observations do not apply only in free markets: when we trace the interactions of planners and politicians, Poles and Soviets, architects and economists, and ultimately, visions, plans, and outcomes in Nowa Huta, it seems that the totality of the process escaped the control of any one party, including the Communist party itself.

The chapter will thus consider not only the competing national, historical, and ideological visions that shaped Nowa Huta, but also the underlying factors that complicated the translation of visions into plans, on the one hand, and plans into realities, on the other. Most significant among these were the pressures generated by Nowa Huta's enormous size, which exacerbated inefficiencies and contradictions already inherent in the state socialist economy. When Warsaw understood the full costs (financial, administrative, and, ultimately, political) of building this worker's paradise, it effectively withdrew its sponsorship for all but a stripped-down version of the original urban plan. Stalin's death in 1953 further eroded Warsaw's political will to build an urban utopia. Thus, a great deal of what was ultimately built in this planned city was, paradoxically, unplanned, while much of what was planned remained unbuilt—another way in which this chapter addresses the limits of ideology under state socialism.

Practical Romantics

There were Poles, once upon a time, who believed in communism—although what exactly that meant was not a straightforward matter. The writer Tadeusz Konwicki, brought up in a patriotic, middle-class family, had fought in World War II together with many educated Poles of his generation in the Home Army, the underground military force of Poland's government-in-exile that was opposed to Nazi and Soviet power alike. As a participant in the Warsaw Uprising, he had witnessed his city's defeat and destruction in the autumn of 1944, during which Warsaw was reduced to rubble by the Wehrmacht as the Poles' erstwhile Soviet allies looked on. In light of this betrayal, not to mention the many crimes committed against Poles in Soviet-occupied eastern Poland in 1939–41 and the Communists' subsequent persecution of Home Army veterans once in power, Konwicki's postwar embrace of a belief system associated with Soviet power seems anything but inevitable. And yet Konwicki was far from the only member of his generation to make this move. Years later, he struggled to explain that communism seemed, at the time, the only alternative to nihilism, to the orgy of death and killing that surrounded him. Besides, Konwicki argued, the end of the war was something unbelievable—

> that . . . moment when we entered into a new life. Sun, blooming orchards, the hope of building something, of doing something; that it would be different, better. . . . Yes, we were naïve; it was a function of our age, of our very intense wartime experience, . . . and of our civic upbringing within the conventions of Polish romanticism.[10]

In 1949, Konwicki joined a volunteer youth brigade bound for Nowa Huta. He soon published a fictionalized work about his time there; its hero "finds the joy of life in collective work" and the book "finishes with the obligatory 'happy end': the plan is fulfilled, the project delivered on time."[11] Konwicki had exchanged the conventions of Polish romanticism for the conventions of socialist realism.

Konwicki came of age in a society deeply inflected by those romantic traditions. The Polish Second Republic had imbued in Konwicki and his peers an ethos of military service and sacrifice, itself a legacy of more than a century of Polish statelessness. During this period of partition by Austria, Prussia, and Russia, the descendants of the Polish nobility had fought in repeated doomed uprisings against the partitioning powers, notably in 1794, 1830, 1846, and 1863. Although they had failed disastrously, the uprisings had created an enduring mythology of Poland as the "Christ of nations" and glorified the idea of self-sacrifice on behalf of the fatherland.

Over time, however, some Poles sought to reinterpret the form such sacrifice should take, convinced that spilling Poland's best blood in armed struggle was self-defeating. In the second half of the nineteenth century, such pragmatists, among them the so-called Warsaw Positivists, argued that Poles should accept their Russian, German, or Austrian rulers in the short run but prepare themselves for a future time when they would again be free. Based on the idea of the nation as an organism, the term "organic work" came to suggest a pragmatic, gradualist approach to strengthening the nation in body and spirit. The agents of such work were to be the intelligentsia—educated Poles with the skills and knowledge needed to uplift the country's impoverished, largely peasant majority and put the country on the path to modernization and development.[12]

Implicit in such ideas was a causal link between Poland's presumed economic backwardness vis-à-vis the West, on the one hand, and its vulnerability to foreign subjugation, on the other. In this regard, progressive Poles of the nineteenth century (and beyond) worried not only about the military implications of underdevelopment but also about the divisive legacies of Poland's semifeudal social structure. The last remnants of serfdom had been abolished only in the 1860s, and more radical thinkers questioned the viability of a nation internally divided between (former) serfs and their masters. In order to narrow the wide gap in mentality and civilization between the *lud*, or populace, and educated, more urban Poles, therefore, progressive nationalists laid emphasis on improving the masses' health, welfare, and education.

Industrialization, in this regard, offered both promise and peril. On the one hand, progressives saw industrialization as necessary for modernizing and enriching the country. On the other, they feared the creation of a proletarian underclass, weakened both morally and physically by dreadful conditions in the new urban factories and slums. The Warsaw Positivists, among others, therefore favored an ameliorated industrialization, to be supported by social welfare and the just distribution of wealth.[13] This vision of industrialization was just one of the Positivists' legacies for future generations of Polish progressives. They bequeathed to qualified professionals—whether doctors, engineers, or architects—an understanding of their everyday work as essential to national revival. Furthermore, they offered patriotic justification for temporarily accommodating a politically hostile regime with a view to contributing to the nation's welfare and independence in the long run.

These ideas were tested after the restoration of Polish independence in 1918. With the creation of Europe's sixth-largest state in the aftermath of World War I, Polish hopes soared: "We are the heirs to everything. We will enter the dreamed-of valley and we will plow, sow, and reap," proclaimed novelist Stefan Żeromski, with uncharacteristic optimism.[14] A key question was what role the independent state—no longer the representative of a hostile foreign power, but the Poles' "own"—should play in cultivating the new landscape. Żeromski's own work expressed deep ambivalence toward state power and its potential abuse: in *The Coming Spring* (1924), for instance, he foretold a visionary leader who would build sparkling "glass houses" for the multitude, but also warned against authoritarian tendencies within the national state.[15] Throughout the interwar period, Polish progressives shared Żeromski's ambivalence, both attracted and repelled by the increasingly authoritarian regime of Marshal Józef Piłsudski and his successors. At the same time, in a country as capital-poor as Poland, it was clear that state planning and investment would be essential for progress in the sciences, technology, and industry.[16]

Two examples of state-led development between the wars would later have special resonance for Nowa Huta's planners. Both were closely associated with the economist and politician Eugeniusz Kwiatkowski, who variously held office as the Second Republic's deputy prime minister, minister of the treasury, and minister of industry and trade. Kwiatkowski believed that Poland was exceptionally rich in both human and natural resources and that with vision and willpower, it could "match the tempo" of Western economies. He thus called for a campaign to imbue "all of Polish society" with what he called "the ambition of competition [*współzawodnictwo*] in productive, everyday work."[17] While reflecting the era's obsessions with time and efficiency ("tempo"), the global race for economic and military dominance, and individual competition, Kwiatkowski at the same time echoed Positivist calls for everyday efforts by all Poles to strengthen the nation. Kwiatkowski thus threw his weight behind two ambitious projects—the new port city of Gdynia on the Baltic Coast and the Central Industrial Region (*Centralny Okręg Przemysłowy*, or COP) in southeastern Poland—that proved, in their respective ways, that the state could effectively mobilize willpower and resources for visionary development projects.

The port and new town of Gdynia, built between 1920 and 1939, were intended to provide Poland secure access to the Baltic Sea in the face of concerns about access to shipping facilities in the Free City of Danzig. Built on the site of a small fishing village, the new national port, initiated by the Ministry of Defense in 1920 and supported by state investments of 88 million złoty, ultimately became the largest and most technologically advanced on the Baltic Sea, handling 47 percent of Polish foreign trade on the eve of World War II. Planning for Gdynia's urban development was overseen by the Ministry of Public Works; working to a general plan drawn up by the ministry between 1926 and 1936, private developers built housing for a mixed population of manual and white-collar workers, which grew to almost 122,000 by 1939.[18] Gdynia was thus quite possibly the largest European "new town" east of the Urals to be realized between the two World Wars.

The speed of Gdynia's success seemed to many a confirmation of Kwiatkowski's optimism, and discussions of the port city in official pronouncements and the press echoed many of Kwiatkowski's keywords: tempo, national pride, competitiveness. Many also stressed Gdynia's "youthful," hard-working, and modern character ("a sparkling modern city, with a verve and bustle usually associated with countries farther to the West. Her streets are broad and straight. Her buildings shiny and new"). The message surrounding Gdynia was that "it would bring economic prosperity and political security, providing opportunity for all and enhancing the country's international standing"; as Bartholomew Goldyn points out, the same would later be said about Nowa Huta.[19] Gdynia's success, above all, lent credence and patriotic luster to the pursuit of ambitious development projects and demonstrated to Poles the viability of building a new city—the ultimate symbol of civilization and modernity—from scratch.

A highly coordinated plan for state-led development of industry in Poland's southeast, the so-called Central Industrial Region, also created precedents for postwar planners. Piłsudski allegedly once commented that Poland was like an *obwarzanek* (a crispy, round pretzel)—full at the edges, in other words, but empty in the middle. Piłsudski was referring to an issue that occupied considerable attention among Polish economists and policymakers during the interwar period, namely, the economic disproportion between the relatively industrialized (Western) border regions and the country's underdeveloped agrarian heartland.[20] On the one hand, the dynamism and modernity of a place like Gdynia contrasted radically with vast swathes of countryside where land hunger, underemployment, and underinvestment had left a population seemingly mired in hopeless stagnation and isolation.[21] On the other hand, the Polish military raised concerns about the concentration of Polish industry near the country's borders, particularly in Silesia, where it would be especially vulnerable in the event of an invasion.[22]

A proposed "security triangle" in southeastern Poland, bounded by the Vistula and San rivers and protected by the Carpathian Mountains to the south, thus became the centerpiece of the government's Four-Year Plan (1936–40) for industrial development on the eve of World War II. What was now called the Central Industrial Region, or COP, was earmarked for extensive development through state investment and tax credits (in the end, however, private investment never reached hoped-for levels, and funding overwhelmingly came from the state).[23] For Kwiatkowski, COP would kill several birds with one stone: it would strengthen national security; generate employment in some of Poland's poorest regions; and provide the focal point for a coordinated nationwide campaign, even more ambitious than Gdynia, for modernization and development. At the outbreak of World War II, COP had become the largest industrial area in Poland outside of Silesia and constituted one of the highest concentrations of state-owned industry in Europe, including major production facilities such as the Stalowa Wola steelworks and the Dębica chemicals plant and tire factory.[24]

COP, unlike Gdynia, also advanced the idea of a coordinated approach to economic and urban planning by earmarking funds for housing, including ten free-standing workers' settlements adjoined to newly built factories. Two, Stalowa Wola and Dębica, became "new towns" in their own right.[25] For the first time, the Polish state took up through COP the mantle of interwar Polish urbanism, which thus far had been the province of left-wing architects working privately or with small cooperative associations.[26] Like their modernist colleagues elsewhere in Europe, functionalist architects such as Szymon and Helena Syrkus, who had designed several model housing settlements in Warsaw, viewed urban planning as a holistic endeavor: they conceived of architects as social engineers whose expertise must extend into areas, such as health or hygiene, well beyond those of classical architecture. As Szymon Syrkus put it, "Architecture changes the social pattern, as the social pattern changes architecture." Reflecting architecture's new status in independent Poland, between 1918 and 1928, the number of registered architects in the country grew by a factor of ten.[27] Until COP, however, progressive architects' efforts to develop social housing were hobbled by a lack of resources and limited to a few model developments. COP raised the possibility of a radical expansion of the social housing agenda and suggested there could be harmonious coexistence between progressive architecture and large-scale, state-supervised development.

The outbreak of war in September 1939 put an abrupt end to such hopes, as it did to COP's projected expansion of the steel industry. In December 1938, Kwiatkowski had presented before the Polish parliament a proposal for a further fifteen-year plan, to be broken into three-year increments. One phase would prioritize steel: despite the construction of Stalowa Wola, Polish steel production in relation to population had actually declined since independence and was insufficient to support projected growth in other branches.[28] After the war, COP's interrupted plans would loom large in discussions of building a new steelworks, and Polish planners would in many ways pick up where COP had left off.

COP prefigured Nowa Huta in other respects, as well: both formed part of a military–industrial complex; both were located in the southeast, Poland's least industrially developed region; both adopted a coordinated model of urban and economic planning, building housing for the workers alongside new industry. As with COP, moreover, many architects and planners who in other ways opposed the state found common ground with the regime in Nowa Huta, particularly in its model of "industrialization with amelioration"—a vision that many Poles were prepared to embrace in the postwar era. Finally, Polish

Stalinists turned Nowa Huta into the focus of a national campaign, echoing Kwiatkowski's calls for a new ethos of competition or *współzawodnictwo*.

In the end, Nowa Huta would appeal to both the romantic and pragmatic legacies of Polish nationalism. As one man who worked in Nowa Huta put it, he was following in his father's and brother's footsteps: while his father, at the age of seventeen, had joined the ranks of insurgents fighting for Polish independence in 1918, he and his brother had joined youth brigades—his brother to clear rubble in Warsaw, he to build the new town. But this time, he added, the weapons were different: "We, his sons, exchanged rifles for shovels, because after 1945, Poland was soaked not in blood, but in work and sweat."[29]

Make No Little Plans

If the tasks of reconstruction that confronted Poles in 1918 were momentous, those they faced in 1944–45 were almost beyond imagining. The furious violence of the dual Soviet and German occupations from 1939 to 1941, and the Nazis' genocidal war of destruction on Polish soil thereafter, caused the highest per capita losses in Europe: 22.2 percent of the prewar population was dead. Approximately 35 percent of national agricultural wealth had been destroyed, along with 32 percent of assets in industry, 30 percent in housing and office stock, and 60 percent in schools and scientific institutions.[30] And yet, as Jan Gross writes, in Poland, as elsewhere in East Central Europe, "after several years of living in limbo or insecurity or horror . . . people yearned for involvement and an active life constructively engaged with the community."[31]

The challenges of reconstruction called forth a huge outpouring of energy. The rapid rebuilding of Warsaw—80 percent of which lay ruins in 1944—was a case in point; a *New York Times* corresponded commented in 1948 that "the reconstruction achieved in [the last few months] takes one's breath away. . . . Warsaw is only faintly recognizable now as the ruined city left by the Germans in 1945." Architect Helena Syrkus assured another foreigner that Warsaw would soon become "one of the most modern, pleasant, and human cities in the world. Come back in a few years," she challenged him, "and see for yourself."[32] Like Syrkus, many Poles were determined to wrest victory from the jaws of defeat: they would rebuild Warsaw—and Poland—not as a replica of what it had been before the war (apart from Warsaw's meticulously reconstructed Old Town), but as something better. The totality of destruction had one silver lining: it offered a tabula rasa upon which to inscribe the wholesale transformation that modernist reformers had long sought.[33]

After World War II, many Europeans pinned their hopes on an expanded role for the state, empowered not merely to manage but also to engineer change in the social and economic spheres.[34] Such hopes were evident across the political spectrum in wartime policy statements by Polish parties and interest groups: the right-wing National Party, for example, advocated a "system of planned economy" like the one it said Franklin Delano Roosevelt had introduced in the United States.[35] An organization of exiled Polish planners and architects also praised the New Deal, citing FDR's housing policy as an example of a "principle [that] is becoming all the more generally recognized": the right of citizens to demand from the state an optimal standard of living. Summing up the necessity of a maximalist approach to human welfare, the authors admiringly quoted Chicago architect Daniel W. Burnham's motto: "Make no little plans. They have no magic to stir men's blood."[36]

The New Deal, of course, was not the only available model of a planned economy in 1944. Poland's first postwar government was established that year when the Red Army marched into the city of Lublin, backed by the NKVD and dominated by Polish Communists, many freshly returned from exile in the Soviet Union. Among them was Poland's new minister of industry, Hilary Minc, who had spent the war teaching Marxist economics at the University of Samarkand; clearly, postwar Poland, unlike the interwar Second Republic, would look East as much as West for models of modernization and development. Initially, however, the Lublin government pursued not a Soviet model, but rather, a mixed program for recovery and development under the auspices of a the Central Bureau of Planning (CUP), headed by respected prewar socialist economist Czesław Bobrowski and staffed by members of the wartime government in exile.[37] The Three-Year Plan for recovery (1947–49) emphasized raising living standards through foreign credits to be obtained through trade with the West; only toward the end of the period did it foresee a shift in priority from consumer to investment goods.[38] The plan thus represented a compromise among various political interests, including the Communists, Socialists, and peasant parties, while at the same time reviving elements of Polish economic policy of the 1930s. Indicative of this backward glance was the appointment of Kwiatkowski to supervise naval reconstruction.[39]

The idea of a major investment in steel production—a new steelworks, with the cryptonym "The Giant"—had continued to be discussed in underground planning workshops during the war. When the war ended and the government began to seek credit for a series of major imports from the West, these included the components of a *kombinat*, a large-scale facility combining all phases of steel production. In June 1946, the state engineering firm Biprohut sketched a proposal for such a facility to be built with equipment imported from the United States; the plans foresaw a workforce of five thousand people, of whom roughly half would live in a new worker's settlement. In July 1947, the Ministry of Industry's Central Management for Steel Production (CZPH) placed an order with Chicago's Freyn Engineering Company (which had helped build the Magnitogorsk steelworks in the Soviet Union in the 1930s) for a complete set of plans based on Biprohut's proposal.[40]

Rising cold war tensions, however, soon derailed these negotiations. On the one hand, a new United States licensing program served as a de facto embargo on American exports to the Soviet bloc, and Polish efforts to negotiate an export license for a blooming and slabbing mill, carried on throughout 1948, were in vain.[41] On the other hand, momentous political changes in Poland soon forced a radical shift in economic policy. In 1948, the Communists embarked on the elimination of their opponents in the "Democratic Bloc," culminating in the forced unification of the Socialist (PPS) and Communist parties (PPR) under the umbrella of a Polish United Workers' Party (PZPR) in December of that year. That summer, first party secretary Władysław Gomułka—who had suggested that Poland was not yet ready for socialism—had been replaced by the bland and thoroughly Moscow-loyal Bolesław Bierut. Bierut would preside over Poland as a "little Stalin" until his death in 1956. Meanwhile Gomułka, though spared the terrible fate of purged leaders elsewhere in Stalinist Eastern Europe, remained in curious limbo, together with his idea of a "Polish road to socialism."

Symptomatic of this change was the disbanding of the CUP and its replacement by a National Commission for Economic Planning (PKPG) charged with overseeing the Ministry of Industry and Trade's new Six-Year Plan (1950–55), adopted earlier that year. Unlike the Three-Year Plan's strategy of seeking short-term improvements in living standards while laying the gradual foundations for further economic growth, the new plan, based on Stalin's forced industrialization of the Soviet Union in the 1930s, aimed at the quickest possible development of industry, and prioritized heavy producer industries (metallurgical, electrotechnical) over consumer branches. The ministry's theses, adopted in December at the first congress of the PZPR, projected a doubling of all industrial output, with a growth of 250 percent for metallurgical industries and 300 percent for chemicals. In the version ultimately enacted into law, the period between 1949 and 1955 was to see investments grow by 40 percent, employment by 60 percent, national income by 12 percent, industrial output by 58 percent, agricultural output by 50 percent, the standard of living by 50 to 60 percent, and real wages by 40 percent. In 1951 and 1952, in response to the outbreak of the Korean War, targets were yet again increased, owing to added investment in defense-related areas.[42]

Throughout the cold war, Western economists puzzled over the Six-Year Plan's "ambitious" and even "unrealistic" targets. Why were the "glaring disproportions" between targets and resources not detected? Why, given "early signs of strain," were these "compounded by escalating investment targets"? According to one Western observer, "The planners seem to have overestimated the so-called undisclosed reserves and overestimated the mobilizing power of plan targets."[43] Indeed, "undisclosed reserves" were key to understanding how such a seemingly irrational plan could be adopted. As Minc explained in 1950, the spectacular advances projected in the Six-Year Plan would never be achieved without a significant increase in labor productivity—in short, through the mobilization and application of an extraordinary human effort.[44] In a political arena that demanded constant demonstrations of loyalty, production targets played not just an economic role but also a symbolic one: a demonstrated willingness to pursue apparently unrealistic production targets could be a marker of devotion, while, as the Soviet experience had shown, expressions of doubts and reservation could result in accusations of "wrecking." Planning, in this sense, was a leap of faith: faith in the leader, faith in socialism, and—in the case of Poland's emulation of Stalin's Five-Year Plan—evidence of unquestioned loyalty to the Soviet model. In this way, Polish policymakers found themselves pushed down a road—sometimes, it even seemed, against their own better judgment—from which it would be difficult, if not impossible, to return.

A New Steelworks for Old Kraków

It was in this atmosphere of intensified rhetoric and heightened expectations that planners began to look for a signature investment to represent the Six-Year Plan, a focal point for popular mobilization and a showcase for socialist productivism. And so the new steelworks that economic planners had once hoped to import from the United States now became the embodiment of a Soviet-directed industrialization policy—a "giant" indeed, swollen into a massive *kombinat* capable of producing 1.5 million tons of raw steel annually, more than the output of all Polish steelworks in 1939. Over the next few years, this target would be increased twice more, ultimately to the previously unimaginable figure of 5.5 million tons. The *kombinat* would contain halls a kilometer long, 150,000 tons of machines, and 150 kilometers of internal railway lines—a veritable city within a city.[45] The new steelworks—now generally written in capital letters as "Nowa Huta"—would be a perfect expression of Soviet-style gigantomania, a colossus demonstrating the supposedly Promethean powers of socialism to transform the human and physical landscape.

Having cancelled its dealings with Freyn in early 1948, CZPH turned to the Soviets, who offered blueprints, equipment, advisers, and cadre training under the Six-Year Plan. Negotiations between the Polish and Soviet sides over Nowa Huta's specifications had been ongoing for some time already; it was during such talks, in November 1947, that the production figure of 1.5 million tons had first arisen.[46] According to the *kombinat*'s later director of investment, this "proposition from the Soviet side" was met with widespread opposition by the Poles, who doubted their country had the manpower or expertise to operate such a formidable enterprise.[47] But there was no gainsaying Stalin: allegedly, it was the Great Leader himself who in January 1948 had questioned the original size of the Polish projections, commenting that it had been a long time since such "small plants" had been built in the Soviet Union.[48]

Besides magnifying the *kombinat*'s scale, Soviet involvement resulted in another critical revision of plans. At first, planners spoke of situating the steelworks on the Gliwice Canal at Dzierżno, in the heart of industrialized Silesia; indeed, as late as April 1948, Minc himself had confirmed Dzierżno as the location of choice. In January 1949, however, a delegation of Soviet specialists arrived to explore other potential sites. Biprohut proposed eleven possibilities—nine in Silesia, and two in southeastern Poland. Among the latter was Pleszów, a village on the northern banks of the Vistula, 9.5 kilometers to the east of Kraków's Main Market Square. It was in visiting Pleszów during this trip that the head of the Soviet team allegedly declared, "Here one can best develop a steelworks." Despite a last-ditch effort by Kraków's regional planning board to present alternate sites slightly farther from the city, the Soviet delegation's determination to build a steelworks in Pleszów was announced on February 17, 1949. With dizzying speed, the decision was confirmed by the Polish government on February 23.[49]

The area of Pleszów, comprising fourteen villages in the rural administrations of Mogiła, Ruszcza, and Wadów, plus parts of Branice and Przewóz, had long been a prosperous microregion, thanks both to its fertile soil and its position along historic trade routes linking the medieval kingdom of Rus', Kraków, and the salt mines of Wieliczka. While Nowa Huta was being built, archaeologists found woolly mammoth remains and evidence of human settlement in the area dating back to Paleolithic times; in another much-publicized discovery, they found traces of copperworking from the Neolithic period, suggesting that it was one of the oldest sites of metallurgical industry in Poland. Metallurgy was also practiced in the area during the Middle Ages: in 1223, Bishop Iwo Odrowąż moved a Cistercian order to Mogiła that fostered both paper and copper smelting industries. The order also built a splendid monastery (its oldest parts date to the thirteenth century), which, along with the fifteenth-century wooden church of St. Bartholomew, would later provide a place of worship for Nowa Huta's faithful.[50] Among other historic monuments on Nowa Huta's terrain was the early medieval "Wanda's Mound," a 14.5 meter high, most likely pagan, burial mound, said to contain the remains of Queen Wanda—she who had thrown herself from the ramparts of Wawel Castle to avoid marrying a German prince. When her body washed up on the banks of the Vistula by Mogiła—literally, "mound"—she was buried, according to legend, under this tumulus.

How important a role did politics—in particular, Stalin's desire to punish Kraków for its perceived anti-communism—play in the Soviets' choice of Pleszów for building Nowa Huta? As of yet, no evidence has come to light that could offer a conclusive answer to this question. However, as the historian Jacek Salwiński has pointed out, other, non-political factors may have played a role in the decision. For example, Stalin shared a belief in industrial deconcentration with Polish planners of the interwar period, and may therefore have favored southeastern Poland, with its large, underemployed rural population reserves, for the same reasons that COP's planners did. Placing the steelworks near Kraków also provided housing stock, office space, and institutional resources (such as the Academy of Mining and Metalworking) during Nowa Huta's start-up period. And Kraków lay at the confluence of railway routes connecting Silesia's raw materials and the destination for many of Nowa Huta's finished products, the Soviet Union.[51]

We might also speculate that a desire to legitimate Nowa Huta through association with Kraków's ancient history and monuments helped make Pleszów an attractive choice for the new town. It seems no accident that the Soviet expert who declared, "Here one can best develop a steelworks," allegedly did so from the top of Wanda's Mound: the sweeping bird's-eye view from this ancient outcropping, with all its romantic-nationalist associations, remained a favored cliché in socialist realist descriptions of Nowa Huta throughout the Stalinist period. Meanwhile, the most famous novelistic account of Nowa Huta from the period, Marian Brandys's *The Beginning of the Story* (1952), contains a scene in the village of Prądnik Biały to Nowa Huta's northwest; according to legend, the national hero Tadeusz Kościuszko spent the night there before the triumphal Battle of Racławice (1794), in which local peasants helped insurgents defeat Russian forces. In the book, Nowa Huta's first team of surveyors spends the night in the very same house where Kościuszko slept in 1794, a heavy-handed allusion to the new "battle" for Poland's future.[52]

In their wish both to endow Nowa Huta with an aura of romance and to deflect attention from its Soviet sponsorship, Polish leaders may ultimately have hoped that some of Kraków's patriotic-nationalist associations would rub off on its new neighbor. Whatever the reasons for locating Nowa Huta near Kraków, however, the fates of the two towns were now inextricably linked. The relationship between them, as we shall see, would not be an easy one.

Modeling Socialism

Following the choice of a site for the steelworks, the first references to a "socialist city" to house its workers began to appear in the press—and often, the features ascribed to the future new town were explicitly contrasted with those of old Kraków. As *Dziennik Polski* put it, "Outside the bourgeois breast of old Kraków a new, beautiful, socialist construction is being born to spite the remaining proletarian basements and old slums."[53] Whereas earlier projections had been for a population of seventy thousand, reports from this period began to cite the figure of one hundred thousand. The words *Nowa Huta* were now used more often to refer to this future workers' settlement than to the steelworks. Although Nowa Huta was not, like sister cities Stalinstadt and Sztalinváros in East Germany and Hungary, respectively, being named for the "Great Leader," its *kombinat* was christened in honor of Vladimir I. Lenin on January 21, 1954. "Huta im. Lenina" (HiL) it would remain until 1990.[54]

What should a socialist city look like? In 1934, socialist realism had been declared the obligatory style for all creative fields in the Soviet Union, including architecture and urban planning, and at their national conference in 1949, Polish architects had pledged to join in the struggle for socialist realism as against "cosmopolitanism, constructivism, [and] formalism."[55] Socialist realism was to be "nationalist in form, socialist in content," incorporating references to national historical styles within an overall framework of stylistic continuity: the latter was to stress classical and Renaissance forms, monumentalist proportions, and highly legible symbolic content—as Richard Stites puts it, "hugeness, order, symmetry—all associated with solemn and unchallenged authority."[56] While generally true, however, such characterizations fail to account for considerable range within socialist realist architecture, including occasional elements of stylistic continuity with earlier architectural styles that were theoretically anathema to the new idiom.

One architectural historian sees in such variation the possibility of "deliberate resistance" by architects in the People's Democracies, most of whom had been deeply committed to modernism/functionalism at the onset of Stalinism.[57] Indeed, while some eminent Polish functionalists went into emigration or even committed suicide, others, working within the "new reality," managed to design buildings, even at the height of Stalinism, that are now upheld as models of postwar modernism.[58] Others created designs that, while undeniably socialist realist, were innovative, functional, even beautiful. Some would say this applies to Nowa Huta.

In 1949, Tadeusz Ptaszycki won a closed competition to develop Nowa Huta's comprehensive plan. Ptaszycki came to Kraków (where he established the offices of Miastoprojekt, the state firm that would draw up plans for Nowa Huta's urban components) fresh from supervising the reconstruction of Wrocław, the largest city in the Western Territories annexed from Germany after the war. No doubt the successes of this massive endeavor, on display at the Exhibition of the Recovered Territories a year earlier, had helped persuade party leaders that Ptaszycki was their man. But Ptaszycki also had great personal charm.[59] A former champion athlete and scout leader, and a successful architect in independent practice before the war, Ptaszycki had fought in the September campaign and spent the war in captivity. In Wrocław, he had been a popular figure, fondly dubbed "Engineer Wrocław" by locals.[60] Ptaszycki's charisma, combined with the stature gained from his achievements in Wrocław, served him well: according to the architect Stanisław Juchnowicz, the older man knew not only how to reach out to the public but also "how to talk to those in power." Or as Juchnowicz delicately put it, "It was often necessary to take risks and to engage in the appropriate sort of politics so that we could realize our plans."[61]

Among the risks, according to Juchnowicz, was reassuring Warsaw that Ptaszycki would take "personal responsibility" for those he hired at Miastoprojekt. Ptaszycki surrounded himself with both young and more established talent, hiring without regard to political record or social background. The team that projected Nowa Huta thus contained many "inconvenient" people, including prewar army officers and veterans of the Home Army and General Anders's forces, as well as many who had studied and held fellowships in the West.[62] Tellingly, when Juchnowicz showed up for his first day of work at Miastoprojekt, the personnel officer, glancing at his documents, chattily asked to "which of the Juchnowiczes" he belonged—a quintessentially "bourgeois" conversational opener.[63] Protected by the powerful mediator figure of Ptaszycki, Miastoprojekt was a perfect example of what the sociologist Janine Wedel identifies as *środowisko*—a community based on traditional social, class, and, in some cases, professional solidarities that protected its members psychologically from external ideological pressures.[64] "There were no ideologues" at Miastoprojekt, insisted Bohdan Bukowski, a draughtsman who worked for Ptaszycki; for Juchnowicz (who would later work on the Nigerian new town of Abuja), Miastoprojekt was "an island of happiness in those hard times, a place where we felt, to a certain extent, free."[65]

Apart from technical directives, the architects received no direct orders about what the new town should look like; nonetheless, they knew their plans would have to withstand close scrutiny by Warsaw. The planning process was treated as top secret: a silent security officer, whose permission was required to take photographs, sat in the corner; all bags were checked before employees left the office. Ptaszycki traveled regularly to Warsaw, sometimes by plane (quite a novelty in those days) to meet with officials; once he was summoned to present his plans before Bierut. Realizing the president would not know what to make of sketches or blueprints, he ordered that a cardboard model of Central Square be made, painted in realistic detail and in bright colors like a child's toy. On returning from Warsaw, according to Bukowski, Ptaszycki, exhausted from the ordeal, announced that Bierut wanted no church in Nowa Huta, but he wanted a "tower" because "it might remind people of a church." (Bukowski claimed this was the origin of plans for Nowa Huta's never-built town hall.) According to Juchnowicz, the architects unofficially designated two sites, known only amongst themselves, where churches could be built at some future date.[66]

Juchnowicz claims that building Poland's "first socialist city" did not bother him: "There was among us the conviction that this city would outlive us," he explains, "and probably the system" as well. Infected by Ptaszycki's energy and enthusiasm, the architects and designers stayed up late, sketched plans on improvised drawing boards in the field, dreamed, and imagined, recognizing their once-in-a-lifetime opportunity to build a city entirely from scratch. In 1950, Ptaszycki enthused to the magazine *Sztandar Młodych* about providing built-in radios in each apartment and a telephone in every entry stair. Apartments were to have parquet floors, elevators, and domestic conveniences such as cooling cupboards and common laundry areas. There would be preschools, shops, cultural centers, sports halls, cinemas, libraries, and theaters—"the complete range of recreational opportunities, to allow [working people] to improve their physical fitness, ensure the best possible conditions for health, enable their intellectual development." Nowa Huta would be, above all, "the first city without cramped courtyards and dark hovels." To achieve this goal, Ptaszycki and his colleagues were willing to accommodate Warsaw's occasional intervention. Far more frustrating, however, was the fact that Warsaw wanted Nowa Huta, while "monumental," to be built on the cheap: "You can fool people with ideology," Ptaszycki supposedly fumed in private, "but to take away people's dreams of a comfortable home is criminal."[67] In fact, the architects were increasingly fighting a losing battle with cost cutting, which forced many of their visions into the filing cabinet.

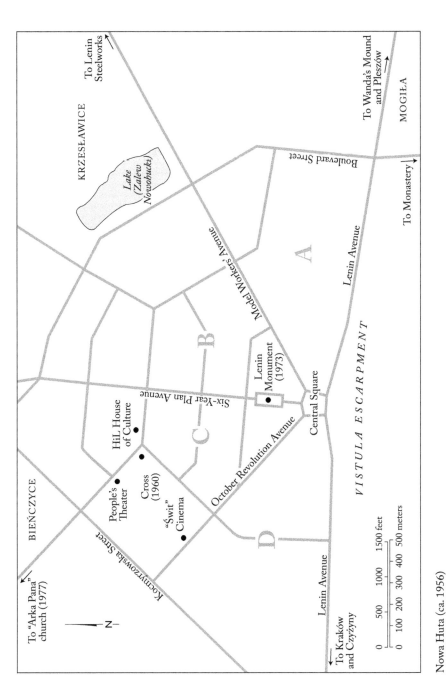

Nowa Huta (ca. 1956)

Miastoprojekt completed Nowa Huta's comprehensive plan in March 1951; it was confirmed by Warsaw in 1952. In 1954, the steelworks director Jan Anioła produced one of the best descriptions of the plan:

> The main axis of configuration is the line between the two most important centers: Central Square and Town Hall Square. Central Square is a giant pentagon, from which the main streets radiate outward—modern ones with a width of 55 meters. On the southern end, it is closed by a magnificent theater and on either side the impressive buildings of the Palace of Culture; the center of the square is filled with a patterned carpet of green, crowned by an obelisk. From Central Square we proceed via a wide street to Town Hall Square. Here a beautiful, harmoniously styled town hall with an 80-meter tower is projected. Around Town Hall Square are planned representative buildings designated as the seats of political, social, and youth organizations, administration and offices, the bank and court.
>
> Around the main axis particular settlements are laid out, which form to a certain extent autonomous organisms. Each settlement contains everything necessary for completely meeting the social needs of inhabitants. There are, therefore, shops, services, recreational centers, a school, preschool, daycare center, movie theater. Each settlement possesses its own common garage for private automobiles. Without leaving their own settlement, residents can fulfill all their daily needs. . . .
>
> Spreading out to the south of Central Square is the vast painterly landscape of the Park of Culture and Repose, leading down all the way to the Vistula. Among the wonderful greenery one will find here a massive sports stadium, gymnasia, and a man-made ice-skating rink. On the Vistula and near the man-made basins in its vicinity will be a marina and a large swimming pool.
>
> On the outskirts of town, low, two-story multifamily houses are being built. Moving through the three- and four-story houses of the settlements we come next to the multistory buildings of the city center and to the tall buildings, among which the slender tower of the town hall dominates—the town's highest point. The style of Nowa Huta's buildings links to the architecture of Kraków and the rich historical monuments of the area.

In Nowa Huta, Anioła echoed Ptaszycki, there would be "no division between rich districts and working-class penury; all people [would] have comfortable apartments and social services, enjoying sun and greenery."[68]

Anioła's description helps us to see why Nowa Huta has come to be called "the largest and most significant city in the history of European urbanism

The tram stop at the Lenin Steelworks, where thousands began their working day. Note the "Doge's Palace" (one of HiL's twin administrative buildings) with its faux-Renaissance details. Courtesy Muzeum Historyczne Miasta Krakowa.

to be based on the theory and practice of socialist realism."[69] With its semi-octagonal shape (also a feature of several contemporary Soviet new towns), Nowa Huta's plan stressed regularity and scale, symmetry and perspective;[70] emphasizing the importance of the town's administrative and cultural center through the progressively rising height of buildings, the planners created long, converging perspectives along wide boulevards, the better to add visual drama to mass rallies in its large central squares. Nowa Huta conformed to Stalinist theories stressing the city as a backdrop for political ritual; East German planner Lothar Bolz, for example, had attacked the Anglo-American concept of the "garden city," which allegedly had as its aim turning "the working man into a rabbit breeder or cauliflower planter, but under no circumstances a participant in political demonstrations."[71]

Architecturally, many buildings in Nowa Huta also offered a primer in socialist realist styles. In their decorativeness, classicism, and historicism, for

Shoppers inspect handmade goods at Cepelia on Central Square. Courtesy Muzeum Historyczne Miasta Krakowa.

example, HiL's two main administrative buildings, straddling the gates of the *kombinat*, are among the most fully realized examples of socialist realism in Poland. Popularly nicknamed the "Doge's Palace," their Renaissance-style attics, similar to those of the Cloth Merchants' Hall in Kraków, and their opulent interiors—fitted with marble, parquet, and chandeliers—made them seem like regal residences (if not for the people, then certainly for the so-called technical intelligentsia). Equally iconic, but less orthodox, are the Świt Cinema and the People's Theater; the latter, with "its squat massing, stripped down, flattened pilasters, expanses of unarticulated blank walls, and bizarre capitals on its columns," has been described as looking like "some strange Mannerist version of Stalinist architecture."[72] The pentagonal Central Square, one of the city's other recognizable landmarks, is marked by large colonnades around the periphery, first-story elevations of over four meters, and, according to critics, a vast, "dead" emptiness at its center used mainly as a transport hub.[73]

Nonetheless, the overwhelming impression created by Nowa Huta today is not (or not only) one of monumentality, but rather of contrast: contrast, that is, between those sections of the district built to Ptaszycki's plan and those added between the 1960s and the 1980s—the sprawling tracts of cheap, prefab high-rises with their "blind," windowless kitchens and reduced allocation of square meters per inhabitant.[74] By contrast, the so-called Old Huta can strike visitors with "the practicality and rationality of its urban plan, the graciousness and human scale of its architecture, and the greenness and intimacy of its neighborhoods," as one foreign scholar described it.[75] While Nowa Huta's aesthetics are not to everyone's taste, many inhabitants praise their neighborhoods or "settlements" (*osiedla*) for their green, open spaces and their apartments for their solid walls, high ceilings, and large windows; "living in Nowa Huta," writes one local enthusiast, "is like driving a Rolls Royce among the Trabants and Maluchs" (cheap cars produced in Communist East Germany and Poland).[76] No doubt they would argue that Ptaszycki's vision, echoing other, earlier dreams for a humane, egalitarian, forward-looking society, can still be felt pulsing beneath the surface of the district's façades—dreams for a city putting *technē* in the service of human needs.

Work in a New Tempo

In 1949, the socialist city could not wait for its architects. Developing the general plan would take time, and time was not a permissible luxury for those building socialism. Just as an extreme "sense of urgency" accompanied the completion of the First Five-Year Plan in the Soviet Union (1929–33), as Moshe Lewin writes, in Nowa Huta, too, "the pace imposed suggests a race against time, as if those responsible for the country's [or city's] destinies felt they were running out of history."[77] Echoing Kwiatkowski, "tempo" was the new keyword—*tempo warszawskie, tempo zetempowskie* (the "ZMP tempo," named for the volunteer youth brigades that took part in work on Nowa Huta). In May, work began on a railroad spur of the Kraków–Kocmyrzów branch to facilitate the transport of labor and materials to Nowa Huta; on June 23, excavation work began (despite the absence of a comprehensive city plan) on Nowa Huta's first settlements, A-0 (later "Wanda" and "Villa Settlements") and A-South ("Settlement on the Escarpment"). The houses were built using blueprints imported from Warsaw's Mariensztat district by Franciszek Adamski—two- to three-story, simple peaked-roof buildings in a park-like area. The effect was thus architecturally and spatially distinct from later settlements with their higher elevations, blocky shapes, interior entryways and enclosed green spaces. Like most of Nowa Huta's first apartment blocks, these were initially put to use as "worker's hotels," each one housing hundreds of construction workers in room after room of tightly packed iron bunk-beds.

The *kombinat* was to consist of eight divisions, some five hundred individual elements (or "objects") in all. During the first phase of building, comprising about two-thirds of all projected work and intended to last until 1954–55, basic productive divisions of the steelworks would be made partially or wholly operational; the second phase, lasting to 1958, would see completion of the remaining objects. Exploratory surveys commenced in September 1949 and construction work began in September 1950. At the end of that year, the Industrial Association for the Construction of Nowa Huta (Zjednocze-nie Przemysłowe Budowy Nowej Huty, or ZPBNH) was established as the main body responsible for building the *kombinat*, under the oversight of the ministries of metallurgy and industrial construction. Nowa Huta's first object, a workshop for steel construction at the repair division, was completed in December 1951. By summer 1954, construction was at its most intense, with work underway on five hundred objects by a workforce that peaked at 29,500 in June.[78]

On July 22, 1954—the ten-year anniversary of Poland's first postwar government—the first molten steel emerged from Blast Furnace Number 1 as hundreds of onlookers sang the patriotic anthem, "Jeszcze Polska nie zginęła" (Poland is not yet lost).[79] The furnace's ignition the day before had been attended by notables including the secretary of the Party Central Committee, the vice premier of the Council of Ministers, the ministers of metallurgy and industrial construction, and Soviet guests, including the steelworks' chief designer, Chryzant Dymitriewicz Zybin. In the accompanying radio broadcast, an experienced steelworker was asked to share his thoughts with listeners. Greeting his colleagues across the country, he spoke of being "moved by this great moment of launching this blast furnace, the likes of which does not exist anywhere else in Poland," adding, "It is all the more important for us because we are starting it up on the holiday of July 22, just as we promised."[80] To all appearances, it was indeed an occasion for celebrating the triumph of the "socialist tempo."

Some insiders, however, indicated doubts about the costs of this achievement. Signs that all was not well had been apparent to industry observers for some time; for example, the economic historian Aleksander Bocheński, then director of a brewery in Okocim, remembered that one of his most talented foremen returned only a few days after being recruited to Nowa Huta: "That's not work [in Nowa Huta]," he allegedly declared—"that's a botch up."[81] Around the same time that the nation was celebrating Nowa Huta's first production of raw steel, the journal *Industrial Construction* published two articles that openly discussed serious errors committed in building the steelworks. The first article was written by none other than the minister of industrial construction Czesław Bąbiński, while a second and more damaging one, entitled "On Mistakes in the Building of the Lenin Steelworks and Means for Their Elimination," was written by ZPBNH's director Michał Rojowski.[82]

Rojowski named several initial planning errors in Nowa Huta that had had far-reaching consequences. One had to do with a problem mentioned in almost all eyewitness descriptions of Nowa Huta in the 1950s: mud. Nowa Huta's soil was particularly loessic, or clayey; when wet, it turned into a glue-like morass capable of swallowing up workers' boots and stopping construction vehicles in their tracks. As Rojowski pointed out, this damaged vehicles and equipment, held up work, and demanded twice the physical effort from workers, costing untold sums in lowered morale. Planners ought to have taken the qualities of Nowa Huta's soil into account before construction began; a simple measure like leveling the terrain before building roads, thus making roads the highest (not, as they currently were, the lowest) points on the building site, would have kept them dry and prevented an enormous waste of resources.[83]

Rojowski ascribed such mistakes to "particularly acute" errors in coordination at the management level—such as when, in May 1953, intricately detailed timetables [*harmonogramy*] for work on the *kombinat* were developed before the arrival of technical blueprints from Moscow. The timetables, which rapidly became invalid, soon had to be entirely redone.[84] This kind of dissimultaneity was, in fact, rife on the construction site, as other reports also noted: one activist responsible for the work of youth brigades in Nowa Huta complained, for example, that "more than once it has been necessary [for the youth] to destroy whole walls, chimneys, or even to complete underground pipes and [then] start all over again from scratch, doubling the work and delaying the completion of the plan."[85] Mistakes such as these were not, as Rojowski delicately suggested, the result of ignorance, but rather an expression of the new Stalinist managerial ideology. Premised on the idea of building a shortcut out of backwardness, Stalinism valorized shortcuts in daily practice as well—"the knowing violation or circumvention of rules and procedures," as Stephen Kotkin puts it, "in the interest of 'getting the job done.'"[86] Hence the disregard, in Minc's words, for "all manifestations of conservatism and routine," for any conventional practice (such as holding up work to wait for necessary documentation) that might hold back the tempo of production.[87]

Successful completion of the Six-Year Plan was dependent, as its originators well knew, on many simultaneous improvements in efficiency, including technical advances. As Minc pointed out in 1950, completion of the Six-Year Plan would be inconceivable without increased mechanization, a point he illustrated with a quote from Stalin about trying to "empty the sea with a teaspoon."[88] Unfortunately, Poland lacked the foreign credit to import construction equipment, and in the initial phase of construction, Nowa Huta was built largely with shovels and, optimally, wheelbarrows; where there were no wheelbarrows, workers transported materials on their backs (hence the quip that Nowa Huta was built with the same technology as Kraków's fourteenth-century St. Mary's Church). More machines began to appear on the building site around 1954, but mechanization remained erratic. One engineer recalled using an assortment of cranes from France, Germany, Poland, UNRRA, and the Soviet Union, many of which lacked documentation; "people worked by feel" and hoped for the best.[89]

The constant shortages that were endemic to state socialist economies plagued production in Nowa Huta at all levels, including in supply of basic materials. Bricks, both the literal building blocks of Nowa Huta and the iconic symbol of "building socialism" (as depicted, for example, in Aleksander Kobzdej's socialist realist painting, "Pass the Brick"), were first imported from the ruined cities of the Western Territories. Later, they were produced on-site, but their quality was poor, and masons continually complained about having to work with "powdered bricks."[90] With deadlines ever looming and materials scarce, however, turning back supplies, however inferior, was not an option. Nor was refusing to work without proper safety equipment: the first workers at HiL wore wooden clogs and ordinary denim overalls that quickly caught fire from stray sparks. Accidents, sometimes fatal, were frequent: there were at least three work-related deaths in 1953, and two in the first four months of 1954 alone.[91]

Other problems arising from the "disproportions" of the Six-Year Plan were rife.[92] The shortage of skilled labor never abated throughout the period, while labor of every kind was hoarded by firms, leading to its irrational distribution.[93] The productivity of labor in the building trades—slated to rise by a minimum of 85 percent (as compared to 66 percent in industry as a whole)—was premised on the introduction of a piecework wage scale based on accurately calibrated norms.[94] As economists have shown, however, the maintenance of such a system of norms is extremely difficult, and worker dissatisfaction around norms and their recalibration was an ongoing source of labor conflict throughout the period.[95]

As the issue of norms indicates, underlying Stalinist industrialization were certain assumptions about the individual's productive contribution to socialism. Officially, dedication, innovation, and initiative were portrayed as fundamental characteristics of the new attitude to work in a socialist system. As one commentator put it, the "socialist style of work . . . requires from the technical personnel and workers a great contribution of independent initiative. Each assignment must be treated as important, and each deadline as utterly bind-ing."[96] Statements like these urged individuals to take personal responsibility for production in a system that was effectively dysfunctional, a requirement further propagated in practices like labor competition, thriftiness campaigns, and the so-called rationalization movement (encouraging workers to devise cost-saving production methods). As we shall later see, the costs of such in-dividualization were ultimately very high, both for individual workers and for the system as a whole.

And yet, for some "technical personnel" and workers, the "socialist style of work" offered opportunities as well as costs. The challenges of overcoming in-surmountable obstacles and beating impossible deadlines—spending, perhaps, upwards of thirty-six hours on the job when a deadline drew near, eating meals from a field kitchen on-site, barely sleeping—could become a source of pride and esprit de corps. Work at such moments, according to one engineer, was performed "with wholehearted enthusiasm and without bureaucracy."[97]

The absence of routine and established practice in the workplace and the consequent emphasis on flexibility and improvisation also removed some of the more traditional constraints on career advancement. One graduate from a technical high school, whose prior work experience amounted to a year in mechanics, was assigned a position normally requiring engineering qualifica-tions upon his arrival in Nowa Huta. When he protested that he was not an engineer, the personnel officer curtly retorted that he, too, was not an engineer, but someone would have to do the job. Later, when he applied for work at HiL, he was appointed assistant director of technical-economic planning on the basis of his supposed engineering background. Once again, his protests fell on deaf ears: "A person was needed and I would have to learn. . . . So I learned technical-economic planning" and, as he later reminisced (with more than a touch of irony), "the 'pioneering work' went on."[98]

Poland's First Socialist District

Despite the fact that foreign economists considered Poland's gains in steel production under the Six-Year Plan "very impressive,"[99] Polish specialists' ini-tial doubts about the scale of investment in Nowa Huta seemed borne out by evidence of waste, irrationality, and inefficiency. It was not simply a matter of trying to build too much, too fast: the inordinate demands of building Nowa Huta also exacerbated already existing weaknesses in the system. Nowa Huta neatly embodied inherent tensions in state socialism between what political economists call "accumulation" (of the means of production) and "distribution" (of its products): the steelworks represented accumulation (that is, of producer industries) and the city distribution (that is, of social goods). According to Katherine Verdery, state socialist regimes sought power through accumulation and legitimacy through distribution. The problem was, "Once a consumer got hold of something, the center no longer controlled it; [thus] central power was less served by giving things away than by producing things it could continue to control." Hence the tendency of regimes to favor accumulation, which, however, created more shortages (both for producers and consumers) and undermined legitimacy.[100]

In Nowa Huta, everyone knew that accumulation (namely, the steelworks) was Warsaw's top priority; the rest (housing, cultural, and recreational facilities) was mere distribution, second in line for resources.[101] This did not change even after the Six-Year Plan was adjusted in 1954 to increase investment in consumer goods;[102] on the contrary, the cost-cutting so keenly felt by Ptaszycki only increased. Stalin died in March 1953; we can only speculate to what extent de-Stalinization motivated Warsaw's announcement that much of Nowa Huta's general plan was to be scrapped. The large theater and two buildings of the House of Culture that were supposed to flank it, closing off the southern end of Central Square, were eliminated on the basis of "unconvincing aesthetic and compositional considerations."[103] Ostensible concerns about flight lines into the small airport at Czyżyny motivated the cancellation of a tall obelisk planned for Central Square. The entire ensemble of administrative buildings on Town Hall Square, including the large Town Hall itself, was also eliminated. It was now no longer necessary, it could be argued, because Nowa Huta had been administratively annexed to Kraków in 1951.

It was also "the time of cost cutting" in construction techniques, of ersatz materials and lowered standards: stone facing on façades was replaced with plaster; only one in three apartments would have a balcony; elevators were eliminated; the number of washbasins was reduced; parquet floors were eliminated for some settlements.[104] "In conception palaces," as one critic writes, "and in reality a dormitory for the working class—unfulfilled dreams of a beautiful city. That is Nowa Huta today."[105]

The full extent of the gap between planners' visions and final outcomes in Nowa Huta became apparent only recently, thanks to two exhibitions at the Museum of Kraków–Nowa Huta drawing liberally on blueprints and drawings long hidden from view. Especially after 1956, when they were liberated from the constraints of social realism, Miastoprojekt's architects and designers continued to put forward new ideas for Nowa Huta's development, but most remained on paper only.[106] The exhibits demonstrated that Nowa Huta had been an important teaching laboratory and workshop—for example, in interior design: photographs of interiors demolished long ago, like those of Nowa Huta's first post office and the Giant restaurant, illustrated innovative efforts to bring design to the masses, and showed continuities with interwar Polish design traditions. A fully resurgent modernism, meanwhile, returned to Nowa Huta in 1957 with the completion of Settlement B-32 (or "Glass Houses," in homage to Żeromski) by Janusz and Marta Ingarden: the settlement's sleek commercial interiors, fittingly, housed a motorcycle shop and a branch of the Orbis travel agency, suited to their streamlined international style.[107] Nowa Huta and the seeming possibilities it offered continued to fire the imagination of Polish architects and designers, independent of Stalinism as a political or aesthetic movement. Perhaps some of these unrealized plans may yet, as Stanisław Juchnowicz puts it, "play an educational and inspirational role, helping in the process of making decisions" about Nowa Huta's future.[108]

Writing of Nowa Huta's history of antiregime protest after 1956, one commentator concluded that "it is not possible to build something torn asunder from national traditions."[109] This chapter has shown the statement to be equally valid for Nowa Huta in the period prior to 1956. From the outset, plans for Nowa Huta were shaped by powerful traditions of Polish economic, social, and national thought emanating from the nineteenth century and the early part of the twentieth, and by models of interwar urbanism and etatism. Between the end of the war in 1944 and the onset of Stalinism in 1948, planning for Nowa Huta continued more or less along tracks laid down by Eugeniusz Kwiatkowski immediately before the war and elaborated during the war in underground planning workshops. The onset of Stalinism represented a sudden change in course, with the Soviets exercising direct decision-making power in key areas. Nonetheless, even during this phase, individuals and groups steeped in earlier traditions attempted to realize their visions within Stalinism's constraints.

Those constraints were felt unevenly. On the one hand, the Soviets (perhaps even Stalin himself) intervened heavy-handedly where Nowa Huta's size and location were concerned, and blueprints for the steelworks came straight from Moscow. On the other hand, political control was more diffuse in the sphere of urban planning and architecture. Ptaszycki's surviving collaborators insist they treated Warsaw's intervention as an unfortunate annoyance to be circumvented, and that Ptaszycki succeeded in carving out a space for maneuver in which core professional and cultural values could be preserved. Nowa Huta's planning professionals perceived their own behavior in terms of what Polish socialists label "*przystosowanie się*," or "adaptation"[110]—pragmatically conforming to external political constraints without internalizing the prevailing value system. The extent to which they succeeded lies in the eyes of the beholder.

More broadly, Sovietization offered no blueprint for how Nowa Huta's physical environment should shape the human material to be transformed into socialism's vanguard proletarian class. Indeed, Polish Communists never seemed to show much utopian verve. In his study of Warsaw housing, David Crowley notes that President Bolesław Bierut's description of the "socialist home" as "comfortable, sunny, dry, aesthetic and adequately heated" was "hardly shot through with ideological elixir."[111] Similarly, Polish political leaders were apparently unable or unwilling to articulate visions of socialist urbanism. It was architects, in the end, who promoted ambitious visions of Poland's first socialist city, ones Warsaw ultimately showed little enthusiasm for funding. The 1951 decision to annex Nowa Huta to Kraków also raises questions about Warsaw's taste for radical social engineering: where was the ideological elixir, after all, in the notion of Poland's "first socialist district"? In the center's overwhelming preference for accumulation over distribution, the Polish regime shared more with economist Kwiatkowski's interwar aspirations for economic and military development than with novelist Żeromski's dreams of shining glass houses for the people. The radical concept of Nowa Huta as a new kind of urban entity, a self-contained and self-governing proletarian city, was unceremoniously dropped like the hot potato it was.

In conclusion, the case of Nowa Huta suggests that liberal critiques have exaggerated the supposedly hyperrational, hyperlinear relationship between plan and practice in totalitarian regimes. Karl Popper famously argued that adherents of utopianism must respond to any unorthodox divergence from the "blueprint" with violence. (A blueprint, even more than a plan, provides a highly detailed map of the desired end result, offering little scope for alteration or improvisation.)[112] More recently, James Scott has identified new towns like Brasília as examples of "authoritarian high modernism," an ideology and practice of power characterized by a commitment to making reality fit the plan, rather than vice versa.[113] But what was the actual relationship between planning and practice in postwar Eastern Europe? How did contemporaries themselves conceive of the relationship between blueprints and outcomes?

Pace the economic historian Aleksander Bocheński's claim that "the plan was everything" under Stalinism, in Nowa Huta planning (defined as a form of rational decision-making, a "sequence of acts which are mutually related as means" toward specified ends) was honored as much in the breach as the observance.[114] Much work was unplanned, starting before plans were ready; many blueprints—including much of Miastoprojekt's general plan—were unrealized. (Ptaszycki, meanwhile, is said to have insisted "that a city must be drawn [by hand], and can't be counted out by centimeters.")[115] In any system, plans are fragile things, as Anne Mosher points out, and visions more so. But according to the cultural theorist Vladimir Paperny, "paper architecture" (unrealized designs), "the uninterrupted demolition of architectural construction," and "construction according to continually changing projects" were defining features of Stalinism.[116] In conforming to such a pattern, the case of Nowa Huta suggests the need for a more nuanced understanding of the multiple functions—political, cultural, and ideological—of planning in state socialism.

How, for example, did the saturation of public discourse with constant references to plans and planning (particularly under Stalinism) affect the dynamics of planning itself? What was the effect of rhetoric linking each worker's individual contribution to the overall completion of planning goals? In this sense, it may be that Nowa Huta's builders and inhabitants lived planning in a way that was extreme but also typical of many East Europeans' encounter with "Stalinism as a civilization." One way to understand the narrative of subsequent chapters is as an exploration of moments when planning escaped bureaucrats, economists, and architects and entered onto the plane of social conflict and negotiation, and of demands by Nowa Huta's builders and inhabitants to participate in the planning, broadly conceived, of their city.

2

New Men

Aﬀter World War II, Poland was a country on the move. Between 1939 and 1950, some one in four Poles changed his or her place of residence.[1] During the war, millions had been deported or displaced; after the war, those who returned were joined by millions more fleeing territories ceded to the Soviet Union under the Potsdam agreement, which shifted Polish borders hundreds of miles to the west. By 1945, some 5 million surviving inhabitants of interwar Poland—roughly 20 percent of the prewar population—found themselves outside Poland's new borders.[2] The movement of these groups back into Polish territory was counterbalanced by the expulsion of more than 5 million ethnic Germans from the newly acquired "Recovered" (or Western) Territories acquired from the former Reich.[3] Poland's experience was not, of course, unique: the aftershocks of Hitler's attempt to redraw the map of Europe turned its central and eastern regions into a vast transit camp. Waves of ethnic cleansing, sanctioned by the victorious Allies, swelled the numbers of camp survivors, displaced persons, POWs, and exiles who crisscrossed Europe, either returning to or fleeing from their prewar homes.

Historians have conventionally assumed that the traumatic upheavals of World War II induced a craving for normalcy among most Europeans—a desire for domesticity, traditional gender roles, stability, and, above all, peace.[4] And yet sometimes a stone set in motion continues to roll. World War II had forced millions of ordinary people to leave their homes as soldiers, prisoners, or slave laborers, including many from isolated rural areas who otherwise might not have left their villages. Although their wartime exposure to a wider world had often been compulsory and far from pleasant, this did not necessarily make it easier to settle down again at home with the return to "normalcy."

Edmund Chmieliński, for example, came from a poor village in the Przasnysz district, a tiny hamlet without electricity or plumbing. Shortly after the occupation began, Chmieliński's family's farm had been seized by the

Germans. In 1944 when Chmieliński was eleven, his father was killed and he himself was sent to work as a slave laborer on a German farm. Chmieliński escaped when the front approached and returned to his mother and siblings; they reclaimed their farm at the war's end, but it was devastated—livestock dead, equipment ruined. Chmieliński was thus forced to work as a herdsboy for other peasants in the village. Chmieliński later remembered this time with bitterness. Comparing his Polish employers to the Germans who had held him in captivity, Chmieliński considered himself now a slave in his own country, subjected to beatings and forbidden to eat or sleep in the house—a privilege granted even the family's dog.[5] Chmieliński was especially bitter about not being able to complete his schooling, which had been (as for so many of his generation) interrupted by the war. Every spring, he had to quit school to go to work in the fields while his employers' children continued their studies. The entire world of the village seemed poised against him. The better-off children teased and bullied him while the teacher (another of Chmieliński's employers) turned a blind eye, and the village priest told him, essentially, to accept his station and be grateful.[6]

But then everything changed: at the age of seventeen, Chmieliński heard of a youth brigade headed for work in the new town of Nowa Huta, and he instantly resolved to volunteer. As he later wrote, "I wanted to live and work like a human being, to be treated the same as others and not like an animal. . . . There was no force or might that could keep me in the village that I hated so much." This chapter explores what happened to Chmieliński and thousands like him as they left the countryside for the "great building site of socialism." Considering both the push of the Polish village after World War II and the pull of what migrants imagined Nowa Huta to be, it asks what happened when imagination and reality collided under the impact of Stalinist industrialization in the 1950s.

The vast majority of migrants to Nowa Huta, like Chmieliński, were under thirty and rural in origin. About 40 percent of those who passed through Nowa Huta between 1950 and 1960 settled there, working in the factories and living in the apartment buildings they had, on occasion, built with their own hands.[7] In later years, Nowa Huta would provide the stability that, according to the "normalcy" theory, postwar Europeans sought. But in the town's first half-decade, Nowa Huta's attraction was something else: chaotic, unfinished, at times anarchic, Nowa Huta was, as one sociological study put it, a "synonym of the 'wider world,' of something completely different from the landscape of their birthplace, of another life."[8]

This chapter demonstrates that, for Chmieliński and other rural migrants like him, Nowa Huta represented a glittering mirage of modernity. The fact that newcomers would face any number of hardships and trials in the new town did not, ultimately, change this. Even though the harsh realities of daily life in Nowa Huta were a far cry from what many urbanized Poles considered a bare minimum of civilization, Nowa Huta offered an environment that was supremely modern in two senses. First, its newness meant freedom from the ascribed status of region, family, and caste; on Nowa Huta's anonymous streets, newcomers fashioned new identities through their choice of career, friendship, ideology, fashions, or preferred music—or through the very fact of living and working in Nowa Huta itself. Second, migration to Nowa Huta offered hopes of civic enfranchisement for rural Poles who historically had been politically and economically marginalized. Through their collective participation in "building socialism," Nowa Huta's pioneers claimed their place in a national struggle to liberate Poland from poverty and backwardness—just as in the past, nobles had fought to liberate their country from foreign domination. Nowohucians' pride in the "little fatherland" they would build on the banks of the Vistula was part, in this sense, of a broader patriotism.

Leaving Home

Poland's cities had been especially hard hit by World War II. City dwellers had disproportionately lost their lives in the occupation: almost 80 percent of Poland's wartime fatalities were among this group. Overall, occupation, genocide, and ethnic cleansing had caused a 50 percent decline in the urban population. But these losses would be made up in the war's aftermath by 1.5 million newcomers from rural areas.[9] In addition, hundreds of thousands of Poles flocked to the Western Territories (some 817,000 had already done so by the end of 1945), taking the place of German expellees in cities like Gdańsk, Szczecin, or Wrocław. By 1950, the urbanized share of Poland's total population (36.9 percent) had not only reached, but slightly exceeded prewar levels, owing mainly to rural-to-urban migration.[10] In a country (and region) where the peasant masses had long been seen by urban elites as a lower order of civilization, this demographic upheaval constituted a real social revolution.

Which of these wandering souls made their way to Nowa Huta, and how? Between two-thirds and three-quarters of those who settled in Nowa Huta were rural migrants fresh from the village, overwhelmingly from Kraków province and those neighboring it.[11] The remainder generally fell into one of two groups: intellectual workers (that is, specialists such as architects and engineers, managers, political activists, or cultural workers) and skilled manual workers. Recruitment of the first category to Nowa Huta was conducted by relevant ministries in Warsaw or central offices of political organizations like the Union of Polish Youth (*Związek Młodzieży Polskiej*, or ZMP).[12] This was the group most likely to come involuntarily to Nowa Huta: university graduates, especially those with degrees in fields like engineering, were in high demand because of the postwar shortage of skilled personnel and would sometimes receive work orders to Nowa Huta upon completing their degrees.[13] Some skilled professionals, however, chose work in Nowa Huta. This was often based on a simple calculus: an extreme housing shortage throughout Poland made the prospect of finding an apartment in one of Nowa Huta's new buildings alluring. As one newcomer (arriving in 1953) remembered, "I came to Nowa Huta because I heard that [here] one could most easily find work and an apartment."[14]

Skilled manual workers were also highly sought after by Nowa Huta's employers. While some had roots in the prewar urban working class, this group was in the minority; many more had been living in villages in 1939 but had acquired qualifications either as forced laborers in German factories during the war, as migrants to the Western Territories, or as refugees in the West. Their reasons for coming to Nowa Huta were varied. Some were put off by harsh conditions in the Western Territories and saw Nowa Huta as a chance to return "to Poland."[15] Direct recruitment (usually involving the promise of an apartment in one of the new blocks) could also be used to lure highly skilled workers to Nowa Huta, particularly from the steel centers of Silesia.[16]

In other cases, skilled or white-collar workers came to Nowa Huta as a refuge from political persecution. Journalist Dorota Gut's father, a grinder in the Western Territories, had been accused of sabotage when the machine he was working on broke down. Under investigation by the secret police, he fled to Nowa Huta, where he rightly guessed he would be able to lose himself in the crowds of newcomers.[17] The artist Elżbieta Borysławska's family moved to Nowa Huta after her father was imprisoned on political charges. Pregnant and evicted from the family's apartment in Kraków, Borysławska's mother found a bookkeeping job and one room with a kitchen in Settlement B-32. When her father was finally amnestied in 1956, this was the home he returned to. "Every place that exists," Borysławska reminds us, "has its painful secrets."[18]

For the majority of migrants, however, the path to Nowa Huta was more straightforward. They were motivated by a desire to gain skills, housing, or cash, or to escape boredom, marginalization, and the back-breaking toil of farmwork. They came as recruits to one of the youth brigades or, more often, simply by turning up, tattered bundle of possessions in hand, at one of the new town's employment offices. They first learned about the new town from the radio, in school, from posters, from their local youth organization, or from friends who had gone before them. "The poster spoke of the possibility of getting work in Nowa Huta and advancing one's studies at the same time," wrote one man who came to Nowa Huta in 1951, adding: "To be sure, I'd heard of Nowa Huta in school and on the radio, that it was the biggest investment of the Six-Year Plan, but still I couldn't really picture it."[19] Another, recently demobilized from the army, made some quick calculations:

> Obviously I was a bachelor, so it was a question of honor to be well dressed and have some change in my pocket. Of course, there's work enough in the village, but the money. . . . I think to myself that I've completed the third year of mechanics high school so maybe I could find some suitable work, moreover one must think seriously already about the future, about a house and a bit of property for a wife. Without thinking very much about it, I betook myself to Nowa Huta. . . . Already at that time a lot of friends from my village were working in Nowa Huta and boasted that the wages were good, and that's what interested me.[20]

Others were driven to Nowa Huta by boredom. For Kazimierz D., a feeling of unbearable restlessness overtook him upon completing his army service: "The lack of activity [in the village] put me at my wits' end," he wrote. He made his way to Nowa Huta in 1953.[21] An autobiographer who went by the pseudonym of "Elf" admitted "a kind of inborn disgust for work in the fields. . . . I persuaded myself that I had to go out into the world," he wrote. "I wanted to go to the city at any price."[22]

The world of the village that these rural migrants left behind was, in many ways, a world apart, isolated economically, politically, and culturally from urban Poland. Long after the withering away of feudalism in Western Europe, the East European peasantry remained locked in personal servitude to the nobility, bound to the land, burdened by service obligations, and subject to their lords' jurisdiction. Peasants were excluded from the early modern *natio*—those of "birth" (hence the word "nation"), or nobles, who claimed the privilege to govern. Only after Poland's partition by Austria, Prussia, and Russia in the eighteenth century did some Polish reformers argue that emancipating the peasantry was essential to creating a united modern nation, one capable of defending Polish sovereignty. However, the Constitution of 1791—which guaranteed, among other things, freedom of speech and religion—upheld feudal privileges, denying civic equality to some 85 to 90 percent of the population.

It was thus left to the partitioning powers to emancipate Polish peasants in the second half of the nineteenth century. Legal equality did not, however, address the peasants' economic woes, above all increasing land hunger. This problem was especially acute in the south and the east; in the Austro-Hungarian province of Galicia, an area that would later contribute large numbers of migrants to Nowa Huta, the average size of peasant plots decreased from 10 morgens of land in 1850 to 4.5 morgens in 1898.[23] As Polish cities became more modern, moreover, the gap between urban and rural life only widened. By 1919, when Poland recovered its independence, and despite a new constitution guaranteeing universal manhood suffrage, society remained deeply divided. As one observer put it, "Two closed worlds lived side by side: haves and have-nots [*góra i doły*]."[24] Compared to his or her French counterpart, the interwar Polish peasant had less than half of the sugar, one-twentieth of the coffee, half of the coal, and a third of the cotton cloth.[25] But the gap between the "two Polands" was not determined only by material differences. It was bolstered by a sense of almost racial otherness, and by deep-seated attitudes of scorn and mistrust: well into the twentieth century, the categories "peasant" and "gentry" constituted a "status and self-concept [that] were not easily eroded."[26]

The Second World War both deepened the Polish peasantry's plight and heightened its importance for national survival: the countryside would have to be the source of the nation's regeneration. But even if rural Poles had fared comparatively better than their urban counterparts, the peasantry had also been both physically and psychologically ravaged by the war. The American journalist Edward S. Kerstein described his impressions of a village he passed through en route to Szczecin from Warsaw in 1947, noting that when his car pulled up, the village children ran away screaming, thinking that the visitors were yet another invading army:

> I closely scrutinized the clothes of the peasants and found them to be ragged. Many of the peasants were in bare feet. The shoes worn by the others were all hand made and old. . . . The row of peasant huts stood in sharp contrast to the landowner's fine, white brick and frame mansion. These peasants' huts were frail and small. The floors were either of a thin layer of cement or hard clay. The peasants' sanitation facilities were near nil, and their furniture was homemade. The beds had no mattresses. The peasants slept on heaps of straw with worn-out sheets over it.[27]

A mission from the United Nations Food and Agriculture Organization reported in 1947 that "food, agricultural, and forestry conditions in Poland are in a state of emergency";[28] Poland's total agricultural production in 1946 amounted to only two-thirds of its value in 1937.[29] Land reform was one of the first items on the new government's agenda, but the reform of September 1944 varied in effectiveness from one region to another. In eastern and southeastern Poland, where land hunger was greatest, the reforms tended to create new plots of only two or three hectares[30]—"too large to be buried in, and too small to live on," as the saying went.[31]

At the onset of Stalinism, rural society was in a state of flux. An estimated 50 to 60 percent of inherited farms had undergone expropriation by the occupiers, war damage, or land reform since 1939. Approximately 305,000 farms were in new hands; in many villages, the wheel of fortune had turned, new forms of social differentiation had emerged, and communal tensions were running high.[32] New farmers—formerly landless peasants who had been granted smallholdings under the reforms—often experienced difficulties starting up and tended to be worse off than those long established on their land. Many resented the better-off peasants and the traditional mindset linking social status to the value and size of one's holdings. Tensions also sometimes arose between locals and refugees.[33] In other words, romantic visions of village society—as solidaristic, organic, and stable—if ever accurate, certainly did not apply in a countryside reeling from the impact of total war.

The experiences of Edmund Chmieliński, with whose story we began earlier, illustrate many of the destabilizing effects of wartime upheaval on postwar rural society. His family was one of those whose fortunes had plummeted while others' had risen during and after the war, and this might help explain his acute sensitivity to the perceived injustices in village society.[34] Chmieliński's story also suggests that breaking free of that society's bonds and obligations was no simple matter. It was Chmieliński's uncle, an organizer for a local chapter of the Communist youth association, who brought him news of the brigade and the new city near Kraków. But his mother begged him not to go, "[wringing] her hands and [crying] to God." When Chmieliński insisted on leaving, she cursed her son, hoping he would "break his neck and both legs" on the journey. For Chmieliński and others like him, leaving the village marked a dramatic break from family and community and a great leap into the unknown. It was often the first time they had defied parental wishes and, by extension, the entire social code of rural life. In such cases, the desire to escape the confines of the village and seek out something new and better was overwhelming.

As Chmieliński's story demonstrates, the push of the village as a motivating force could be as strong as, or even stronger than, the pull of Nowa

Recreation on the building site. A merry-go-round in Settlement B-32, 1950s. Collection of T. Binek.

Huta (which, in any case, was a fairly abstract concept for most of the young people described here). As with all great waves of migration, economic conditions at home were a primary cause for seeking out one's fortune in Nowa Huta. But economic motivations always have a cultural dimension, and in this case, they were intimately bound up with a sense of what was wrong with rural life. Young people, especially, were all too aware of their limited opportunities in the village. Looking into the future, they saw a life of relentless drudgery and cultural marginalization and found the prospect intolerable.

Meanwhile, like any big city beckoning to the provincial, small-town boy or girl, Nowa Huta held out the chance of a new beginning—of anonymity, freedom, adventure, and limitless possibilities. Few, however, could understand what awaited them. "I didn't consider the fact that I'd be participating in a great endeavor such as history has never known, or what Nowa Huta would become," wrote Edmund Chmieliński. "I didn't know then that work building Nowa Huta would be still harder, more backbreaking and dangerous, and life in the brigade no bed of roses."[35]

Human Steel

For those who, like Chmieliński, could not even afford a third-class rail ticket to Kraków, Universal Organization "Service to Poland" (*Powszechna Organizacja "Służba Polsce,"* or SP) offered a ticket out of the village and into the great unknown. The widely publicized role of SP labor battalions in Nowa Huta, who allegedly dug the first shovelfuls of earth at the construction site, helped to cement the propagandistic linkage between Polish youth and "building socialism." Media images of Nowa Huta were conspicuously populated by brigade members, or "*junacy,*" lean, raffish teenagers in khaki uniforms and red ties energetically carting earth away or laying bricks. Nowa Huta's moniker "city of youth" was embodied by these young volunteers and suggested the dynamism and growth that the new regime wished to project onto a country rising from the ashes of World War II. The writer Marian Brandys elaborated on this connection by arguing that Nowa Huta's youth was to be considered "the most precious raw material of the Six-Year Plan," whom the party would "purify on this great building site of all friable alloys and process into refined, stainless human steel."[36]

The inseparable partnering of youth and Nowa Huta in the socialist realist idiom was a legacy of Lenin's belief in youth as the natural ally of revolution.[37] For Polish Communists after World War II, like Bolsheviks after the civil war, youth held the key to national rebirth. According to the text of one educational "chat" for young people, sport and physical education were especially important for young Poles after the enfeebling effects of the Nazi occupation: "We were forced through several years to live in the worst conditions, working often beyond our strength, eating whatever was at hand, and deprived, moreover, of proper medical care by the occupier. A large section of the population's health was weakened by being in prisons or concentration camps or from wandering through the forests. In addition, the Nazis intentionally tried to destroy our youth, encouraging them to use alcohol, smoke cigarettes, etc."[38] Over two million children had lost one or both parents;[39] thousands of underaged combatants had fought in the resistance; and untold numbers of young people had witnessed unspeakable violence at close range. Schools had been closed during the war, but "everyday life taught that that which before [the war] was good was now bad, and vice versa."[40]

The official response to this crisis came in 1948 with the creation of a national service corps for youth aimed at binding "the broadest mass of youth with the new Polish reality, rooting them in the new relationship with work, [and] strengthening their conscious social discipline," as articulated in a proposal put before the Sejm. Placed under the ideological leadership of the

ZMP, which was modeled on the Komsomol and envisaged as an elite organization for the most politically active and committed youth, SP was intended to reach the remaining 3.2 million unaffiliated Poles between the ages of fifteen and twenty-five. At a time when only half a million young people were enrolled in secondary or vocational schools, SP was to propagate its message about the "new reality" to this crucial constituency.[41]

From the outset, then, there was no question about the ideological purposes for which SP was intended. The reality, however, was more complicated. Spontaneous youth labor brigades had first sprung up just after the war when former resistance leaders had gathered groups of orphans and young demobilized partisans to help with reconstruction efforts. The brigades provided needy young people with food, clothes, a place to sleep, and sometimes the chance to continue their schooling.[42] These early groupings provided a template for activists like Feliks Białkowski, a former army officer and official in the new government's Office for Physical Education and Military Training. Białkowski, who had organized a custodial brigade for homeless youth on the Baltic Coast in 1948 before working in Nowa Huta as a cultural instructor, felt that SP's custodial mandate remained more important than its indoctrination function, even in the new town; in Nowa Huta, he later remembered, SP brigades sometimes provided a home for young people who had nowhere else to go.[43]

Warsaw, in fact, complained that SP was not successfully fulfilling its ideological function; allegedly compromised by the presence of so many pre–World War II military officers among its cadres, SP was criticized by the Politburo as early as 1950 for its "right-nationalist tendencies." SP was dissolved as high Stalinism waned in 1955, mandatory conscription having been abandoned two years earlier. In the end, SP's effect at the national level was probably minimal: although, in theory, every Pole between the ages of sixteen and twenty-one was obliged to serve two months in the organization (exceptions were made for married or pregnant women, family breadwinners, and other categories), only 30 to 40 percent of those eligible to serve ever did so.[44] Its impact in the sphere of propaganda, on the other hand, was enormous. While SP lasted, its *junacy* (singular: *junak*) were to be found at work on many of the Six-Year Plan's largest projects—building shipyards in Gdańsk and Szczecin, car factories in Warsaw and Lublin, chemical plants in Silesia, and, above all, the town and *kombinat* of Nowa Huta.

The "special relationship" between Nowa Huta and youth dated to January 1949, when the Organizational Bureau of the Party Central Committee had stipulated that one large investment should be designated as a "banner assignment for Polish youth," under the oversight of the ZMP. With the official decision to build Nowa Huta in February, Poland's first "socialist city" became the obvious choice. Nowa Huta was therefore most often portrayed in propaganda and recruitment materials as a pedagogical project—both in the practical sense (as a kind of giant vocational school offering training for all) and also, more abstractly, as a site of personal formation and transformation. As Marian Brandys enthused, "It was wonderful, beautiful, and wise that in Nowa Huta, along with the walls, arose new people. . . . People raised the walls. The walls raised with them people. That was Nowa Huta."[45]

In May, the first three-year ZMP brigades (the 51st, 52nd, and 53rd) were formed to work in Nowa Huta, along with nine SP brigades. On July 28, 1949, the 60th SP Brigade completed the first work by *junacy* on Nowa Huta's terrain, scything about a hectare of wheat. The mythology of the youth brigades' pioneering role worked its way into one former *junak*'s recollection of the speech given by his brigade leader before their first day of work: his troop was reminded that they were about to build the biggest steelworks in Poland, and perhaps in all of Europe. "*Junacy!*," he exhorted, "You are the first, the ones to dig the first foundations for the apartment buildings in which you and the first workers will live. So be proud that this honor fell to you! History will write about you! Don't spare any effort for the good of your country! Show what you're capable of!"[46] Later, the 60th was credited with completing the first finished object in Nowa Huta, an apartment building in Settlement A-1. It was put to use as a workers' hostel; its first inhabitants were the *junacy* themselves. Similar achievements by *junacy* were widely publicized, for example, those of the 37th SP Brigade, which was credited with completing the foundations for the *kombinat*'s first blast furnace in just a month and a half, well ahead of schedule.[47] Such brigades were formed with the explicit intent of training youth for future work in the *kombinat* or elsewhere in Nowa Huta,[48] and volunteers were recruited with slogans like "*Służba Polsce* is the new school for life" or, "If you want to acquire professional training, enquire at your SP command post—they'll help you."[49]

Throughout 1949 and 1950, further brigades were organized in Nowa Huta with the arrival of new recruits, as well as two-week summer brigades of high school and university students.[50] By 1950, these seasonal brigades comprised more than 8,000 *junacy*,[51] and in April of that same year, 2,169 volunteers were employed in the three-year ZMP brigades. The origins of recruits were overwhelmingly poor and rural: in one brigade, 55.9 percent of the young men were identified as being of a working-class background, which in this case largely meant farmhands and agricultural laborers; another 34.4 percent were from peasant families with small or medium-sized holdings; while the remainder were listed as "wealthy," "working intelligentsia," or "other."[52] In one brigade, around 80 percent of the recruits had lice; 7 percent were unfit to serve on health grounds.[53] Fewer than 2 percent of new members in one brigade had completed more than seven years of schooling.[54] Nowa Huta's *junacy* hailed very substantially from the bottom rungs of society.

One of them was Edmund Chmieliński, who arrived at the SP camp dressed in shabby clothes and wooden clogs. For him, as for many new arrivals, the unquestioned highlight of induction into the brigade was being issued his SP uniform—a khaki shirt and trousers with military-style cap and red tie, which was by consensus "truly smart."[55] After a haircut, a medical exam, and his first shower, Chmieliński burned his old clothes—marking the break with his old life.[56] He felt transformed: "Sometimes I looked at myself furtively in the mirror," he remembered. "I couldn't get over how different I now appeared." Chmieliński also savored his first meal in the brigade, a piece of *kiełbasa*, and approvingly noted that portions were weighed out equally for everyone. Wearing the same clothes, eating the same food, and sharing the same quarters, he recalled, "all of us [in the brigade] were equal." For the first time, Chmieliński writes, he fell asleep "completely happy."[57]

As we know from high desertion rates, however, not all new recruits reacted to their first days in the brigade like Chmieliński. To stem these losses (sometimes as high as 20 percent), brigade leaders engaged in targeted "chats" with newly arrived *junacy* to raise morale.[58] More than the difficult living conditions (tents or barracks, mud, cold) or monotonous diet (no fruits or vegetables), a major cause of desertion seems to have been the initial lack of vocational training courses and the nature of the work itself. "There prevailed a great dissatisfaction," remembered one former *junak*. "Everything was promised us at the time of signing up—that there'd be some kind of schools, that we'd be able to choose our profession, etc. In reality it turned out these were fairy tales for well-behaved children. Outside of work and the movies once a week, there was nothing. Boredom and no point to it all."[59] Brigade commanders noted with exasperation that recruiters had promised prospective *junacy* they could study forestry, haberdashery, radio mechanics, watchmaking, and even pastry making in Nowa Huta.[60] Upon their arrival, newcomers quickly learned the absurdity of such promises: work for most of them would be grueling physical labor on the largely unmechanized construction site.

Still, most stayed. Elf's friend, for one, was embarrassed to return home because his head had been shaved for lice.[61] Chmieliński decided to stay after his first meal in the brigade, a "dream come true": "for the first time in my life, I became sick from overeating."[62] The old rags had been burned, the mother's curses resounded, and turning back was out of the question. Besides, however bad it was in Nowa Huta, things could always—indeed, could only—get better.

City of Mud

Nowa Huta's population continued to grow rapidly: from 16,000 in 1950, to 90,000 in 1957, to 100,000 in 1960.[63] The typical profile of the newcomer was young, male, and rural-born;[64] by 1955 only a little under one-third of those living in Nowa Huta were women.[65] About a third of the population was under the age of eighteen, and almost another half was between the ages of eighteen and forty-nine.[66] In August 1950, eighteen state firms were employed in building Nowa Huta, and were responsible for everything from laying rails to installing blast furnaces; together they employed 18,479 people, of whom about 1,700 were intellectual, or white-collar, workers and another 5,000 were members of *Służba Polsce* brigades.[67] Until mid-decade, almost everyone who worked in Nowa Huta was engaged in construction; gradually, however, the Lenin Steelworks took over from the state construction firms as the single largest employer. In 1954, 68 percent of employees at the Lenin Steelworks were classified as youth; 47 percent were of peasant origin.[68]

Until at least the mid-1950s, those arriving in Nowa Huta for the first time were often surprised by its physical appearance, its changing but always anomalous landscape. Those who arrived in 1949–50 were in for the biggest surprise: anticipating a "great socialist city" and massive steelworks, they found an all-too-familiar landscape of fields, orchards, and peasant huts.[69] In 1950, for instance, Szczepan Brzeziński arrived in Kraków *en route* to Nowa Huta. Unable to squeeze himself onto the overcrowded bus bound for the new town, he decided to make the 7 kilometer journey on foot. After hours of slogging along country roads, his spirits rose when he glimpsed a red banner in the distance. On it was written "Nowa Huta" in large letters; but as he approached, he saw that it stood alone in a vast expanse of fields. It was another kilometer before he reached the next sign of development, a worker's hostel in a converted prewar cigarette factory hall, also surrounded by farmland.[70] Another newcomer remembered that his first impression of the new town was of peasant cottages in Mogiła "painted a sun-bleached turquoise. . . . Ripe fruit: pears, apples, plums, leaned over beds of flowers. . . . The gardens were almost empty; only clay pots hanging on the fences gave a hint that people were living here."[71]

Edmund Chmieliński had never seen a town, let alone a city, before leaving for Nowa Huta; he had only foggy notions of what "a great steelworks" or "socialist city" could look like but expected something marvelous. The train journey only heightened his expectations: "Only now did I perceive the beauty of our country . . . and my heart beat loudly with joy and happiness. . . . When I arrived in Warsaw, the city drowned in lights. I thought I was in the land of fairy tales, but it was reality." By contrast, Chmieliński's first glimpse of Nowa Huta was an anticlimax: expecting a great "socialist city," Chmieliński found himself back in the village; his brigade's encampment was in Ruszcza, a village that much resembled the one he had left.[72] Another SP recruit spent his first few days wandering around the area of his barracks, looking for the steelworks—which, of course, did not exist yet.[73]

Increasingly, however, Nowa Huta took on a new look. In the village of Mogiła, Chmieliński remembered, "the ground was ploughed up by the excavations and sections of future streets and roads as well as dreadful mud, which remained through the whole period of building. From a hillock one could see among the corn fields many cut-out squares of varying shapes, deep excavations under the foundations of buildings. Among the corn fields, along with poppies, there were stacks of red bricks, boards, and thousands of building materials."[74] Nowa Huta soon presented a chaotic scene of bulldozed earth and scaffolded red-brick walls that grew taller day by day. As buildings in the new settlements were completed and filled, occupants found themselves living amidst the chaos of a massive construction site—in neighborhoods without sidewalks or street lights, confronted at every step with piles of construction materials and gaping foundations. By 1953, only the first few settlements (A-0, A-1, and A-2) had the semblance of an urban infrastructure, with greenery, park benches, and shops.[75] "Supposedly a new town," one observer remembered thinking at the time, "yet lacking in the basic things— no street names, traffic signs, modern lighting, or coherence among the buildings. . . . Our very own Nowa Huta! A few houses smeared with plaster, and that's your city."[76]

Wherever there was no grass in the new town, moreover, there was mud. In the absence of playgrounds, children played with it; planks formed makeshift sidewalks across it.[77] And it was not ordinary mud: it was a viscous, sticky substance that lay ankle-deep across the terrain. It sucked and held everything in its grip, from rubber boots to heavy construction equipment.[78] Mud dictated fashion in Nowa Huta—not only the universal denim work pants, *kufajka* (a thick jacket made of cotton batting), and cap, but also the tall rubber boots worn by everyone at all times.[79] In this sense, mud was a social leveler because, as Józef Tejchma recalled, everyone "from the general director to the bricklayer" dressed much the same.[80] Stanisława Siudut, Nowa Huta's health and social welfare czar from 1952, went through twenty pairs of rubber boots in

A demonstration of internal plumbing in Settlement A-11, around 1955. Wiktor Pental, Imago Mundi Foundation Collection.

ten years. Once her boots got stuck so fast in the mud that she had to leave them and continue barefoot.[81] In such conditions, boots meant to last a worker six months started to fall apart after only one, causing "embitterment" among those forced to wear boots with holes, or none at all.[82]

Despite the initial confusion between Nowa Huta's urban and rural landscapes, as in the Book of Genesis, chaos soon gave way to differentiation. The new settlements and construction sites became visually distinct from the villages at their margins, and although the boundary between them was permeable, it was marked by an invisible wall of mistrust. Peasants like Maciej Kardas of Mogiła mourned the end of an era: before construction began, he remembered, "there wasn't a spot in the [night] sky without stars. We had clean streams, rivers, and the Vistula was pure. [Later] the smoke from those smokestacks obscured everything."[83] Most newcomers, themselves of rural background, were all too aware of what having one's land taken away meant to a peasant. Local villagers whose land or homes had temporarily escaped expropriation haunted the margins of the construction site like a collective bad conscience, and rumor had it that lone workers had sometimes been attacked by unknown assailants armed with pitchforks.[84] Chmieliński remembered how his troupe would march to work through surrounding villages singing, "We ZMP aren't afraid of reaction or work, no, no!" or, "Youth and SP, inseparable sisters we—SP, hey SP!" while watched in hostile silence by locals over their fences. "It was no cause for wonder," he pondered, "that people didn't want to part with earth that had nurtured them for centuries, where every square foot was the history of their life."[85]

Although unofficial commerce between peasants and workers (especially in the sale of *bimber*, home-brewed alcohol) was widespread, so, too, was the "expropriation" by *junacy* of fruit and vegetables from local gardens to supplement their monotonous diet.[86] On the other hand, *junacy* sometimes demonstrated solidarity with the locals, as when two young men (who, according to the state prosecutor, showed "an inappropriate relationship to the present reality") intervened in the arrest of peasant women who were selling meat illegally, or when others protested against peasants' eviction from their homes.[87]

However, Nowa Huta had a bad reputation among peasants in the surrounding area that reached well beyond its boundaries, as the worker Szczepan Brzeziński discovered on weekend trips around the area. On a bus ride to visit a friend, Brzeziński struck up a conversation with an older woman whose priest had threatened any parishioner who left for Nowa Huta with eternal damnation. She and the other passengers, he found, had heard only negative rumors about the new town. Trying to overcome their mistrust, Brzeziński tried to explain about internal plumbing and central heating, but found it hard to get his point across. More often Brzeziński just kept quiet about where he was from.[88] A tour guide who used to show members of agricultural cooperatives around Nowa Huta also found that her rural clients were unimpressed with the new town's technological advances: farmers would grab handfuls of Nowa Huta's rich soil and exclaim disbelievingly, "A factory on such land! Whose idea was that?"[89]

If anything, however, Nowa Huta was even more divided from its urban neighbor than from its rural surroundings. At first, only an unreliable bus service linked Nowa Huta and Kraków. With the establishment of regular tram service in November 1952, it became easier for workers to spend their Sundays off touring Kraków's legendary sights—the Wawel, St. Mary's Church, the Old Town Square—or visiting its famous cafés and restaurants. Kraków's fairy-tale mystique as Poland's medieval capital, the place where its kings and queens were buried, was enormous, and for some migrants, its proximity was part of the new town's draw. "I imagined to myself that Kraków was the most splendid city in the world," one wrote, "that every house and street was grand and bound up with history, that people there were very posh and cultured and did nothing but visit these splendid houses and streets, beautifully dressed."[90]

But such enthusiasm was not widely reciprocated, and Nowohucians visiting the medieval capital often felt unwelcome. Some club bouncers denied entrance to those in *kufajki* or rubber boots,[91] while workers pursuing degrees in Kraków's schools often met with hostility from other students. "When did you take off your rubber boots?," one student remembers being sneeringly asked.[92] According to journalist Barbara Seidler, the song "O Nowej to Hucie piosenka" (A Song about Nowa Huta) originated in a Kraków cabaret, where it was intended as a satire of socialist realist clichés. But with its lilting melody and catchy lyrics, it was soon taken up with unironic enthusiasm by *junacy* and other workers in Nowa Huta, who sang it, Seidler recalled, defiantly, "like a hymn."[93] Krakovians' rude name for Nowohucians of "*Hutasy*" (a punning combination of *huta* and *kutas*, a farm tool but also a slang word for "penis") reinforced an identity that was separate and sui generis.[94] Indeed, Nowohucians were literally marked out as other: even when women dressed up for a day out in Kraków, the chafe marks on their shins—left by the tops of their boots—showed through their stockings and gave them away.[95]

The Hygiene of Communal Living

"I walked around the room and counted the beds. There were 74. It boggled the mind to think how we would live here. Would we all get along?

Wouldn't there be theft?" These were the thoughts that raced around Szczepan Brzeziński's head when he first saw the workers' hostel he would call home in Nowa Huta. It was daytime, and most occupants were out: "The room . . . was a large factory hall, divided by walls of insulating board. The plaster on them was fresh. The walls had just been painted. Three o'clock approached. . . . At this time workers started to open the door and come in. . . . I jumped out of bed. I sat at the table. With my eyes, I measured those who came in. And they me. At first no one spoke to anyone. Everyone was a stranger to the other. . . . But time did its work. Already that same day our tongues slowly began to loosen."[96] For everyone in Nowa Huta but top-level skilled, technical, or managerial personnel, life in a hostel (or "workers' hotel," in official lingo) was an inevitable rite of passage, often spanning several years. Hostels could be converted structures like the factory hall at Czyżyny, but typically they were located in the new apartment blocks. Living conditions were rudimentary at best: in one hostel designated for workers with children, there could be up to

A woman and child in Settlement A-1 South (Wanda's Settlement), one of the first to be completed. The large trees on the left once lined the old road from the village of Mogiła to Kraków. Miastoprojekt—Wojciech Łoziński, collection of A. Sitarski.

six people living in a room, "while in the kitchen a married couple with children or two women with their offspring would be quartered: married women, widows, divorcées, or unmarried single mothers. The furniture consisted of iron bunk beds and simple wooden equipment (tables, stools, cabinets, and pegs). A bathroom, perhaps without warm water, was shared on average by seventeen people. Sheets came from the hostel and were changed every two weeks. The interiors were gray and shabby."[97] Nonetheless, as the woman quoted here noted, for the majority of residents the standard of living was a step up from what they had known in the village. "Some were seeing a bathtub for the first time; for the first time they enjoyed some comfort."[98]

While this may have been true, inspectors' reports frequently sounded the alarm about worker accommodation that failed to meet basic requirements, stressing overcrowding, poor hygiene, and malfunctioning plumbing and heating. In an apartment block similar to the one described above, inspectors found forty-five workers in a room intended for ten.[99] In Czyżyny, roughly three thousand SP recruits slept sixteen to twenty to a room in a building with cement floors, no showers or baths, and an insufficient number of cold-water sinks and toilets.[100] In 1951, an inspection of a women's barracks at Prądnik Czerwony allegedly discovered eighteen women living in a room of four by four meters; the tenants complained that their straw mattresses, which had not been changed for a year, contained fleas and bedbugs and that the room was infested with rodents.[101]

Health workers in Nowa Huta battled furiously to raise awareness about the health risks posed by overcrowding and poor hygiene. Typhoid fever was not uncommon in Poland in the early postwar years, and in 1947, the incidence of tuberculosis was ten times that in the United States.[102] The new wonder chemical DDT was one weapon in health officials' arsenal; in his memoirs, Dr. Zdzisław Olszewski described the disinfection of the hostel at Czyżyny as a "dangerous" job, although whether because of disease-bearing insects or the inhabitants themselves is not clear:

> Night. Cold like the devil. . . . The massive hotel block. Lights shine here and there. . . . Militia officers silently warn us against such a nighttime action. It could end badly. . . . We had no choice. . . . Time to enter. I stood before the microphone. . . . I started to speak about pediculosis, about spotted fever and other diseases carried by insects. . . . One could hear curses against [those] who would disturb the sleep of hardworking people. . . . "Who is this 'doctor,' anyway?" . . . "Some kind of Bolshevik." . . . I myself entered a room in which various insults were hurled at me. I stood face to face with them. . . . And somehow, I spoke their [hostel residents']

language. . . . The white DDT powder—as if we were in some macabre flour mill—destroyed the greatest danger that truly threatened Nowa Huta at that time.[103]

At the same time, miasmatic theories of infection were still widespread, and lectures on the "hygiene of communal living" exhorted hostel dwellers not to hang damp work clothes in their bedrooms to dry (which some believed would reduce the amount of "breathable air" in the room) or lie in bed with their shoes on.[104] Despite their efforts, inspectors routinely found workers "fully clothed and in dirty, muddy shoes" lounging on their bunks after work.[105] Analysts from the Housing Institute noted that without purpose-built showers or cloakrooms, workers inevitably brought mud and dirt from outside into their living quarters.[106]

While authorities' concerns about living conditions in the hostels focused on hygiene, residents themselves complained especially vociferously about inadequate (or nonexistent) heat. Central heating was a novelty in Poland at the time, and in part because of builders' lack of experience with the new technology, it was several years before central heating systems could be made to work properly in the completed settlements. The District Council received a flood of letters of complaint; in 1953, for example, one group of workers threatened to quit *en masse* if the central heating in Settlement C-1 (where about a third of the hostels were located[107]) was not fixed. As one worker wrote, "SOS–SOS–SOS. Save our health! Save the health of the people who must realize the postulates of the Six-Year Plan," adding that some saboteur was probably "counting on people getting sick . . . in order to destroy the postulates of the Six-Year Plan."[108] Without even the warm stove of a peasant hut to snuggle up to, long winter days became a true hardship. "Cold was our enemy," remembered Chmieliński. "After work I returned to the hostel with the hope that maybe I'd just lie for an hour on the bunk in a warm room, [but the hostel] was as cold as a dog kennel. . . . I raised the matter . . . several times at ZMP meetings and with [brigade] leaders, but without results."[109]

The rough living conditions in Nowa Huta's hostels, similar to those in hostels elsewhere in Poland at the time,[110] did not represent unbearable discomfort for most. "We had guaranteed room and board. What more could a young person like me expect? From youth I hadn't been accustomed to luxuries," one young man from the countryside remembered. Besides this, "young people in Nowa Huta had fun." One made friends, met people from all over Poland, heard dialects—Kashubian, the *gwar* of the Tatra Mountains.[111] One "Jontek from Nowy Targ" used to improvise vaguely insulting tunes in *górale* dialect while looking longingly out the window: "From Nowa Huta the winds blow, and far away the Tatras glow. Stuck among you lot of sheep, I play my pipes to help me sleep."[112] In the best cases, roommates formed surrogate families, sharing meals and looking out for one another. "We were a well-matched bunch," writes Brzeziński of his eleven roommates, "We got used to each other like members of a single family." They pooled their money to buy an electric heater and shared meals cooked on an improvised device made out of a board, nails, box of paste, and denatured alcohol.[113]

Some rooms developed sophisticated forms of internal governance that helped smooth over potential differences in habits or social background. One woman described how her six-person room was presided over by an older woman known by all as "Grandma," a widow who worked as a cleaner and had been "drawn to Nowa Huta by the desire for financial independence." The other inhabitants included both physical and intellectual workers:

> "Grandma" was strict with us. . . . In the evening [the girls] sang religious
> and secular songs (singing was one of the few forms of entertainment
> in many rooms), or talked. Money was tended carefully; each person fed
> herself, cooking in the mornings on a hot plate, in the afternoons in the
> common kitchen. Breakfast was onions fried in lard, bread, and the free er-
> satz coffee. Dinner—soup or potatoes with some side dish. Sometimes they
> went to a dance. They didn't drink or make trouble. They went to bed early.
> They were indignant at the behavior of some residents who led an immoral
> life. All went to church every Sunday. Two of them stayed in Nowa Huta,
> got married and had children.[114]

By general consensus, the rooms in women's hostels tended to be more orderly and cared-for than those in male hostels, their walls frequently decorated with religious pictures.[115]

Not all rooms, of course, were so well-regulated. One young man remembered of his hostel roommates in Settlement B-2 that "the dirt and the fleas were bearable . . . but this bunch of people . . . seemed to me worse than the worst plague of insects." On his first night in the hostel, the man's roommates kept him up all night with their drinking, swearing, and fighting.[116] Even where group relations were harmonious, peace and privacy were rare commodities in any room. Many hostels, for one thing, were subjected day and night to a barrage of music and announcements from their loudspeaker systems (except when these were silenced by a blow from a rubber boot).[117] In spring and summer, one could at least retreat to the surrounding fields with books or daydreams, but in the long, muddy autumn and winter months, there was no escape.[118] Szczepan Brzeziński's anxieties about theft were well-founded, moreover, and it was habitual to sleep with one's valuables stashed between the sheet and mattress.[119] Elf quickly learned that Nowa Huta helped those who helped themselves. When first issued his SP uniform, "I was so enthusiastic about getting changed . . . that I didn't notice when my field cap 'vanished.' In a flash, however, I adopted the customs prevailing here and, saying nothing, began to circulate among the beds. It didn't take more than an hour before I had another one."[120]

Living Wild

A particular ideal of domesticity lay at the heart of Nowa Huta's potency as a symbol of a new life. Between 1949 and 1958, 14,885 new apartments were built in Nowa Huta, 6.1 percent of all new housing created in Poland during this period.[121] Print media, film, and music propagated images of workers' families ensconced in bright, modern apartments, of children happily at play in their new homes. Images like these stood in stark contrast to the acute realities of Poland's postwar housing crisis. While millions of Poles were left homeless by World War II, the housing shortage was most severe in the years between 1950 and 1956, when Europe's highest birth rate combined with rapid urbanization to put inordinate strain on existing stock.[122] Overcrowding, unsanitary conditions, and intra-family strains were the norm. It was not just Nowa Huta's promise of central heating and indoor plumbing, therefore, but also of privacy and a modern, dignified home life for the nuclear family that led many to try their luck in the new town.

Studies conducted in the mid-1950s by the Housing Institute (IBM) emphasized the dire living conditions that generally preceded (and motivated) a family's move to Nowa Huta. A typical case was that of a fitter in the Lenin Steelworks who had lived with his nine-member family in a 24 square meter room in a ramshackle peasant's cottage; this family was able to move into a new three-room apartment in Nowa Huta of 49.7 square meters. Researchers found that one-quarter of the unskilled workers surveyed had previously lived in homes without any modern conveniences, that is, electricity, gas, running water, or indoor plumbing.[123] Such conditions took their toll not only physically but also psychologically, as evidenced by floods of desperate letters from citizens begging authorities to help them find adequate housing in this period; interpersonal strife and emotional stress could indeed turn home, as one petitioner wrote, into a "purgatory."[124]

Despite the rapidity with which Nowa Huta's residential settlements grew, the demand for housing grew even faster as the new town's labor force expanded. As one self-described model worker, a long-distance commuter to his job in Nowa Huta, wrote to President Bierut: "I know that it's not possible to guarantee all workers an apartment in such a short time, but I see new blocks rise up every day and every hour, and already 30,000 people live there. I envy my colleagues who have attractive and comfortable apartments and after work find rest and entertainment in the midst of their family."[125] For this worker and many others like him, Nowa Huta became the focal point of an intense longing for a new kind of domestic existence. And yet, four years after work on Nowa Huta had begun, roughly 21,600 of the town's 37,000 inhabitants were still living in workers' hostels.[126] The shortage of family housing would soon turn into one of the greatest crises Nowa Huta's authorities would face before 1956.

Indeed, far from being able to reassign or close down workers' hostels as more residential settlements were completed, planners soon found it necessary to build more. The construction of a workers' settlement in Pleszów, nicknamed "Mexico" by inhabitants because of its far remove from the center of town, was a forced acknowledgment that many workers would occupy temporary housing for longer than originally planned. These monotonous rows of barracks, housing some thirty-six hundred single men far from Nowa Huta's urban amenities (such as they were), and crisscrossed by muddy and inadequately lit byways, gained notoriety for their inhabitants' reputedly legendary drinking, fighting, and theft. Although one party inspector noted in 1955 that crime seemed to be on the decline in the barracks, vigilante justice seems to have had as much to do with this as law and order: one group of residents told how, after a pair of gloves went missing from their room, "the occupants found the perpetrator within twenty minutes and, as they explained . . ., perhaps that resident won't be stealing anything more."[127] Mexico would ultimately provide inspiration for the so-called black legend of Nowa Huta that we will explore in chapters 4 and 5.

Along with Mexico, the wooden barracks at Łęg were another sore spot on Nowa Huta's landscape. Built in 1949 for youth volunteers, they had been evacuated when an inspection in 1951 declared them unfit for habitation.[128] Nevertheless, in response to a desperate demand for family housing, the buildings—though riddled with mold, lacking plumbing or electricity, and a declared fire hazard—were soon home to more than one hundred families, who complained "often and en masse" to authorities about the unhygienic and dangerous conditions in their living quarters. In 1954, authorities noted that one-quarter of that year's typhoid cases in Nowa Huta had occurred in Łęg, tracing the outbreak to a nearby drain ditch swimming with feces. Despite fears of how such facts could be "used propagandistically by the enemy,"[129] however, the families remained. No fewer than forty-three commissions had investigated the barracks by 1955, the secretary of the Kraków Party committee complained, "and all had determined that unsanitary conditions predominate there, even calling the situation a 'small Auschwitz.' But unfortunately," he went on acerbically, "Minister Jędrychowski feels that our position is not correct, and I was called a dictator and found no support."[130]

By the spring of 1956, only a little over one-third of workers at the Lenin Steelworks had been allocated family apartments, and housing problems were offered as the main reason for workers' resignation.[131] When they were able, workers often chose to commute long distances in order to live with their families, but the costs could be high. For instance, Walter N. (whose letter to President Bierut was quoted earlier) lived in a village that was 42 kilometers from Nowa Huta. Because he had to leave so early in the morning and came back so late at night, he hardly ever saw his young son: the boy was asleep both when Walter N. left home and when he returned.[132] Others lived in Nowa Huta's hostels throughout the working week, going home on the weekends. But the hostels housed not only migrant male workers with families in the village; increasingly, they were also home to young people who had been single on their arrival in Nowa Huta but who had married while living in the new town. Many had children. Needless to say, romance and reproduction failed to follow the constraints of housing availability.

A 1954 exposé in *Gazeta Krakowska* of "The Suffering of Young Couples in Nowa Huta" accused authorities of malign indifference toward such workers as the Więckowscy, two young metalworkers who had met, married, and had their first child in Nowa Huta, living all the while in separate, sex-segregated hostels. Krystyna Więckowska struggled to get the newborn to sleep in the noisy, cigarette-smoke-filled room she shared with six other women. One estimate put the number of families like this one at six hundred.[133] In addition, the hostels housed numerous single women—widows, divorcées, women living apart from their husbands, and unwed mothers—with children. Hostel administrators, on the whole, lacked precise statistics on any of these groups; all that was certain was that their numbers were rising, and their plight was highly visible.[134] As a committee of activists sent by Warsaw to investigate the situation reported in 1955, "The matter of mothers with children and broken marriages . . . is on the tongues of everyone in [Nowa Huta and is] raised at every meeting."[135]

As that report also noted, authorities' attempts to address such problems had been largely ineffective. An order of the Government Presidium of July 1955 had provided for finding between seven hundred and nine hundred rooms for families, but the plans had not been realized, a fact the committee blamed on inaction by the management at HiL.[136] In late 1955, some families were transferred to apartments or to special hostels in Pleszów, and plans were made to convert the House of the Young Steelworker, a former hostel, into housing for married couples by spring.[137] Nonetheless, as a District Committee report admitted, "despite critical voices in the press and complaints about this state of affairs, finding a radical solution for these problems will be difficult at the moment, and the initiatives undertaken are only half-measures that partially mitigate this serious social problem."[138] Local officials, too, openly expressed their frustration with what they perceived as a lack of support from Warsaw in dealing with the ongoing fallout: as a local party leader bitterly complained, some comrades in Warsaw seemed to "think you can build the *kombinat* without building apartments for the workers."[139]

Meanwhile, frustrated couples took matters into their own hands by cohabiting illegally in single-sex hostels or squatting in half-finished buildings—as officials put it, "living wild." Although workers had to sign a declaration when moving into the hostels promising that they would not bring their families to live with them, some families had set up house in hostels as early as 1950, sporadically harassed by hostel administrators but largely tolerated.[140] Such was the case, for example, of Stanisław and Irena W., rent-paying hostel dwellers who were threatened twice with eviction by the DRN, and once even had their furniture thrown out onto the sidewalk by the hostel director. Although at the time of their writing to the DRN for help the threatened eviction had not yet materialized, they lived in constant anxiety, afraid to use the gas or electricity. Although Stanisław W. had worked in Nowa Huta since 1950, in November 1953 his name was still only twenty-eighth on his division's waiting list for a family apartment.[141]

Alternatively, families seized the opportunity provided by Nowa Huta's many poorly secured building sites to create squats, either in hostel basements or in as-yet-unallocated apartments. In the absence of precise figures, we can only guess at the extent of squatting from documents like one report on settlement B-2, where 18 out of 105 inspected apartments were partly or wholly occupied by individuals not meant to be living there.[142] The chaotic administration of the housing allocation system only exacerbated the problem. Officials complained that the housing divisions at firms were not only slow in assigning completed apartments—providing all-too-tempting opportunities for families to move in illegally—but also sometimes did not even know which apartments were under their jurisdiction, allowing squatters to escape notice more easily.[143]

As of January 1952, confronted by indications that some three hundred families were living in hostels meant for single workers, authorities began to use harsher measures, including fines and evictions. But most squatters simply paid the fines without moving, and carrying out evictions was difficult.[144] At a discussion of the district party executive in early 1954, Commander Oleksy of the Citizens' Militia (*Milicja Obywatelska*, MO) claimed that his men had intervened in 264 cases of squatting in 1953 but that citizens and local officials alike refused to cooperate with them. For example, guards who were meant to prevent people from moving into partially finished buildings frequently turned a blind eye to squatters, "explaining that they would do the same if they had no place to live." The district prosecutor also complained that local officials were reluctant to "exert repression" against squatters; for example, the district administration had refused to implement a directive from the Kraków province party secretary to evict all squatters within three hours, demanding that there should first be a guarantee that the families would be provided with alternate housing. Beyond whatever ethical concerns they may have had about throwing families with children out on the street, local authorities may have been reluctant to carry out their orders for another reason: those attempting to evict such families had been known to be slapped, attacked, or otherwise openly humiliated by squatters and their neighbors.[145]

New Men

Despite these brewing problems, the *tempo nowohuckie* did not flag. Nowhere was this more evident than on the building site of the Lenin Steelworks, or HiL. When construction was at its peak in summer 1954, it presented a mind-boggling vista. Covering an area the size of a small town, some 29,500 workers were busy erecting a staggering five hundred buildings and components within its perimeters. Here the heavy machinery—too precious to waste on the construction of mere apartments—was concentrated: cranes, excavators, bulldozers. Szczepan Brzeziński, now an electrician, was fascinated by the large machines and used to visit friends who worked at the *kombinat* in order to get a closer look. Climbing a towering crane, Brzeziński saw a breathtaking panorama: "From the crane you could see the whole *kombinat* like the palm of your hand. Józef explained to me how all the different constructions would be linked to one another, what they were called, where the raw [steel] would be smelted. . . . When I looked in the direction of the rolling mill, all I saw was dug-up earth. Trucks were bringing in building materials like cement, bricks, boards. Less than a year ago there were fields on this land, through which a country road led." Although, by his own admission, Brzeziński was not much interested in politics, he *was* deeply impressed by the ceremony marking the *kombinat*'s first production of steel in October 1952. From one of the girders, he looked down at the proceedings: "I won't forget the moment when, to the sounds of the "Internationale," a white thick substance flowed from the furnace. . . . Heat radiated in all directions, white sparks scattered. I was moved. The effort of hundreds of workers had produced its first results."[146] Onlookers sang the patriotic anthem "*Jeszcze Polska nie zginęła*" as the first molten steel poured forth. Some had tears in their eyes.[147]

Something remarkable had happened: the green fields of 1949–50 had grown the giant smokestacks of 1954–55. For those who had helped accomplish such a Promethean transformation, it was a source of individual and collective pride. Dramatic changes in other aspects of their lives, moreover, often paralleled those in Nowa Huta's landscape; country rubes no more, the Chmielińskis and Brzezińskis were on their way to building independent adult lives in the new town. For one thing, by mid-decade the demand for skilled labor at HiL had enabled many to make the transition from unskilled construction to stable, well-paid work at the steelworks. The long-awaited vocational training courses had finally arrived; even though there were sometimes more students than seats, and even though the very desks they used sometimes had to be hand-built by the participants themselves, the thirst for training did not abate. If necessary, students took turns sitting on the floor.[148]

For those with exceptional perseverance and aptitude, Nowa Huta opened doors to schooling or university studies that had been firmly closed to generations before them. Elf, who forged his primary school certificate in order to gain entrance to a part-time technical secondary school, had what was in many ways a typically atypical educational career among his Nowa Huta peers. After high school, he completed a one-year preparatory course that enabled him to enter the military academy in Warsaw. Not liking military discipline, however, he returned to Kraków and enrolled at the Academy of Mining and Steelwork. But without the means to support himself in school, Elf decided to move back to Nowa Huta and worked full time while attending night school. He completed his university degree in 1958. Another worker-student, Kazimierz D., switched jobs so that his working hours would not clash with his course schedule, although it meant a pay cut of about 50 percent. "There were hard times," he recalled, "when I had to buy books [and] even a dry roll was a delicacy. . . . [But] the material loss was nothing compared to my inner satisfaction. . . . It was always before my eyes: not marriage, but study, high school, and graduation." When he finally achieved his goal in 1957, he was one of only two to graduate out of an entering class of fifty-six.[149] Chmieliński, however, was one of those who fell by the wayside: despite excellent marks in history, literature, and contemporary politics, he struggled with math and failed his entrance exams to technical university.[150]

Despite the fact that Communist policies of "social advancement" had offered unprecedented opportunities for Poles from formerly disadvantaged backgrounds, successful individuals like Kazimierz D. could justifiably claim to be self-made men, to borrow from a capitalist idiom. Their educational achievements required tremendous discipline, self-sacrifice, and determination; no one got an easy pass. Such individuals' stories have an analog in the building of Nowa Huta as a whole, also a story in many ways of success against the odds. Nowa Huta's builders might well have wondered to whom the achievements of the town's first years were owed: to communism and the party, or to those who had labored daily to make its plans a reality?

Between 1955 and 1960, Nowa Huta's population of hostel dwellers dropped from twenty-one thousand to eight thousand, and living conditions in the hostels improved considerably.[151] Thousands of former hostel residents were moving into apartments in the new settlements; the birth rate, a full 21 percent higher in Nowa Huta than in Kraków as a whole, surged.[152] Life in Nowa Huta was beginning to achieve normalcy. Surveying residents in 1964, one sociologist concluded that for the "decided majority" of Nowa Huta's inhabitants, "settling there was seen as a life success."[153] One suspects that for many, such satisfaction reflected not just where they had arrived in their lives, but also what it had taken to get there—a journey that had required sacrifices as well as brought gains.

A few months after joining SP, Edmund Chmieliński went home for a visit. Like many young workers on their first trip back home (one usually postponed until they had earned enough to buy their first "citified" clothes),[154] Chmieliński thought keenly about the kind of impression he would make. "I prepared myself very carefully. I couldn't sleep or eat at all. I counted the days, then the hours until the moment finally arrived. On the day of my departure I got a new, pressed uniform, coat, and shoes. To my uniform I pinned my shining medals and awards. Deep in my pocket were several hundred złoty withdrawn from my savings account." At first, the visit went well. "My mother turned me around and couldn't get over how good I looked. . . . Guys came over to see me and talk with me; some envied me when I told them about how I had won the medals. . . . Girls who at one time would never have spoken to a herdsboy now asked me to dance." But the honeymoon was short-lived. On his second night back home, Chmieliński was attacked and beaten by some (presumably anti-Communist) youth in the village. And, he added, "the atmosphere at home was very bad. My home was now in the brigade. There, I was among colleagues and good friends."[155]

Chmieliński's experience confirmed another sociologist's findings in 1961: not only did a majority of those surveyed express "contentment with work and life in Nowa Huta," but an overwhelming number of respondents (84.7 percent) was "negatively and even categorically opposed to the possibility of returning to the village." "This," the researcher wrote, "constitutes its own sort of road of 'no return' to the old life." In addition, an "overwhelming majority" described their original motivations for coming to Nowa Huta not only in utilitarian terms (better work, housing, earnings) but also in terms of "a decided desire to *break away from their previous social milieu.*"[156] Those expressing contentment with life in Nowa Huta embraced the notion that they had embarked on a life-altering adventure, one in which the traditional and familiar were willingly traded for a new and modern existence.

The road of no return that led from impoverished village to socialist city was paved with high expectations, of course, and such expectations were easily disappointed. Many passed through Nowa Huta and did not stay, for precisely this reason. Others, however, developed a fierce emotional attachment to the new town that reflected the nonutilitarian dimensions of their quest for a different life. "I'd rather have one room with a kitchen in Nowa Huta than three in Kraków," confessed one respondent to sociologists in the early 1960s. "I can't imagine life outside Nowa Huta, which is literally growing before my very eyes," said another. "I'd like to avoid pathos, but I fell in love with this city and I'm one of its fervent enthusiasts." Another commented, "I feel myself to be an owner [*gospodarz*—literally, "land-lord"]. When I came to Nowa Huta, there were still no streets or houses. I like the town. We built it so we could live here. Those who criticize it don't have a clue. . . . There's nothing like it anywhere else in Poland." If, God forbid, the new town were to burn down, said another respondent, "I'd sit on its ashes."[157] The "hope of building something, of doing something" infected many living in East Central Europe after World War II. In the historiography emphasizing Europeans' craving for normalcy and private life, this dimension of postwar European experience—the urge to participate in meaningful, productive work, and the conscious or semiconscious conviction that doing so could make life better for oneself and others—is lost. And yet the continent's remarkable postwar recovery, east and west, depended on such energies being channeled and mobilized by political and economic actors of various kinds.

The extent to which Nowa Huta satisfied a need for constructive engagement in the world is apparent in many memoirs by its builders. One resident, on the eve of leaving Nowa Huta to begin his studies in another city, recalled climbing Wanda's Mound for one last look at his new home: "I wanted to enjoy a panoramic view of the Huta, to bid farewell to her. My thoughts ran backward to the first days and, like a film in my mind's eye, I saw all the hardships and the fruits they had borne. I looked as though at my own creation, and I was overcome with regret at the thought of leaving."[158] The young man promised himself that, as soon as he could, he would return to Nowa Huta "for always." Memoirs like these should be forgiven a touch of pathos. We can imagine that, atop Wanda's Mound, their authors may have felt a little like gods—a little closer to heaven in the city they had built with their own hands.

3

The Poor Worker Breaks His Legs

Piotr Ożański was one of a family of nine from the tiny village of Mołodycz, nestled in the Carpathian foothills near the border with Ukraine. In 1949, Ożański made the fateful decision that would lead him from this remote region to the heart of postwar Polish power and politics: following a stint of army service, he volunteered at the age of twenty-four for the 51st Union of Polish Youth Brigade. Thus, he set off to work in Nowa Huta, the "great building site of socialism," the future "socialist city" just outside Kraków. In the brigade, he trained as a bricklayer. As his skill with the trowel increased, Ożański later told journalists, he began to dream of "a new exploit by youth" in construction—an effort to hasten the completion of housing for Nowa Huta's growing workforce. He dreamed of laying twenty-four thousand bricks in a single shift, using the so-called troika or three-man method developed in the USSR. Unable to sleep from excitement, the story goes, he woke up his friends in the middle of the night and urged them to join him: "When I go forward, boys," he told them, "I'll be pulling you up after me. And we'll lay those twenty-four thousand bricks."[1]

The newspapers reported that on July 14, 1950, Ożański's team, working eight hours, exceeded its goal, laying 34,728 bricks—a staggering 525.6 percent of the norm (the base unit meant to correlate with an ordinary day's work)—and breaking the national record. Ożański went from strength to strength. During the commemoration of Poland's first postwar Communist government on July 22, his image appeared in the news and on banners; fellow brigade member Sławomir Mrożek (later to become a famous antiestablishment playwright) penned a song in praise of the young hero. A subsequent record-breaking achievement (66,000 bricks in one shift) was followed by Ożański's pledge to complete a three-entry building in record time, in honor of the October Revolution's thirty-third anniversary. Each of these feats was staged with maximum fanfare, with onlookers, orchestras, and banners.

Ożański was chosen as a delegate to the second World Congress of Defenders of Peace in Berlin and to the Rally of Labor Heroes in Warsaw. "There was a march past [Premier Bolesław] Bierut, a tour of Warsaw," Ożański's fellow delegate, the electrician Szczepan Brzeziński, later remembered. "After the return to Nowa Huta—meetings, meetings. We walked from rally to rally in our rubber boots, drowning in the mud."[2]

Mud and meetings: the story of Ożański's achievements as a model worker (*przodownik*) is one of Nowa Huta's founding myths and, by extension, of Polish Stalinism as a whole. Like all myths, it has proven to be both enduring and elusive: subject to multiple interpretations, the narrative of Ożański's rise (and fall) has been repeatedly rescripted over time, with each retelling pointing to a different moral. The most famous of these by far is Andrzej Wajda's 1977 film, *Man of Marble*, inspired by an article about Ożański that Wajda's collaborator Aleksander Ścibor-Rylski had once read in the newspaper. The film's version of the Ożański myth hinges on a single dramatic moment, which in historical time occurred on September 26, 1950. In the course of his record-breaking attempt for the thirty-third anniversary of the October Revolution, an anonymous worker (the perpetrator's identity was never established) passed Ożański a hot brick, evidently meant to burn Ożański's hand. Officially, it was an act of sabotage by the class enemy aimed at slowing down the pace of construction in Nowa Huta. Unofficially, it was read as an expression of widespread resentment among rank-and-file workers against so-called model workers like Ożański and their record-breaking achievements.[3] For Wajda, it is the beginning of the man of marble's fall, the first in a chain of events revealing the true colors of those unscrupulous party and union officials who placed him on his pedestal—and the beginning of his rise to true heroic martyrdom.

Labor competition was a pillar of Stalinist strategies for "building socialism" in the Soviet Union of the 1930s, and was exported to all the countries of the Soviet bloc after World War II. To achieve "the utmost activity of millions of toilers," Stalin had explained, communism would rely not on the capitalist strategy of competition, but rather on the motivating principle of emulation; under socialism, work would no longer be "a drudgery and a heavy burden," but "a matter of honor, a matter of glory, a matter of bravery and heroism."[4] Besides popularizing norm-busting worker-heroes like Ożański, this meant encouraging all workers to undertake voluntary pledges to perform additional labor (for example, by completing certain tasks on their time off), promoting competition among work teams for the highest productivity, and offering prizes to innovators and "rationalizers" for discoveries that could realize the slogan "faster, better, cheaper." Eventually, such practices came to be known as "labor competition" (in Polish, *współzawodnictwo*) and were obligatory in every socialist workplace. Before 1956, the organization of labor competition consumed an enormous share of firm-level party and labor union activists' time; management, too, was charged with fostering labor competition at every level of production.

This chapter explores the dynamics of labor competition at the height of Stalinism (ca. 1948–56) and at the heart of Polish Stalinism's mobilizational enterprise: Nowa Huta, the steelworks and new town constituting the flagship investment of Poland's Six-Year Plan. In particular, it considers the relationship among labor competition, ideology, and political control. This relationship was one that concerned not just party ideologues, but has long occupied analysts and critics of communist regimes. In 1955, for instance, Isaac Deutscher argued that labor competition was "as essential as political terror, if not more so," for maintaining party control over society; noting that Trotsky himself called emulation a form of "labor compulsion," Deutscher proposed that such "primitive Taylorization" pitted workers against one another even more effectively than the capitalist labor market. Thus, Deutscher wrote, workers' energies under socialism were "easily made to flow into molds operated by a single party," limiting the scope for coordinated dissent.[5]

One year after Deutscher's essay was published, however, the near-revolutionary events of 1956 in Hungary and Poland seemed to defy his bleak picture of an atomized socialist proletariat. And yet, subsequent studies have tended to agree with Deutscher that state socialist workplace regimes did not "form a basis for the development of worker solidarity," as historian Mark Pittaway put it. On the contrary, labor competition and norm-based wages "exacerbated the tendencies towards atomization that existed on the shop-floor," whether of gender, age, skill, or experience.[6] To understand the instabilities of state socialism, such studies have focused, instead, on the unintended consequences of such labor regimes (in particular, on the emergence of informal shop floor bargaining of norm-based wages),which, they argue, undermined party control at a structural level and generated long-term instability throughout the system.[7]

A careful analysis of labor competition in Nowa Huta supports many of these findings. But, as this chapter also proposes, a glimpse beyond Nowa Huta's shop floor offers a broader panorama of labor competition and its legacies. Among these was the ambiguous but enduring myth of the labor hero—a myth that bespeaks the troubled linkage between Nowa Huta's origins as a "city of work" and Stalinism's promise to redefine the very meaning of work in a worker's state. Stalinism's productivist rhetoric and mobilizing practices, I argue, helped to shape new ways of talking, thinking, and acting about work and citizenship by Poland's new working class as it came into being after

World War II. While labor competition indeed heightened particularization at the site of production, it simultaneously contributed to other forms
of worker solidarity. In particular, it reinforced Nowa Huta's self-image as a
moral community of labor, based on a certain understanding of work itself.
It was a community from which, as we shall see, the party and its ideological
allies would increasingly be excluded.

New Workers, Old Workers

The protagonist of *Man of Marble*, like most migrants to Nowa Huta, is a
peasant by origin: early in the film, we learn that before arriving in the new
town young Mateusz Birkut has known only, as he puts it simply, "the land."
Birkut's peasant background is typical not only of migrants to Nowa Huta
but also of the larger cohort that swelled Poland's postwar working class. In
the first two decades after World War II, millions of rural migrants flooded
into depopulated Warsaw, the former German cities of Gdańsk, Wrocław,
and Szczecin, the mines of Silesia, and the new factories of the Six-Year
Plan—in short, wherever work might be found. By 1962, just 17 percent of
Poland's industrial workforce had its roots in the prewar working class and its
distinctive identity and traditions; for the remainder, the formative experience
of industrial labor occurred in the period just after World War II and in the
mass mobilization and industrialization of Stalinism.[8]

Contemporary observers noted that rural migrants stood apart from more
established working-class communities in this period, mixing little and exhib-
iting distinct patterns of behavior. Between 1949 and 1951, for instance, long-
time residents of the old working-class center of Łódź told sociologist Hanna
Świda-Ziemba that rural migrants drank too much, were undisciplined, and
lacked pride in their work. Migrants were often known by scornful epithets
that stressed their rural origins (e.g., "cowherds"), and in large urban centers
such as Warsaw or Wrocław, they remained a group apart, living and social-
izing with other migrants from their village or region.[9]

In his comparative study of workers and Communists in the cities of Łódź
and Wrocław between 1945 and 1950, Padraic Kenney stresses that the frag-
mentation and isolation of new worker communities in Wrocław created
factory-floor relations that were different from those in the old worker centers of Łódź. A formerly German city annexed at the end of World War II,
Wrocław was in effect a new town, its population a seething hodge-podge of
migrants from across the country, many of them recent migrants from rural
areas. By contrast, Łódź's population had remained relatively stable, its urban,

working-class roots stretching back generations. Working-class community and traditions in Łódź—where family, neighborhood, and workplace ties over-lapped and reinforced one an-other—gave rise to strong repertoires of col-lective protest, and conflict with party and union officials was often expressed through strikes. In Wrocław there was no equivalent culture of factory-floor solidarity. While workers in Wrocław were no more content with their lot than those in Łódź, they tended to engage in passive and individual, rather than ac-tive and organized, resistance—not least, by "voting with their feet" and leaving town.[10] New workers, moreover, were more likely to join the Polish Workers' Party (the precursor to the Polish United Workers' Party, or PZPR), and more likely, like Birkut, to engage in labor competition. In Łódź, for instance, ten-sions between old and new workers often coalesced around early forms of la-bor competition such as the "multimachine" or "work race" movements; these often pitted younger, less-experienced, or migrant workers against their more established colleagues. Given their exclusion from informal networks within the factory and their reduced access to traditional forms of apprenticeship, new workers had the most to gain from labor competition, which opened alternative doors to income and advancement.[11] Considering these various fac-tors (lower strike rates, higher party membership, and greater enthusiasm for labor competition), historians have characterized rural migrants' attitude to-ward political authority as one of "indifference" or "conformism."[12]

And yet, such descriptions of new workers leave a number of questions unanswered. First, they tell us little about workers' perceptions of their own actions. By extension, they do not tell us much about new workers' relationship to Stalinist ideology and propaganda, which they would have confronted on a daily basis in the workplace and in the public spaces of their towns and cities. Did such workers really care little who was in power, as long as they collected a decent paycheck—as the idea of indifference implies? As for conformism, historians have tended to portray new workers' participation in labor compe-tition as largely instrumental: in other words, they participated if and when it contributed to higher earnings. Yet such voluntarism seems at odds with the idea of conformism and its implied lack of individual choice. Moreover, historians suggest that at some times, in some places, among some workers, labor competition elicited genuine enthusiasm.[13] A more nuanced exploration of where, why, and how such enthusiasm appeared could help us better under-stand emerging new worker identities.

To do this in a context as demographically fluid as postwar Poland, as Ken-ney's comparison between Łódź and Wrocław suggests, we must pay special attention to processes of community formation within particular working-class milieus. In considering Nowa Huta from this perspective, a few observations are in order. As we saw in chapter 2, Nowa Huta's social landscape resembled Wrocław's far more than that of Łódź; yet Nowa Huta's emerging society was less differentiated than Wrocław's, and better integrated. For instance, the percentage of urban, skilled workers was lower in Nowa Huta, and apart from the small group of privileged cadres immediately allotted family housing, workers from all different backgrounds and regions lived jumbled together, cheek by jowl, in the workers' hostels. When they ultimately moved into permanent housing, moreover, it was the vagaries of firm housing allocation rather than regional ties that determined residential patterns in the new settlements. We can speculate that Nowa Huta's patterns of urban development may have more quickly fostered new ties and solidarities.

Two less tangible factors, though, are also critical for understanding Nowa Huta's interlocking labor and communal identities. First, the Six-Year Plan (1949–55) projected an enormous increase in skilled labor throughout Poland: in 1948, the party spoke of increasing numbers of industrial workers in the country by some 250,000 to 300,000 by 1955.[14] In Nowa Huta, it was clear to planners that the majority of workers for the Lenin Steelworks would have to be drawn from the construction labor force, which was largely unskilled.[15] Expectations of mobility, then, were central to newcomers' understanding of what work would entail in the new town.

Second, a particular idea of work also informed the official rationale for Nowa Huta's existence; intersecting planning and political discourses dictated that Nowa Huta was to be created not only by, but also *for* workers. On the one hand, it would address underemployment in Poland's rural areas, giving work to its surplus labor force. On the other hand, Nowa Huta would "work" for all of Poland: its steelworks would produce raw materials enabling workers in other industries, in turn, to produce more of the goods needed by society. (Less was said about the steel that would be siphoned off to Soviet defense industries.) The individual benefits of working in Nowa Huta (a better standard of living and social advancement) were thus explicitly linked in this discourse to broader, societal ones (economic development and rising standards of living). Work in Nowa Huta was simultaneously an opportunity to transform one's own life-chances and those of the community at large; it was, in short, a civic endeavor.

The power of such an idea is evident in the traces it left behind in many memoirs and recollections of Nowa Huta's first decade, where the experience of work is granted a status and importance all its own. Memoirs can be otherwise full of ambivalence toward life in Nowa Huta yet focus on work as a transformative experience, portraying it as the basis for a new, collective identity transcending politics or ideology; often, the first day of work in Nowa

Huta is described as a watershed moment in the authors' lives. During his first day in the youth brigade, for example, Edmund Chmieliński was set to work digging a vast hole in the muddy earth, which, he was told, was to be the foundation of one of Nowa Huta's future housing settlements. Although Chmieliński remembered being "very puzzled that we were to build a powerful plant and great modern city with shovel and pickaxe," he set to work with zeal. After a short time, his palms were covered with blisters, but Chmieliński, who was small for his age, wanted to prove himself. At the end of the day, he elatedly received his reward: the handshakes and congratulations of his colleagues and platoon leader. He had been initiated into a fellowship of labor.

A similar example appears in the memoir of an anonymous worker, who, unlike Chmieliński, had come to Nowa Huta unwillingly: an orphan, he had been sent by his state guardian to Nowa Huta upon graduating from school, an assignment that had filled him with the opposite of enthusiasm. But something unexpected happened during his first day of work at HiL. Randomly assigned to a group that would be taught how to install electric lights, he experienced a minor revelation. "After eight hours of our first work together, the first eight lamps shone with a bright light. For the first time," the author writes, "I felt satisfaction and a tremendous zest for life."[16] As in Chmieliński's memoir, the moment is a rite of passage, an initiation into a fellowship of labor—one in which working together imparts luminous satisfaction.

One can certainly see in this passage a reflection of socialist realist tropes of enlightenment and mastery over the powers of the natural world, according to which the bright light that shone out after a day's labor represented the Promethean powers of socialism. But this trope would have been a powerful one for rural migrants who came from villages where electricity was rare or nonexistent. For the young man quoted above or others like him, such a sudden and unanticipated mastery of technology could, in fact, be personally electrifying. This suggests another possible meaning of the term "work": literally overnight, newcomers like Chmieliński had moved from the margins of Polish economic life to its epicenter—from being backward toilers, unproductive surplus people, to workers. Work defined not only one's relationship to the natural world, but also one's relevance within a community of labor and, more broadly, within a national community. Induction into Nowa Huta's hard world of work could potentially seem like a passage from backwardness to modernity, dependency to adulthood, isolation to fellowship, and disenfranchisement to citizenship.

Chmieliński, who dreamed of becoming a model worker and having his picture in the newspaper, had quickly and eagerly absorbed labor competition's message of collective effort and common reward. As he remembered, he "firmly believed that with a common effort we would build in a few years a splendid

Members of a Służba Polsce brigade building an apartment house, 1952. These *junacy* have been trained as bricklayers, like Piotr Ożański. Miastoprojekt—Wojciech Łoziński, collection of A. Sitarski.

city in which I would live and work. . . . I didn't count the hours of work. I built as though I was building my own house. I believed that I was working for myself and my children."[17] As we shall see later, however, his enthusiasm—the very opposite of indifference or conformism—would ultimately create its own problems for authorities.

Everything Is Agitation

Stalinist "mobilization" (the Bolsheviks adapted the term from its original military context, with its implications of top-down coordination of military, economic, and social resources) is typically understood to mean the channeling of popular energies toward specific goals. The party would mobilize society to complete the Six-Year Plan by encouraging workers to perform unpaid labor on Sundays, the Women's League would mobilize women in the "struggle for peace" by urging members to take part in the National Peace Plebiscite, and the unions would mobilize factory workers to travel to nearby villages to enlighten peasants about the "new reality." As Marcin Zaremba points out, the term was used so widely during the Stalinist period that it could describe "nearly every intensive collective activity" (as, for example, when one provincial party official spoke of "the great mobilization in the line of harvests, which were conducted day and night").[18]

Another word that conveyed a related sense of urgency, activity, and intensity, and that was sometimes used interchangeably with "mobilization," was "agitation." Although, strictly speaking, agitation had more to do with propaganda (for example, the reading aloud of newspapers during workers' lunch breaks), like mobilization, it suggested mass participation in overlapping forms of political ritual, communication, and persuasion.[19] As one activist put it, "Everything in Nowa Huta is agitation. . . . Every activity in all areas of work and everyday life is agitation, is a momentous [kind of] politics."[20]

This "momentous politics" was to be coordinated by Nowa Huta's district party committee, and executed by party cells in the workplace and "transmission belt" organizations such as the labor unions, Women's League, and League of Polish Youth. Activists were at the receiving end of a cascade of directives, originating on high with Warsaw's decision to launch a particular mobilizing campaign. In the second quarter of 1951 alone, for example, Nowa Huta's District Council of Trade Unions directed local branches to organize mass meetings at all workplaces in connection with May Day, the National Peace Plebiscite, International Children's Day, the three-hundredth anniversary of a peasant uprising in the Podhale region, the National Loan campaign, and a show trial of army officers.[21] Activists put in extremely long hours to prepare these campaigns, drafting yearly, monthly, and weekly work plans and meticulously reporting on their fulfillment to superiors.[22] The unrelenting pace of such activity reflected a certain internal logic. As Zaremba points out, Stalinist mobilization was not just about achieving concrete goals or communicating the party's position to the grassroots. It became practically an end in itself, since in the party's eyes, the ability to organize successful mobilization campaigns was equated with possessing social legitimacy. Conversely, failure to mobilize the base was read as a fundamental failure of leadership, because it threatened the legitimacy supposedly proven by society's active participation in such campaigns.[23]

Such logic is implicit in much party and activist discussion of mobilization campaigns in Nowa Huta: many such reports focus nearly exclusively on the organizational level, rather than on what we might think of as the critical question of campaigns' outcome; whether the public was actually persuaded by a given campaign's message often appears as a secondary consideration.

A district-level party report about May Day, 1955, can be taken as an example. The report is full of lists and figures. Eighteen thousand attended the parade and mass demonstration; twenty-five thousand attended "festive assemblies" at workplaces and schools; thirty thousand attended more than one hundred public events such as concerts and performances, sports matches, and children's parties. On the previous day, there had been a parade of schoolchildren, concluding with a bonfire for five thousand young people in Central Square. Buildings throughout the town had been decorated with portraits of local and national party leaders, as well as "classics of Marxism": flags, banners, and so forth. The takeaway message (probably intended for superiors at the provincial and national level) is that local activists had "passed their exam" on May Day, as evidenced by such an impressive range of events. Only in passing does the report mention that "the mood of the assemblies" was "celebratory and solemn," and that "inimical comments or acts were not noted" (even if, as one member of the district executive somewhat wistfully opined in discussion, "there wasn't that enthusiasm that characterized demonstrations before the war").[24]

By contrast, when campaigns went poorly, activists were more likely to start pointing fingers both at organizational failures and at "enemies" in the targeted population. For example, although the elections of 1952 and 1954 were preceded by extensive preparatory campaigns aimed at ensuring good turnout and minimal disruption to the single-slate elections, neither campaign could exactly be judged a success. When party agitators spread out across Nowa Huta to "chat" with people in their homes in 1952, for instance, the embattled agitators had "literally to capture" each settlement "building by building"; stones were thrown at them in Mogiła, one report noted, and elsewhere hot coffee was poured on them from upper-story windows.[25]

Two years later, the situation was not much better. On the one hand, the numbers looked good: attendance by over twenty-two thousand at 216 mass meetings called by the Committee for the National Front; 116 additional meetings for youth (attended by five thousand) of the Union of Polish Youth; and another 69 informal "evenings for young voters" attended by some thirty-five hundred, supplemented with election-themed chess and table-tennis tournaments coordinated by the sports clubs Stal and Budowlani. Even the boy scouts had pledged to educate their neighbors about voting procedures.[26] And yet the campaign foundered. There were multiple logistical problems, including a last-minute scurry to organize meetings and a delay in printing the candidate profiles; a shortage of canvas for making banners and decorations; and, because the photographer from *Budujemy Socjalizm* had overcharged the party (!), insufficient funds for distributing copies of the candidates' pictures to voters. According to party executive member

Skróbiszewski, though, none of this could explain the population's disquieting ignorance about electoral procedures: "Some [voters], instead of depositing their cards, put them in their pockets, . . . there were cases in which voters wrote their own names at the bottom of the list of candidates, and so on. There were some envelopes in which pieces of paper or scraps of newspaper were found, but that was clearly enemy work."[27]

Can documents like these tell us something about the mood, views, or opinions of Nowa Huta's population toward mobilization campaigns? In particular, do they reveal a reservoir of social resistance in Nowa Huta? Similar questions can be asked about mood reports by the secret police—which unlike the party reports discussed above, were explicitly intended as windows onto the views and attitudes of the population at large. Thus, the Office of Security (*Urząd Bezpieczeństwa*, or UB) reported during the elections of 1952 on the following "inimical statements" overheard in Nowa Huta: "They say that it's a workers' government, but wherever they see a worker, they just stuff their pockets" and "The PZPR gathers in its ranks only careerist sons-of-bitches who can't do anything, so they push their way into positions [of power]."[28] Noting further "enemy activity" during the election period, reports mention that inhabitants of some of the villages annexed to Nowa Huta "vilified our candidates," while a seventy-seven-year-old worker at HiL, a known supporter of the Polish Populist Party, had been arrested (apparently as a prophylactic measure, since he was "arrested during every election"). In addition, the children of some party members had been caught vandalizing election posters.[29]

Historians are divided over what, if anything, such reports tell us about popular opinion. Some have suggested that the incidents they describe represent the "tip of an iceberg" of popular opposition; this is based on the assumption that only the bravest (or most reckless) members of society spoke their views openly, but that such views must have been shared by many others who remained silent. Other historians have arrived at the opposite conclusion, contending that because the secret police's raison d'être was to root out enemies of the regime, its agents would tend to exaggerate the extent of popular opposition. Thus, they argue, such documents reveal far more about the inner dynamics and institutional logic of the police state than about society itself.[30]

Taken alone, party and secret police documents are unreliable guides to popular sentiment in the aggregate. We can, however, ask what they can tell us about the parameters, or "discursive boundaries," of grassroots political expression in Nowa Huta.[31] For example, whether or not they were typical of more widely held views and attitudes, inimical statements and rebellious gestures recorded in the archives are important datum points: they help us map out a discursive field in which other social actors operated.

Viewed from this perspective, it becomes clear that this field was one the party had difficulty delimiting and controlling in Nowa Huta. Examples abound of open critique and back-talk, even in face-to-face confrontations with party officials—for example, in reports on those rank-and-file party members who were either expelled or withdrew from the party. Marian B., a carter, was "struck from party ranks by decree of the [basic party organization] for failure to pay dues . . . and participate at meetings and party training. When reprimanded," continued the report, "he explained that he would pay his dues, but that he would not attend meetings because [even] a horse couldn't drag him" to them. A building technician, who refused even to attend his membership hearing, reputedly announced that his decision to join the party had been "a serious error." Other members resigned by explaining more evasively that they had become involved in the party "accidentally," or that they had lost their membership cards but "declined to apply for a new one."[32]

Discussions of party agitators also show the party at a disadvantage when trying to articulate its position, not from the safe position of a stage or podium, but rather "on the terrain." Party leaders expressed dismay at the inability to find good candidates for the role of agitator (rank-and-file members with model personal behavior and ideological consciousness) to reach out to the nonparty masses and educate them politically. After observing agitators at a lecture during the 1952 campaign to popularize the new constitution, for instance, one frustrated official had "the impression that we were not at a gathering of the leading activists, but at a very average meeting of less conscious nonparty members, at best." The unfortunate result was that, when directly challenged by colleagues and neighbors, agitators "did not always succeed in immediately smashing the enemy's arguments." An anecdote made the party rounds about agitator Comrade K. At a meeting with women in one of Nowa Huta's apartment buildings, she asked them to discuss "how the worker lived before the war and how he lives now, and what the people's constitution gives us." One audience member apparently replied that she herself was too young to remember life before the war, but that "how it is now, you yourself know." Instead of responding to this provocation with facts and arguments, Comrade K. seems to have lost her temper and left the room in a huff.[33]

Labor competition was both a form of social mobilization and an everyday part of the labor process. It occurred not on a proscenium, therefore, but on terrain where the party's legitimacy was often explicitly or implicitly contested. We can speculate, then, that workers who participated in labor competition were more obliged to explain their participation to themselves (and quite possibly to hostile work colleagues or friends) than if the party had exercised a hegemonic control of discursive boundaries in Nowa Huta. In other words, workers had to think about how labor competition related to other values and goals outside the narrow idiom of Stalinist discourse.

Labor Competition

"Significant accomplishments should be noted in mobilizing youth to dedicated productive work," wrote one commander of the youth service organization SP of its brigades in Nowa Huta. Some members distinguished themselves as model workers (*przodownicy pracy*) like Piotr Ożański, who was said to perform habitually at 200 percent of norm. Others committed themselves to working extra hours without pay; for example, by working one Sunday in June, the entire 51st Brigade earned money designated to buy a tractor for the State Center of Agricultural Machines, while other sums were intended for civilians in Korea. Youth brigade members, or *junacy*, also took part in savings campaigns: under the slogan "faster and cheaper," the *junak* Kołodziej gathered a group of twenty colleagues and pledged to use all the broken bricks lying about a particular building site.[34] "Frequent examples of devotion to work on the part of youth are well known," wrote an activist from the ZMP in Nowa Huta, contrasting the readiness of young workers to engage in labor competition with the sometime reluctance of their elders. When the foundations of a boiler room in one of the settlements had collapsed, he wrote, a group of young bricklayers had "immediately taken up the work of demolition, while the older workers had refused." The brigade worked thirty-four hours without a break; thus, "the plan was not threatened and the settlement got its boiler in time."[35]

Memoirs, too, contain numerous descriptions of young workers' enthusiasm for labor competition. When labor competition was introduced into his youth brigade, the memoirist Elf wrote, "the brotherhood was simply hot to work," and everyone would hurry to see his production results on the brigade scoreboard at the end of the day.[36] Another worker described his brigade's efforts to meet its "Bierut pledge" (in this case, to finish repairing a digger ahead of schedule) on the eve of the national Rally of Young Labor Heroes: "On April 4, 1952 we're pouring sweat, and so much work yet to do before April 15. After work I bring newspapers to the workshop, everyone picks up *Sztandar Młodych* [The youth standard], our daily paper, whose headline is 'Forward to the Rally of Young Labor Heroes—Builders of People's Poland.' We read the appeal with concentration, and the next day each of us stands at his place and our commitments for Bierut are completed three and a half days ahead of schedule.' 'What helped us here?' the author asked. 'It helped that each of us . . . wanted to be the best in the brigade, so he could go to the rally.'"[37] Leopold Sułkowski, a teacher at the Lenin Steelworks' vocational training center, stressed the incentive power of events like the Rally: "Labor heroes were hung with sashes [on which was written] what percent of the norm they had achieved, of course there was an orchestra . . . and it was all very festive. I looked into the faces of these workers. They were convinced what they were doing was right; they were filled with the satisfaction that it gave them, and worked with unheard-of self-sacrifice. . . . The norms were a fiction but the fact that they were exceeded was a reality, the result of the authentic engagement of these people in their work." Such enthusiasm faded, Sułkowski avowed, only when it became clear that "nothing that had been promised had come to pass."[38]

Enthusiasm for labor competition was dependent on various factors. It was predominantly young, unskilled workers, first of all—those to whom labor

An award ceremony for *junacy*, around 1951. *Junacy* of the 91st and 92nd brigades were stationed in twenty-four barracks (visible in the background) far removed from the building site. The prizes are being distributed by the director of vocational training at one of Nowa Huta's state firms. Wiktor Pental, Imago Mundi Foundation Collection.

competition gave the opportunity "to make up for their lack of experience through their enthusiasm," as one worker in Nowa Huta put it—who had the most to gain from the system. The historian Hubert Wilk also argues, however, that labor competition campaigns in Nowa Huta were most successful early on, when productivity, reflecting the primitive and unmechanized nature of construction work, correlated most strongly with physical effort. Once steel began to replace construction as the dominant form of production and the work process became more mechanized and complex, the economic utility of labor competition declined, as did enthusiasm for it.[39]

Even before this, however, disjunctions between the fiction of norms and the reality of engagement would generate tensions in Nowa Huta's workplaces, and beyond them. As Lewis Siegelbaum writes of Soviet Stakhanovism in the 1930s, the very success of labor competition "undermined its own effectiveness": first, the breakneck speed of Stalinist industrialization, which labor competition itself was meant to increase, heightened bottlenecks and imbalances in the production process, which in turn made it more difficult for workers to achieve high production targets. Conflicts thus arose over which workers would gain access to the scarce materials and good working conditions necessary for achieving high outputs. Second, as in the Soviet case, perceptions arose that foremen and brigade leaders were not recording workers' outputs fairly, which became a target of resentment.[40] Needless to say, the more genuine enthusiasm workers brought to labor competition, the greater their potential for disillusionment when its promises of reward for effort and dedication proved false.

In the 1980s, Piotr Ożański revealed how he had actually broken his first record. The site where he was to perform, he remembered, was meticulously prepared for two weeks before the event. "Engineers, technicians, every day the director came to have a look; everything was made even, neat," because this would guarantee the highest results. All tools and materials were gathered in advance, and most important, his bricks were preselected—they were whole, new bricks, not the irregularly shaped hand-me-downs from bomb-damaged buildings in the Western Territories so widely used on the building site. With bricks like these, one could build much faster. "It wasn't work," Ożański concluded, "it was sport."[41]

The fact that special working conditions were provided for model workers was no secret. When efforts were made to popularize the Lorenc system (a new method for bricklaying) in Nowa Huta in 1954, for example, teams of specially trained workers were deployed on the building site to prove the method's alleged superiority. But as the head of Nowa Huta's builders' union noted, efforts to persuade other workers to adopt the system met with complaints that the demonstration workers were "never short of materials because [the higher-ups] took an interest in them." By contrast, he was reminded, "for everyone else, there's a shortage of materials and of the work front, which makes it hard to complete one's pledges."[42] Indeed, in a shortage economy, the work front itself was a scarce commodity. On the building site, some work set-ups were more conducive to high productivity than others, depending on factors as varied as weather, tools, or labor distribution (too many workers on one job, for example, would lower individual output). Charges of favoritism could easily be leveled at foremen and managers who were perceived as distributing this commodity unfairly among workers. As scholars like Michael Burawoy have shown, shortages in the state socialist economy tended toward the emergence of "a core of key workers, usually male, skilled, and experienced, who bargain[ed] their way to comfort but at the expense of peripheral workers, the unskilled, the inexperienced, and often women."[43]

In Nowa Huta, too, the potentially egalitarian beginnings of its work force soon reflected the particularization of production and remuneration typical of state socialist production.[44] Such problems were especially acute for women and youth, whom managers often treated as reserve labor (apparently assuming that *junacy* would be less productive than so-called civilian workers).[45] Youth brigade members and their commanders complained regularly about cases like that of the 39th Brigade, which in July 1951 was (according to its commanders) continually moved from one place of work to the other by the firms with which it was contracted. This meant that, as a consequence, many youth were unable to complete the work pledges they had undertaken for July. Poor organization of production, moreover, "condemned" certain platoons to perpetually low output, as they had no work to perform for large parts of the day. This group had worked at 180 percent of norm at their previous work site but now was achieving 15 to 30 percent. As a result, the desire of these *junacy* to participate in work competition had declined.[46]

At a meeting called to evaluate productivity on May 13, 1951, members of the 37th Brigade aimed a barrage of complaints at management about problems ranging from inadequate supplies and tools to tardy, incompetent, or absent foremen. Worse still, *junacy* said they often had to wander about the site, sometimes for several hours, actually looking for work—an activity that naturally lowered their output for the day.[47] Sometimes firms provided no work at all.[48] Such "mistakes," wrote one trade union officer, "have a demobilizing effect on exemplary volunteer brigades."[49] Or, as one SP commander put it, "The question arises why on the one hand we have a recruitment campaign, when on the other, participants of brigades have no employment. Moreover, participants in the brigade see the futility of their presence [there], where in connection with this there are concerns that there will be desertions in the near future."[50] In the end, according to one estimate, a full 40 percent of work by *junacy* was performed at less than 100 percent of norm—while about half of all brigade members never took part in work competition at all.[51]

The danger of demobilization, according to activists, also accompanied the introduction of new forms of labor competition such as pledging (*zobowiązania*) in autumn 1951—supposedly voluntary commitments by groups of workers to perform extra labor within the framework of a particular campaign. As one union inspector noted, "One often encounters comments by workers such as, 'the foreman brought [the papers], and he said that we were to sign up for labor competition—we signed our names, and that was that.' When asked what labor competition is, the majority responded that they don't know." Such "administrative pressure, purely formal and mechanical," was to be considered the "greatest error" committed thus far in labor mobilization campaigns: "It forces us to treat with great caution the apparently impressive figures given [in reports]. . . . Observing work on the terrain, we arrive at the proposition that there exists a great disproportion between the level of the leading workers, about whose pledges we read in the press, and that greater number of unskilled or barely skilled workers whose still low level of political consciousness damages the true mass undertaking of pledging, the fundamental form of socialist competition." Because of this, the official provocatively claimed, "the average worker productivity on our building site is one of the lowest among all investments of the Six-Year Plan."[52] Another report opined gloomily that "labor competition on Nowa Huta's terrain is not developing, and we even see certain signs of stagnation of this movement." Participation was hard to measure, because "no one is in a position to provide complete data on the quantity of participants in labor competition," but it was "weakly developed among youth," despite young workers' enthusiasm. Leading model workers, meanwhile, did not receive adequate care and guidance from ZMP. As if to symbolize this, "one often sees mud on portraits of model workers that are hung in front of the apartment blocks, or that they are tattered and worn."[53]

To the extent that labor competition in Nowa Huta was in disarray, this reflected multiple contradictions between the structural inefficiencies of production in the new town, on the one hand, and Stalinism's unyielding productivist rhetoric, on the other. The contradictions of Stalinist productivism escaped few who were closely acquainted with the nature of work in Nowa Huta and fundamentally shaped relations among workers, their supervisors, and political authorities. "Oh Tadek, look how our lives have improved," one worker was allegedly overheard telling his mate in 1953. "Our earnings are being cut all the time and higher norms are being imposed on people—now they think that a human being is a machine."[54]

Dissent over labor competition arose not only among ordinary workers, but also extended into the party and among model workers themselves. During preparations in Nowa Huta for the Rally of Youth to be held in Warsaw, organizers expressed concern about the allegedly bad influence certain party members were having on delegates. One, for example, had stated that youth should be allowed to conduct its own affairs without interference by the party, while another had allegedly caused a "rift between intellectual and physical workers, claiming that pen pushers should not be elected" to the rally. "Propaganda," moreover, "circulated widely to the effect that youth should not undertake pledges, because delegates to the rally are already chosen by the party." Someone had written on a wall, "Who will go to the rally?" and underneath it, "No one." Possibly influenced by such "propaganda," a group of ten elected delegates announced that they did not want to attend the rally, and were persuaded to go only after being "convinced of the inappropriateness of their position." Four other delegates, however, had to be struck off the list as "unsuitable."[55] Despite occasional bouts of enthusiasm and compliance, Nowa Huta's "leading element" was unreliable, unpredictable, and at times uncontrollable.

The Poor Steelworker Achieves the Norm and Breaks His Legs

By his own admission, youth brigade member Edmund Chmieliński was a true believer who wore his ZMP badge proudly and pored over the works of Engels, Marx, and Lenin in his leisure time. Chmieliński "built [in Nowa Huta] as though he were building his own house." Yet many like him were frustrated in attempts to lay claim to their "own house" by Nowa Huta's housing shortage of the early to mid-1950s. Workers' response to this crisis demonstrates how clashing visions of labor and its value generated a growing sense of the boundaries around Nowa Huta's "moral community" of labor.

As apartments were completed, they were distributed by the housing committees of individual firms to their employees. In detailed guidelines issued by Warsaw, committees were instructed to distribute apartments first to the most highly prized categories of employees—political cadres, trained specialists, and "essential" administrative staff—and second to foremen or highly skilled workers (especially those who had distinguished themselves through labor competition). Only 15 percent of the total was to be set aside for all other workers; ordinary workers without qualifications could hope to gain consideration only if they could prove that their present living conditions were health-threatening or otherwise unsustainable. "Underlying the above criteria," stated a report of the party district committee, "lies the principle: 'to each according to his work,' resulting from the deep sense of the just distribution of material goods in proportion to the size of an individual's share and contribution in building a system of social justice."[56]

Such rhetoric was like a red flag to the workers who flooded officials with requests for help. In their letters, apartment seekers detailed their housing woes, stressed their dedicated and productive contributions to the enterprise of building Nowa Huta, and appealed to the laws and guiding principles of People's Poland. In a 1954 letter to Józef Cyrankiewicz, chair of the council of ministers, Anna N. described how she had left her village "the moment work began on Nowa Huta." Her first job in the new town, that of office cleaner, had not satisfied her, as she wanted to find "more productive and fruitful work . . . serving our beloved People's Fatherland." She trained as an engine driver and earned the bronze Cross of Service as a model worker. "I fell in love with my . . . work and I want to give everything of myself in building these beautiful and glistening furnaces that the People's Government is building for us. Looking at them and at my work, . . . I would hate to leave [Nowa Huta]." But, Anna N. wrote, unless allocated an apartment, she would be forced to give up her dreams and return home to her village, because she had a sick mother whom she was unable to care for in the hostel.[57]

Anna N. was lucky; the railway authority put her second on the firm's waiting list for housing. More often, desperate letter writers simply received a form letter stating that as "an ordinary manual worker without special qualifications," he or she was ineligible for housing allocation.[58] The phrasing must have raised questions about how "an individual's share and contribution in building a system of social justice" should be measured: according to a worker's abstract economic value on a bureaucrat's ledger sheet, or according to his or her dedication and efforts on Nowa Huta's behalf? As a disabled worker angrily wrote in 1952:

When I could [still] work I was the first worker, wading up to the knees in the mud and mire, sleeping at night in a field under the naked sky. . . . They were very hard times. . . . Now I've lost all my strength, and have visited every office with the goal of getting an apartment. . . . Let Director Julian Lipski remember his debts and to whom an apartment is owed, namely to the worker, who was first to labor and build the foundations of Nowa Huta, who sank in the muck . . . and slept in wet workingman's rags, who doesn't [work] in an office like he does, where it's all about corruption and favoritism.[59]

This was advice that Poland's rulers would have done well to remember.

Stalinism linked workers' collective efforts to the construction of a new sort of civic community, a "splendid city" or "common home" writ large. In concrete ways, labor competition reinforced a rhetorical linkage for workers between productivity and civic virtue. The distinction between those who worked for the benefit of all—a moral community of labor—and those who worked only for themselves (or didn't work at all, or obstructed the ability of others to work productively through waste, inefficiency, or corruption) would be echoed, many years later, in the reminiscences of older residents interviewed by Dorota Gut in the early 1990s. "People lived by those norms," she was told: "They went to volunteer activities after work; there was enormous enthusiasm. Model workers were idealistic people who believed in what they were doing. Those young people who came to build didn't ask how much they'd be paid, but what was to be done, and whether they'd succeed. Spontaneity and enthusiasm were everywhere." By contrast, "those activists were do-nothings, they talked and wandered around more than they worked. After a year, a guy like this ended up a drunk and a bum because he had too much money."[60] When enthusiasms sparked by Stalinist mobilization began to cool, those representatives of party and state who appeared to have removed themselves from the community of collective effort would increasingly be regarded not as "us," but as "them," excluded from the moral community. Meanwhile, as a popular rhyme remembered by one of Gut's respondents went, "The poor steelworker / Achieved the norm / And broke his legs."[61]

Nowa Huta was a city of work. Production was its raison d'être, and labor was the common denominator of its new inhabitants' daily lives. In the Stalinist worldview, work (as distinguished from toil) was conceived both as a collective effort in pursuit of shared goals and as a vehicle for personal transformation. In both senses, work was understood as a key to realizing and unlocking the essence of socialism. So while work came to define the emerging community of producers in Nowa Huta, conflicts over work in the new town also became conflicts about socialism and its promise.

In the genealogy of worker protest that Andrzej Wajda created in his 1977 cinematic masterpiece *Man of Marble*, the choice of a new worker protagonist was significant. *Man of Marble* depicts a young worker in Nowa Huta—a simple, good-natured country lad—who rises to celebrity as a model worker, and just as precipitously falls. Like Ożański, the fictional Birkut undertakes a record-breaking feat in bricklaying; like him, too, he is injured when an anonymous worker engages in silent protest by passing him a red-hot brick. The incident launches a train of events that reveal the regime's terroristic nature. Birkut then symbolically handles one last brick—heaving it through the windows of party headquarters—before leaving Nowa Huta in disgrace.[62]

In making his protagonist a rural migrant, Wajda accurately identified the peasant origins of most of Poland's working class in the 1970s and 1980s. Provocatively, moreover, this symbolic forefather of worker protest (Birkut's son, played by the same actor, later becomes a leader of Solidarity in the sequel *Man of Iron*) was no hardened anti-Communist at the outset, but a somewhat green-about-the ears, undoubtedly naïve, but thoroughly idealistic—and ultimately truly heroic—adherent of "building socialism." Not only Wajda, but also Polish audiences captivated by the film seemed to feel that Birkut's story spoke to the crisis of late socialism on the eve of Solidarity.

Released on a limited basis and largely unpublicized in Polish cinemas, the film caused a sensation; in Warsaw, audiences (forced to discover where the film was showing through word-of-mouth) lined up around the block to see it. Belatedly realizing the film's damaging content, authorities hastened to pull *Man of Marble* from theaters. That it had escaped censors to that point, it turned out, was owing largely to the strong support of culture minister Józef Tejchma, who had worked as a youth organizer in Nowa Huta in the 1950s. Tejchma later wrote that he felt the film was an authentic portrait of the new town's young builders, one he was personally invested in seeing brought to the screen.[63]

While Mateusz Birkut was explicitly based on Piotr Ożański, however, Wajda took considerable liberties with Ożański's story. In the film, for instance, Birkut's idealism makes him a thorn in the system's side. Ożański's downfall was quite different. He was expelled in 1952 from the party and was fired from the white-collar job to which he had been socially advanced for two reasons, according to a confidential district party report. First, he had allegedly concealed his family's connections with the Ukrainian nationalist movement during the war (raising the interesting possibility that Poland's iconic "man of marble" was actually Ukrainian). Second, he had appeared drunk at several official functions.[64] Ożański left Nowa Huta for three years but returned following the change in local party leadership in 1956, taking a job as an ordinary steelworker. In a later profile, one journalist portrayed Ożański as something of a swaggering fool—an opportunistic conformist, perhaps, but no idealist. By contrast, in *Man of Iron*, Wajda's sequel to *Man of Marble*, Birkut resurfaces in 1970 as a martyred striker on the Baltic Coast—true to his ideals and defending workers' interests to the very end.[65]

But Birkut is fiction, and this is a history book. So let us end instead with Chmieliński—the enthusiastic model worker who was in some ways closer to the real-life Birkut than Ożański, the conformist activist. Like Birkut, Chmieliński was deeply idealistic, stubborn, and inconvenient. At first, he was smitten with the new ideas he encountered in the educational chats of agitators and in the ideological training he received through ZMP. He was elated to know that "every wheelbarrow-load of earth, every meter of completed road, every brick in the wall was bringing us closer to socialism and well-being," and he was awarded prizes and distinctions for conforming to the Stalinist models of behavior. But nothing came easily. After several failed attempts, Chmieliński finally earned a coveted place at a trade school in Kraków and left the brigade. But without a salary or family support, he had no money for books, clothes, or transportation. No one at school, except for some older students from Nowa Huta, sympathized; he was told that "school is not a holiday." Finally, when he missed a payment, he was expelled from the program and kicked out of the dorm.[66]

Now homeless, Chmieliński passed some time wandering about Nowa Huta, sleeping in the cellars of unfinished buildings and eating out of rubbish bins, until a friend arranged a place for him in a training course in Silesia. He returned to Nowa Huta in 1953 and struggled for a while with alcoholism and depression, but finally, like Ożański, married, settled down, and held a stable job as a crane operator at HiL. But unlike Ożański, Chmieliński's story did not end there. Chmieliński found himself constantly at odds with party, union, and management bosses. As in the scenes where Birkut is shown defending workers' interests as a work inspector, he bristled at every instance of "the unkindness, unfairness, bureaucratism, and insensitivity" that he saw around him, and "at every production meeting came out with sharp criticism for the management, firm [union] council, and firm party committee." He earned a reputation as a troublemaker and a personnel folder "fat with reprimands, punishments, docked wages, and letters from the foreman and brigade leader." In October 1956, Chmieliński joined other workers, both in Nowa Huta and throughout Poland, to demand the overthrow of the Stalinist regime and the return of Władysław Gomułka to power. Their hopes for a better deal for Polish workers, however, were not to be realized.[67]

Unlike Birkut, Chmieliński did not return to the barricades when Solidarity erupted in Nowa Huta in 1980; like many of his generation, now reaching retirement age, he remained a passive supporter of the young movement. And yet, these men of marble served an important role as living reminders of Nowa Huta's origins, and of how Stalinism had betrayed its builders' enthusiasm. Some years later, the ethnographer Michael Burawoy found a job at Hungary's

Lenin Steelworks in the city of Miskolc. "The soul of the socialist proletariat lay here," Burawoy wrote, "capable of heroic feats of endurance, celebrated in posters of the Stalinist past, carrier of the radiant Communist future"; but what remained was "a nightmare of coordination" in production, and a work-force steeped in a "socialist 'culture of critical discourse.'" That culture, forged out of the constant encounter with socialist rhetoric and imagery, expressed itself in wisecracks that "relentlessly drew attention to the gap between ideology and reality." Still, in the workers' "outbursts of anger," Burawoy "detected a continuing commitment to [those] socialist ideals" first encountered in the Stalinist crucible.[68]

In 1981, Chmieliński submitted his autobiography to a memoir contest organized by Polish sociologists hoping to study the sources of worker dissatisfaction behind Solidarity. However, the memoir was published only in 1996, after communism's collapse. In their introduction to the collection in which it appeared, the editors took an unflattering view of Chmieliński: The "system of values" from the early 1950s, they wrote, "functioned in the consciousness of the author in relation to all periods of his life," and "the social personality of the author" was "uncomplicated, of a rigid and stable system of values." And yet one could say something similar of Mateusz Birkut: the drama in Wajda's films arises from friction between Birkut's uncomplicated and stable values and the fickleness and conformism of those around him. It is they who adapt their views and behavior as political fashions change. However, the new worker who took at face value Stalinist ideals of justice for working people stays just the same.

4

Women of Steel

On October 9, 1953, workers at the Lenin Steelworks in Nowa Huta stood by to watch as Poland's only all-female team of metal casters performed its high-precision task. "The whole staff of the foundry observed the women bustling about the furnace. . . . When the vat was already full, the caster gave the sign and the gantry started to pass slowly over the great mold. With the help of the mechanism, Jarominowa tilted the vat. Molten metal began to pour in a thin stream into the mold. Enough. Jarominowa again gave a sign of the hand, and the vat moved on to the next mold." With great care, W. Bosak, K. Cyc, M. Jarominowa, and E. Olchowa directed a stream of molten iron into the waiting molds, making sure that not a drop of the red-hot metal was wasted. It was their last chance to show off their mastery of this demanding work; hereafter, they would be transferred to different jobs in the foundry, lighter ones, away from the hot furnaces. It was not that they worked worse than men; in fact, from time to time they had beaten their male coworkers' norms. Rather, their work had been found in violation of health regulations governing women's employment. In the words of one commentator, the brigade had to "give up its ambitions for its own good." Privately, however, the women protested against the brigade's dissolution, insisting "that they could work just like men."[1]

The story of these four women is remarkable for a number of reasons. Of all branches of industry, steel and metalworking has certainly been among the most masculinized worldwide, both in fact and in its cultural associations. Moreover, steel occupied an iconic status in European state socialism, and within the Polish Stalinist universe, the Lenin Steelworks in Nowa Huta was its high temple. Surely no other Polish women have ever penetrated so deeply into the sanctum sanctorum of national industry, and indeed, their story is exceptional in a world context, where female steelworkers are rare. The vignette described above thus illustrates how far Polish women had come in

Poland since the Second World War, while also suggesting some of the obstacles encountered by women pioneering new roles in the workplace and the subversion of their achievements by official and unofficial means. Put more broadly, as we read this anecdote—and the story of women in Nowa Huta more generally—we become painfully aware of the contradictions of Stalinist ends, means, and results with regard to the woman question. Those contradictions are the main subject of this chapter.

The chapter will also consider what is in some ways a parallel case, that of the Roma (Gypsies) in Nowa Huta. Just as the Stalinist regime pledged to productivize and integrate women into the traditionally male workplace in Nowa Huta, it undertook the project of integrating members of this allegedly parasitic ethnic group into the new town. In both cases, the regime pointed to its supposed achievements in assimilating the two groups to demonstrate socialism's break with an archaic prewar past.[2] Moreover, after 1956, official policies toward women and Roma followed similar trajectories: political liberalization during the thaw period and the collapse of the Stalinist system brought, paradoxically, regression in certain gains for both women and Roma. We are thus challenged to consider anew how Stalinism, on the one hand, and post-Stalinist liberalization, on the other, affected distinct segments of the working class in different ways. Far from affecting only women and Roma, moreover, these losses and gains had profound meaning for Polish society as a whole.

Baba and Comrade

Article 61 of the Constitution of the Polish People's Republic stated that "woman in the Polish People's Republic has equal rights with man in all areas of national, political, economic, social, and cultural life."[3] The centerpiece of Stalinist policy toward women in Poland, and the one with the most far-reaching impact on women's lives, was the active promotion of women's entry into the paid workforce. During the interwar period, fewer than one in four Poles employed outside agriculture had been female; by contrast, between 1950 and 1954 women's total participation in the workforce rose from 31 percent to 33 percent.[4] Even more striking were increases in specific sectors. Women's work in industry before World War II had been almost exclusively in the textile and garment trades. In 1931, their participation in the building trades was 2.7 percent, and in transportation, 5.2 percent. By 1950, these figures had risen to 13.7 percent and 13.4 percent, respectively.[5] Women also entered other sectors of heavy industry, such as steelworking and metalworking, where their prewar presence had been practically nonexistent. In steelworking, women's employment rose 760 percent between 1937 and 1949 alone.[6]

Polish Communists had not been at the forefront of the fight for gender equality during the interwar period, when it was mainly Socialist and bourgeois advocates who had pressed for improvements in women's legal status and reproductive rights, the entry of women into the professions, and economic and social changes that would lessen the burdens on mothers and female workers. Women's demands for greater rights were strengthened by their vital role in World War II, both as combatants and civilians. Counterbalancing these tendencies were the church's teachings on women and deeply held cultural beliefs about the natural basis of gender difference that even most Polish feminists shared with their opponents. After the war, the Polish Socialist Party (PPS) again took up the lead in organizing women and advancing issues of gender equality.[7] The Communists, meanwhile, had inherited a mixed legacy on the "woman question." While Marx and Engels had linked women's liberation to the defeat of capitalism, some Soviet Bolshevik leaders saw feminism as a bourgeois movement that diverted energies from class struggle. With the "great retreat" from radical cultural and social experimentation around 1930, moreover, Soviet leaders had abandoned utopian projects of restructuring family life, gender roles, and sexual mores.[8] At the same time, they remained formally committed to a program of gender equality.

Stalinist programs of forced industrialization, moreover, demanded unprecedented levels of female employment. Thus, Barbara Einhorn argues, Soviet policy stressed women's economic activization as "not only the necessary but also the sufficient condition" for their emancipation. Avoiding difficult questions of cultural and sexual patriarchy, Stalinism ignored (among other things) the unequal division of labor in the home, instead relying on public services such as childcare to paper over the contradictions in its partial approach to transforming gender roles.[9]

Such contradictions may also be seen, Eric Weitz argues, in Communists' failure to construct a coherent vision of socialist femininity, one that could compete with traditional gender models "in the way the [Soviet image of the] heroic and combative male proletarian provided a uniform and consistent construction of masculinity."[10] According to Elizabeth Wood, Stalinist discourse represented woman in a bifurcated and ambivalent way. She was either "*baba*," the backward, superstitious, and ignorant "biddy," or "comrade," the active, selfless, and in some senses sexless paragon of the new regime—a knockoff of her male counterpart that had little to distinguish her as specifically female.[11] Polish Communists, too, adopted this dichotomous typology of femininity. On the one hand, there was, as the periodical *Kobieta Wiejska* put it, the traditional village girl, whose consciousness "enclosed itself in the circle of her farm and village. The prayer book, . . . sermon in church, rumors and news told over the fence or in the fields—this was her entire spiritual sustenance." By contrast, her liberated rural counterpart—the iconic female tractor driver—saw a wider world from the perspective of her driver's seat: "Ola's tractor plows a broad field; it will plow the well-being and might of Poland, the well-being and might of the democratic countries; it will plow peace."[12]

Polish Stalinists thus presented women's "'equal rights' as synonymous with paid work."[13] As President Bierut put it in a speech before the Unification Congress of 1948, the socialist woman's advancement was inextricably bound up with her unselfish impulse to submit to the needs and demands of People's Poland: "Polish women already are taking an enormous part in the building of People's Poland; . . . they continually achieve new vocational qualifications and, for the sake of completing the ravishing [*sic*!] tasks of the Six-Year Plan, give of themselves in persistent labor, enlivened by the feeling of their warm hearts."[14] The new woman extended her traditionally nurturing role beyond the sphere of the nuclear family to embrace not only the nation but also the wider family of international progress and peace. This rhetorical strategy of cathexis, what Joanna Goven calls "familialization," suggested that women's equality in the workplace would in no way destabilize their traditional roles as girlfriends, wives, and mothers.[15]

Not surprisingly, the image of the woman-comrade in Polish Stalinist iconography found its perfect vehicle in the "Nowa Huta woman." In 1953, the newspaper *Budujemy Socjalizm* held an essay contest on this theme, and the prizewinning reply celebrated the Nowa Huta woman's fortitude in the face of the new town's pioneering conditions and her willingness to work "on an equal plane with men." However, the (male) author appeared to be at least as interested in Nowa Huta women's looks. First of all, he wrote, they "distinguish themselves by their healthy humor and natural color of skin. No makeup, no artificial hues. In spring the breeze and sun give them color, in winter the frost paints their cheeks." This image of healthy, ruddy femininity was further offset by dress. Contemporaries often commented on the distinctive costume worn by all workers in Nowa Huta, but this was particularly notable in women, because unlike women elsewhere, they "dressed for everyday just like the men [not quite—some women in Nowa Huta actually worked in skirts], in quilted jackets and rubber boots."[16] Even out of costume, though, the "Nowa Huta woman" was instantly recognizable: as one male worker recalled, all the "young ladies" of Nowa Huta had chafed shins where the tops of their rubber boots met the skin, the indelible mark of their labor.[17] This alone would be enough to distinguish them from the elegant Krakovian *bourgeoises* with whom they might mingle on a Sunday stroll in the *Planty*.

"In My Fiftieth Year I Rebelled"

Women came to Nowa Huta for many of the same reasons as men—among them, a longing for independence, adventure, job security, and a higher standard of living. Many women were also escaping village patriarchy and dependence on male relatives. This included pregnant women fleeing the stigma of single motherhood in rural communities, as well as older women like the widow affectionately known to the younger inhabitants of her hostel as "Grandma," who were drawn by the lure of financial independence.[18] "In my fiftieth year I rebelled and set forth to look for work," wrote one woman in an open letter to her grown son in *Budujemy Socjalizm*. "[Now] I work and have my own money, busy up to my eyes with my own work. What a pleasure. I don't need to wait for whatever you might give me."[19] Nowa Huta offered economic independence to middle-class women as well as the majority who were rural migrants. One white-collar worker, styling herself "Victoria" in her autobiography, explained how her three-year stay in a women's hostel had enabled her to leave an unhappy marriage: "In Nowa Huta I recovered a feeling I had lost—happiness and joy in life; I recaptured peace of mind. . . . [Here] I am raising my only treasure, my daughter, in peace; I work and revel in my good fortune."[20]

During and immediately after World War II, many Polish women became accustomed to acting independently from men. As one twenty-eight-year-old single mother wrote to the Kraków provincial party office, asking for work in Nowa Huta, she felt confident in her abilities and had a strong desire for self-fulfillment: "I am known at our firm as a competent and hard-working woman but none of it satisfies my expectations of myself. I want to study—it seems to me that deep inside me is some tremendous potential, with which I could serve my People's Fatherland and society." The letter writer's husband, a soldier, had disappeared when posted to L'viv after the war, leaving her alone to support their child.[21] Another single woman, Barbara S., also had followed a hard road to Nowa Huta: a former slave laborer and Auschwitz inmate, she had separated from her husband after liberation, emigrated to Nowa Huta in 1952, and within a year, parlayed her experience of work in concentration camp kitchens into a job as director of the cafeteria at the House of the Young Worker.[22]

After the war, many Polish men migrated internally in search of work, leaving their wives to take care of farms and extended families back home. When Janina Radwan's husband found a job in Nowa Huta, however, she was not content to stay behind; Radwan, a World War II veteran, explained, "I didn't see any other solution, because there [at home in Wadowice] the conditions were also unlivable." Without her husband's knowledge, Radwan began looking for ways to join him; ultimately, she found work and housing in Nowa Huta with help from the Women's League. When she and her three-year-old son surprised her husband at the end of his shift on their first day in the new town, Radwan got the impression that he was impressed but not entirely pleased at her having taken matters into her own hands. Even married women, it seemed, could lead uniquely independent lives in Nowa Huta: Radwan continued to take the lead in improving her family's living conditions, working as a hostel assistant and eventually securing family housing so that she, her husband, and their children could live together.[23]

For Radwan and others like her, what was important was to be active and occupied, rather than sitting at home in the village passively waiting for one's fortunes to change. For all the difficulties they encountered in Nowa Huta, many women subjectively experienced a vast improvement in their lives in the new town. Indeed, in women's narratives of life in Nowa Huta, as in men's, hardships serve the narrative function of underlining authors' ultimate successes. Women's narratives, like men's, also stress the personal satisfaction derived from work, "the process," as Martha Lampland writes, "whereby a job or means of earning a living became a calling, a satisfying activity, and a moral purpose."[24] As Elizabeth Tobin and Jennifer Gibson argue in their study of German women under Nazi and East German rule, by validating women's work, state socialism gave women a vocabulary and framework within which to describe their life choices, along with actual opportunities to pursue careers. In this sense, socialism affected women's sense of self.[25]

Comrades

Between 1950 and 1956, women's presence in Nowa Huta grew from about 42 percent to almost half of the population.[26] According to one estimate, some 22 percent of the women in Nowa Huta worked outside the home in 1955.[27] There are few reliable statistics for the period, but data for individual sectors offer a snapshot of women's employment patterns: In construction, which employed more than 60 percent of Nowa Huta's workforce in 1954,[28] women constituted 10 to 14 percent of employees, slightly more than half of them manual laborers.[29] Women made up a comparatively greater proportion of employees at the steelworks—about 20 percent in 1952, a figure that probably reflects the growth in clerical and administrative positions there. About 11.5 percent of HiL employees categorized as "physical workers" were women.[30]

The idealized Nowa Huta woman was one who worked in the "new," i.e., skilled, traditionally masculine occupations that had been opened to women during the Stalinist industrialization drive. In construction, this included bricklaying, steelfixing, laying concrete, glazing, electricianship, welding, engine driving, and operating machinery; in steel production, it included work in transport, at the iron furnaces and iron purification unit, and at the electrical plant.[31] Skilled women workers, who often appeared with their pictures and brief biographies in *Budujemy Socjalizm*, were sent as delegates to provincial and national meetings and were pointed to as demonstrations of women's advancement under socialism. These were women like Helena Sandorek, "daughter of a small farmer, [who] has been working four months on Nowa Huta's building site—a model worker who, after finishing a course in servicing machinery, obtained her professional qualifications"—and Zofia Wójcik, "model worker from PPRK Nr. 3. Achieved 197 per cent of the norm. She's one of the first four women who, having completed a course in servicing building machines, services transports on this area of the site."[32]

A woman like the twenty-three-year-old mason Zofia Włodek was Nowa Huta's female answer to Piotr Ożański, the Stakhanovite bricklayer whose achievements were broadcast throughout the country. According to the press, however, Włodek and her female colleagues had not only excelled in production like Ożański, but had also dared to overcome traditional gender barriers to become Nowa Huta's first female bricklayers—at "the call of the party organization," of course. As one member of the group told a reporter, when the women (previously employed as cleaners) had first started their training, they "met with a hearty reception from our foremen, who taught us the trade in the course of three weeks. Many [male] workers, however, thought that only men could build a wall." To prove them wrong, Włodek's brigade, split into two competing sections, resolved to build Nowa Huta's first daycare center in time for the thirty-third anniversary of the October Revolution. Work began with a great deal of publicity and a ceremony, complete with banners and musical accompaniment by the ZMP orchestra. *Budujemy Socjalizm* followed the group's progress as they took on new commitments, such as completing sections of the building ahead of schedule in honor of the Second World Congress of Defenders of Peace. (Although the team had already fallen short of its original deadline for completing the daycare center, the reporter tactfully let that pass without comment.)[33]

Two members of a female plastering brigade, 1953. Wiktor Pental, Imago Mundi Foundation Collection.

Włodek, who joined the ZMP and was elected vice president of the Women's League shortly after "volunteering" for her new career, was made a representative at the first conference of the Nowa Huta Council of Trade Unions, by which time she was also a party member.[34] Women like Włodek and Wójcik—the only woman in Nowa Huta to receive a silver Cross of Service in 1950—were on a fast track to becoming professional worker-activists; indeed, in 1954 Wójcik was no longer working at machines, but rather as an agitator (and, according to the complaints of local activists, was too busy traveling around the country to have time for propaganda work in Nowa Huta itself).[35]

Obviously, few women in Nowa Huta became celebrities like either of the two Zofias. But how many actively sought out work in the new occupations, and how many of those succeeded in gaining entry to these higher-skilled, higher-paid positions? In 1951, the Women's League put the number of qualified women workers in Nowa Huta at only 274—a seemingly unimpressive figure some two years into work on the nation's flagship "socialist city."[36] Generally speaking, the demand for vocational training in Nowa Huta's first years always outstripped supply, and anecdotal evidence suggests this was at least as true for women as for men, if not more so; gaining one of the precious spots in a vocational training course required perseverance, luck, or connections. Thus, regardless of the regime's official affirmative action program, Women's League officials noted, women were often turned away. For example, "Julia R. sought to no avail to be enrolled in a drafting course as she has a talent for drawing—[and] eighteen girls [from the same hostel] asked to be enrolled in a driving course in keeping with their preferences—thus far without result."[37] The majority of Nowa Huta's women workers remained in unskilled positions, working side-by-side with men in physically demanding, unmechanized labor on the construction site.[38]

Yet ordinary women workers also held a place in the pantheon of Nowa Huta's heroines, and in some cases they could earn high wages (although these could vary widely and unpredictably, depending on circumstance). As one agitator explained to "[female] comrades and friends" in a speech prior to the National Convention of Leading [*Przodujących*] Women of the Cities and Villages, such women "complete their assignments on a par with men and even better, as, for example, the brigade of Genowefa T[. . .], composed of twelve women employed in excavation work at ZPB Nowa Huta." The brigade was said to earn an average monthly wage of 1,200 złoty—on a par with many male workers and well above the national average.[39]

Finally, many women in Nowa Huta worked in traditionally feminine occupations. As we have seen, female cadres often filled posts in the cultural or social services; for other educated women, there were white-collar opportunities such as secretarial work or hostel administration. Unskilled women cleaned offices and workers' hostels or worked in the kitchens of the communal cafeterias. With the exception of cadres, for such women, opportunities for earning high wages or premiums through labor competition were few. Secretaries might pull even with or ahead of unqualified female physical laborers; cleaners, on the other hand, could earn as little as 150 złoty per month—little more than pocket money, considering that the official price of bread was 3 złoty.[40] Yet even these workers were assured that they had a vital role in "building socialism" through dedicated and self-sacrificing work—for example, by pledging to save on the use of soap powder, or by promising to "enlighten" the residents of the hostels to value cleanliness, not to gamble and drink vodka, and so on.[41]

O Nowej to Hucie Piosenka

"One wanted to *live* in Nowa Huta—it was so gay. . . . A person enjoyed just going out on the street," remembered Krystyna G. of the town's first years in the 1950s. Young people engaged in labor competition simply because "they wanted to be the best," and the best things in life—dances, music, movies— were free. Life in Nowa Huta, she remembered, was accompanied by "nonstop music," whether it was the sound of men singing on their way to work or songs piped over the loudspeakers. The light, catchy tune "O Nowej to Hucie Piosenka" (A Song about Nowa Huta) was on everyone's lips; "how many pairs of shoes my husband and I wore out, dancing in front of the post office!" After a year and a half of living "wild" (squatting illegally) in an unoccupied apartment, she and her husband moved into their own home with their first child. Her neighbors were "like a family." Nowa Huta had offered Krystyna G., a Roma who had lost most of her relatives in the Holocaust, a new beginning.[42]

Krystyna and her husband, Augustyn, came to Nowa Huta thanks to a concerted government effort to recruit and settle Roma in the new town. This, in turn, was part of a broader policy, first articulated in the early years after the war, of "productivizing" Poland's population of some fifteen thousand Roma.[43] Polish officials began searching for a solution to what they termed the "Gypsy problem" shortly after the war, entrusting first the Ministry of Public Administration, and later the Presidium of the Council of Ministers, with working out the details of integrating Roma into the formal economy. Ending the migratory lifestyle still practiced by some 75 percent of Poland's Roma was considered an essential part of the program; thus, a resolution of the presidium on May 24, 1952, on "assistance to the Gypsy population in making the transition to a settled way of life," called for a range of government ministries to offer supervision and material assistance to Roma who gave up a nomadic lifestyle. The Ministry of Education was to provide Roma families with supplementary income, where needed, so they could pay for books, clothes, and education; the Ministry of Health was to raise the level of sanitation and health among the Roma population; the Ministry of Culture and Art was to organize Roma musical and artistic endeavors and identify gifted youth for admission to art schools; and so on. This policy, which stressed carrots over sticks, remained in place through the early 1960s.[44]

As with gender, Polish Communists came at the Gypsy problem with a contradictory mix of cultural prejudices, ideological imperatives, and ethno-nationalist baggage. During the interwar period, Poland had been one of the most multiethnic societies in Europe; nearly one-third of its population was officially classified as belonging to ethnic minorities.[45] While the Polish political mainstream increasingly gravitated toward exclusivist ethno-nationalism and antisemitism in the 1930s, parties of the Left, including the PPS and the outlawed Polish Communist Party (KPP), opposed racial, ethnic, and religious discrimination. As Nazism rose in Germany, Communist propaganda linked the racism of both the center-right "Sanacja" regime and its prominent far-right opposition, the National Democratic Party, to "Hitlerism" and the growing Fascist threat. By contrast, it depicted communism as the movement most committed to ethnic, religious, and racial equality, traits that Communists proclaimed would characterize a future multiethnic, Communist-led Polish state.[46]

In contrast to these formal ideological commitments, however, was the strongly nationalist stance adopted by leaders of the PPR during and after World War II. Broadly speaking, the postwar Communists attempted to take credit for a fact not of their own making: Hitler, Stalin, and the Allies had ensured that postwar Poland would be, for the first time in history, an almost entirely homogeneous nation-state. The postwar settlement agreed at Teheran in 1943 ceded some 200,000 square kilometers of Poland's eastern territories to Stalin, granting Poland German land to the west in compensation. Thus, Poland inadvertently lost the regions in which a majority of its prewar Ukrainian, Jewish, and Belorussian populations had lived. Hitler, moreover, had substantially eliminated Poland's Jewish question, and those Jews who survived the war were expected to emigrate to Israel in due course. Under the terms that the Allies imposed at Yalta in 1945, postwar Poland would expel the German population of the new Western Territories as well as a sizeable percentage of its prewar German minority. Ethnic cleansing at the new borders with the Ukrainian and Belorussian Soviet Socialist Republics and forced resettlement of Lemkos and other minorities in 1947 in Operation Vistula completed the process of ethnic homogenization.[47] Ironically, in militantly pursuing the goal of a national (not multiethnic or multinational) Poland, the Communists ended up realizing, in large measure, the program of their former right-wing opponents, the National Democrats. At the same time, Communist propaganda, aimed at winning over a population inclined to view the new government as a puppet of the much-hated Soviets, downplayed Communist internationalism, instead noisily depicting the party as the defender of Polish national traditions and aspirations. For the next two decades, the party would be unable to square the circle of these two contradictory ideologies.

The party's nationalism, as one scholar puts it, was never a "coherent doctrine, but rather a conglomeration of slogans and undeveloped concepts,"[48] and its approach to dealing with the small ethnic minority communities that remained in Poland after World War II was similarly incoherent. This allowed ample play for inherited cultural stereotypes to shape policy. In the case of the Roma, such stereotypes held them to be dirty, disorderly, childlike, lazy, superstitious, thieving, and dishonest.[49] Many perceived Roma otherness as a matter of cultural deficits rather than cultural differences, a tendency reinforced by the government's classification of Roma as a mere "ethnicity" rather than a "nationality."[50] Whether benignly paternalist or overtly coercive, state policies toward the Roma assumed a civilizational gap between Roma and ethnic Poles that would be closed only when Roma assimilated to a culture and lifestyle resembling that of their non-Roma neighbors.

Such assumptions dictated the government's decision to direct its initial attention to the one-quarter or so of Polish Roma who already led a sedentary lifestyle. The so-called highlander or Carpathian Roma (sometimes called Bergitka Roma by other Roma, but known among themselves simply as *Roma*)[51] led a settled way of life, mainly in the mountainous Nowy Targ area of Kraków province. Probably descended from fifteenth-century Balkan migrants, they typically engaged in traditional occupations, like coppersmithing and tinkering, that had been hard-hit by economic changes of the interwar years. By contrast, the peripatetic lowlander Roma made a living from music, fortune telling, and (so it was widely believed) theft—sources of income largely unaffected by the transition to a modern economy. Thus, not only were the highlander Roma already accustomed to a sedentary lifestyle, but they also had the most to gain from new forms of economic activity.[52] In concentrating their (somewhat misnamed) settlement efforts on highlander Roma—styled a "gypsy proletariat"—officials hoped to set a positive example for other groups of Roma. In 1950, 112 men from Nowy Targ were thus recruited to work at a state firm in Szczecin; the same year, thirty Bergitka Roma families (about 160

Roma women. They work in the same plastering brigade as the women in fig. 4.1. Wiktor
Pental, Imago Mundi Foundation Collection.

people in all) were brought to Nowa Huta. In 1952, the Roma population of the new town had grown to an estimated 200; by 1956, it was more than 270.[53]

Augustyn G.'s uncle, Walenty, among the first Roma to settle in Nowa Huta, led a cement-laying brigade hailed in the inaugural issue of the newspaper *Budujemy Socjalizm*: "Citizen Walenty G[. . .] is a model worker among a twenty-five-person group of Gypsies at work on building Nowa Huta. His entire team achieves on average 176 percent of the norm."[54] Personally awarded the Silver Cross of Service by Prime Minister Cyrankiewicz, Walenty G., like another Roma labor hero, Stefan Gabor, was held up as an example of how "socialist society has a strong influence over even the most stubborn individuals and groups."[55] (Perhaps poking fun at such rhetoric, an unnamed Roma worker—possibly Walenty G.—showed up late once for an award ceremony at which he was to receive a Silver Cross and give a speech. When urged to the podium, he allegedly declared, "Life is too short for a Gypsy to have to work" and stepped down, to laughter from the audience.)[56] Authorities were well aware of the Romas' propaganda value in Nowa Huta, and noted that foreign visitors touring the new town, for instance, liked to snap photos of them.[57] Unfortunately, Roma visibility was a two-edged sword. Their high profile rendered them a target of considerable official anxiety; the project of "civilizing" the Roma could not be seen to fail.

Roma in Nowa Huta were thus subject to the surveillance and "guardianship" of health officials, Women's League activists, and the Committee for Public Order of the municipal administrative apparatus. Among these, the health services assumed a special role, because it was feared that Roma were vectors of infectious disease owing to their supposedly poor hygiene. Health officials took a paternalist interest in the Roma; Zdzisław Olszewski, for instance, director of Nowa Huta's health services in the early 1950s, recalled having "fought like a lion" to get the first group of Nowa Huta's Roma inhabitants moved from the unsanitary barracks at Wyciąże into apartment blocks—especially after rumors of a typhoid outbreak occurred.[58] Stanisława Siudut, head of the municipality's Committee for Health and Social Welfare from 1952 to 1956, likewise saw her role as one of special guardianship over the Roma, counting as one of her successes the first Roma woman persuaded to give birth in the municipal birthing center—a sign, in her eyes, of the growing trust for authority in the Roma community.[59]

Other officials, however, regarded the Roma primarily as an administrative nuisance. In 1954, the Committee for Public Order of the DRN complained that in Roma apartments, "the lack of hygiene made itself felt at every step" and recommended fining eight inhabitants for "destruction of apartments, dirt, disorder, and starting rows."[60] Some tenants were accused of having pitched camp inside their apartments (Olszewski claimed to have worked mightily to persuade Roma not to "keep rabbits and chickens in the beautiful bathtubs and not to burn campfires on the floor").[61] Rumors of Roma families slipping away from Nowa Huta in the middle of the night, never to return, confirmed a view of the Roma as resisting assimilation to their new lifestyle. So did the appearance of a shantytown on the outskirts of town inhabited by Roma who had abandoned their allocated housing allegedly because in the new apartment blocks, they felt as if they were "in prison." The alternative explanation, given credence by many, was that the Roma were thieves and preferred to live outside town, the better to practice their trade.[62]

For those like Krystyna G., the presence of these other Roma, camped just outside town on the banks of the Dłubnia, gave "model" Roma a poor name, and relations between the two groups were sometimes tense.[63] Even those Roma who aspired to take advantage of the full spectrum of employment and social welfare opportunities in Nowa Huta, however, had serious obstacles to overcome. In contrast to the few who, like Walenty and Augustyn G., attained skilled and well-paying positions at the steelworks, by 1956 most Roma still had unskilled, low-paid jobs.[64] Krystyna G. began work with a group of other Roma women as part of a landscaping crew, but after the whole group was fired without explanation, she sought work at HiL. There, she tended vats of ammonia crystals, a sulfurous byproduct used to make photographic film. The smell was so strong that when she got on the tram after work, passengers would joke, "Here comes the pharmacy!"[65] A long-range study conducted in 1970 confirmed that, like Krystyna G., most Roma in Nowa Huta held undesirable forms of employment (for example, garbage collection) and that overall, "chances for social and professional advancement of Nowa Huta's Gypsies" had been "a great deal less than for other inhabitants of the town."[66]

While good relations sometimes flourished among Roma and non-Roma neighbors, many ethnic Poles still made no effort to hide their prejudices. "People looked at us as though we were freaks," one man remembered; "they were afraid when they saw that we were coming to work in Nowa Huta." Some young Roma men bleached their hair with peroxide in an effort to fit in and avoid trouble.[67] Schoolchildren, meanwhile, were bullied or made to sit on separate benches by their teachers.[68] Roma women complained that the Women's League did not want to work with them, while league activists complained in turn that the Roma were interested only in handouts.[69] The district party executive was vaguely aware of anti-Roma prejudice ("our people say . . . that they wished the Roma weren't in Nowa Huta") but focused on combatting its negative propaganda value rather than on rooting it out (the Women's League, for instance, was instructed to counteract recent press reports "that there was discrimination against national minorities in Nowa Huta"). Officials stuck to formulaic exhortations to "teach [the Roma] and bring them closer to us," suggesting that the solution for overcoming prejudice lay ultimately with the Roma themselves, in their becoming more "Polish."[70]

Some commentators blamed the mixed results of Nowa Huta's Roma experiment on the Roma tendency to "nihilistic freedom."[71] The writer Jerzy Ficowski, who had traveled with groups of Roma for two years, called it their "disinclination to submit to any form of authority, a complete lack of discipline and understanding of how to conform," alleging in 1953 that an "'anarchist' need for complete liberty and independence inclined certain individuals to leave the good living conditions in Nowa Huta." Suggestively, Ficowski quoted certain Roma leaving Nowa Huta as saying, "We are bound for freedom."[72] On the other hand, it was precisely the freedom of Nowa Huta that appealed to someone like Krystyna G.—both its spatial openness and its freedom from the past. A new town like Nowa Huta was, no doubt, easier to integrate into than an older, more established community; here everybody was forced, in a sense, to find his or her place. In Nowa Huta, Krystyna G. created a new life on her own terms, later becoming an advocate and organizer for children and Roma women. Acculturation did not mean giving up her Roma identity.[73]

Notwithstanding some successes, Warsaw began to change its thinking about the "Gypsy problem" in the post-Stalinist period. For one thing, the experiment of Nowa Huta was couldn't be reproduced—and it was effective, in the end, for only a minority of those (the Bergitka Roma) who were themselves a minority within the Roma community. Frustrated by the meager results thus far obtained, in March 1964 the government introduced a new Roma policy that instituted extensive police and administrative surveillance of transient communities, amounting to a de facto strategy of forced settlement. By the late 1970s, administrative policing and harassment had put an end to the Polish Romas' wandering way of life without addressing continuing and widespread discrimination, outbreaks of anti-Roma violence, or pervasive social and economic marginalization.[74]

Gender Unfixed

As Joanna Goven puts it, Stalinism had simultaneously "homogenizing" and "differentiating" impulses. Just as the Romas' otherness was not erased in Nowa Huta despite government attempts to eliminate their cultural distinctiveness, Stalinism's campaign for women's equal rights did not do away with gender difference. Indeed, for a regime intent on establishing stable and unquestioned relations of authority, attempting to erase gender altogether could have been a dangerous undertaking. "Gender and political power are— or may be—mutually constitutive," Goven reminds us. Thus, a wholesale "unfixing" of such a fundamental category of social and political life could have threatened Communism's attempted "construction of a rationalist, authoritarian political order."[75] Indeed, even Polish Stalinism's limited efforts to change gender relations proved destabilizing, provoking "male resistance" (as Donna Harsch writes of women's skilled labor in East Germany) across "every social and political boundary."[76]

Such resistance, "uniting workers, trade union functionaries, Communist officials, foremen, supervisors, and plant directors," was facilitated by the system of norm-based pay, the ambiguous lines of managerial and political authority on the shop floor, and pervasive informal bargaining at the workplace.[77] For example, just as younger workers struggled to be assigned work that would yield a higher percentage of the "norm," women fought not to be placed in unproductive and un-remunerative positions on the "work front." Women's advocates in Nowa Huta complained frequently about women's brigades being moved constantly from one worksite to another or being broken up by supervisors—practices that lowered their wages by preventing participation in labor competition.[78] Similarly, reports noted cases of skilled women workers being assigned to menial tasks. For example, a nine-woman brigade of bricklayers that had once been featured in the newspaper for their outstanding achievements was found unloading materials and digging excavations. The women complained, moreover, that they were harassed by "the boys, and the management made no effort to help them." As in the case of the female steelfixers who were docked 20 to 50 złoty in pay by their foreman—allegedly because they had earned more than their male coworkers—it seemed that the message of women's economic empowerment was just not getting through to the grassroots.[79]

Further examples of hostility from male coworkers and supervisors abounded. Even Zofia Włodek's model brigade complained bitterly that the foreman spoke "vulgarly" to and ridiculed them, to the point where they "lost the desire and ability to work"; the report's author concluded that there were "many similar complaints of the poor treatment of women, and here we see that the women's councils, factory councils, and party cells work together too little or not at all."[80] In another example, a female glazier working at ZBMNH—a model worker with a Silver Cross of Service—claimed she had been told by the chairman of her trade union, the first secretary of her workplace party cell, and the second secretary of her party factory committee that women were ineligible to apply for family housing; they advised her that her husband should put in an application at his workplace instead.[81] As a worker-correspondent for *Budujemy Socjalizm* wrote, not everyone in Nowa Huta understood "the meaning of women's work in industry, . . . [and] that the rights of men and women are exactly equal."[82]

Indeed, it was not clear who would represent women's interests when sexism was so embedded in party and union structures. In theory, Women's Councils at each workplace were to extend their special protection over women workers, supported by the local and provincial branches of the Women's League.[83] Women's League activists, however, complained that their work was impeded by union officials' lack of interest in the councils; some factory council chairmen, they noted, did not know who the chair of their workplace's women's council was, or even that such a body existed.[84] One Women's Council chairwoman ruefully explained that her committee was never invited to factory council or party cell meetings, and "since everything happens behind closed doors . . . we can't complain about it." She added, "The [party cell] doesn't take any interest in us, and that's very sad."[85]

The Women's League itself was another potential advocate for women, and indeed, when complaints of workplace discrimination came up, low-level party functionaries often dodged the issue by passing it along to local league activists.[86] As the only national Polish women's organization following the forced merger or abolition of non-Communist women's groups in 1948, the league's official mandate ranged over a wide area, from nurturing women's athletics, providing legal advice, and mobilizing women in the "struggle with speculation" to fighting alcoholism, prostitution, and venereal disease.[87] Many of the league's activities in Nowa Huta focused on the domestic sphere, such as the "Great Cleanliness Competition" of 1950 directed at residents of the women's hostels: "WOMEN OF NOWA HUTA!," urged the competition announcement, "Remember that a clean apartment demonstrates the culture of a worker. In a light, clean apartment one rests better and more pleasantly after work." Winners received electric irons and curtains.[88] League activists likewise prepared decorations, costumes, and a buffet for a children's holiday party; sewed workers' pillows and children's school pinafores; and prepared tea.[89] And, as one league activist told women in Nowa Huta, "We women and mothers must show all those who wish to destroy the happiness and joy of our children that the peace for which the whole of progressive humanity fights will be upheld through increased work."[90]

At the same time, Nowa Huta's league branch initially focused its most intensive efforts on organizing women through the workplace; by late 1952, the majority of its membership came through its workplace circles, of which some 75 percent consisted of physical workers, 16 percent of white-collar workers, and 9 percent of housewives.[91] In 1952–53, however, Warsaw instructed league branches nationwide to withdraw from all activities in the workplace, including organizing women's councils.[92] This was a double blow: not only did it mean that women's work-related concerns would be wholly overseen by the heretofore unresponsive, male-dominated unions, but it also eliminated Nowa Huta's most active Women's League circles, forcing the organization to rebuild its membership practically from scratch and outside the workplace.[93] In the period that followed, membership levels remained low, and many women seemed confused about the league's role—avowing, for example, that if one belonged to the union, "one didn't need to be a member of the league."[94] If only indirectly, such comments reflected Stalinism's conflicting messages about women's identity in the public sphere: should women be organized (and defined) as workers, mothers and wives, or all of the above?[95] League officials bristled at male party members' suggestions that they should attend to "liquidating rumors and panics" among women in Nowa Huta, which seemed to focus on the woman as *baba,* and not comrade.[96] In reality, league activists realized that without a foothold in the workplace, they were effectively marginalized in a city whose raison d'être was production.

Mother and Child

The incoherence of Stalinist plans for the productivization of women was especially evident in their lack of foresight concerning women workers' reproductive healthcare and childcare needs. On paper, Poland and the other People's Democracies, following the Soviet Union, promised to provide everything necessary for women to reconcile their roles as mothers (or potential mothers) and productive members of the workforce.[97] These included workplace protections for pregnant and lactating women, reproductive healthcare services, and childcare (and, to a limited extent, communal arrangements for housework and food preparation, such as milk bars and laundry facilities). In Nowa Huta, the Stalinist era's stridently pronatalist tone was echoed in ceremonies celebrating the first and thousandth births in the new town's birth clinic;[98] but many women found that once they became mothers, they were left to fend for themselves.

Polish labor regulations guaranteed a pregnant woman's right to work while spelling out provisions for the "protection of [women's] physiological-biological functions" before, during, and after pregnancy. From the sixth month of pregnancy onward, women performing physical labor were to be transferred to lighter duties, during which time they were guaranteed their average wage of the preceding three months. Maternity leave lasted from two weeks before to eight weeks after birth, and after returning to work nursing mothers were entitled to regular breaks for breastfeeding, for which a special room was to be provided.[99] After the fourth month of pregnancy, and through the first year of caring for a newborn, women were also forbidden to work the night shift or overtime.[100] Inspectors' reports from Nowa Huta indicate, however, that such regulations were often ignored.[101] There were cases like Stefania H., whose request for lighter work while pregnant was refused, and who miscarried in her seventh month while performing heavy physical labor. While employers and foremen were accused of taking little interest in their responsibilities toward mothers and pregnant women, on the one hand, on the other, the latter were often not aware of their legal rights.[102]

Given the chronic shortages and organizational chaos that characterized Nowa Huta's first half-decade, it is not exactly surprising that services for families (like other social goods such as housing) fell far short of projected visions of cradle-to-grave social welfare. But contemporaries were exceptionally critical of the lack of provisions for working mothers and their children. As an undated report on "Care for Mother and Child" in Nowa Huta put it, city officials at the "highest levels" had taken an "incorrect approach to this issue," with the result that only one building (a preschool) had as yet been built to serve the needs of mothers and children, while other family services (an outpatient clinic and a birthing center) were housed in temporary spaces and poorly equipped. (There was only enough room in the birthing center, for instance, for one woman to give birth at a time.) The vulnerability of newborn infants and their mothers to infectious disease was a special concern, and the report advised that women be sent to recuperate postpartum at the House for Mother and Child in Kraków rather than return to their crowded hostel rooms, an environment said to have a "fatal" effect on the health of mothers and newborns.[103]

Similarly, the former head of Nowa Huta's health services, Stanisława Siudut, later claimed that "no one had thought about the fact that there would need to be daycare" in Nowa Huta: the first infant daycare, with about forty places, was a stopgap measure hurriedly organized in the same building as the birthing clinic.[104] According to a contemporary report, however the facility served primarily as an infirmary for sick children referred by the Division of Health, and over the course of seven weeks, three babies from the center had died of infectious diseases such as pneumonia and diarrhea. Another inspection criticized the center for its inadequate heating and hygiene. Because the center had too few places and was far from many workers' hostels, moreover, the report concluded that "the problem of productivizing women on the terrain of Nowa Huta has not been solved in the slightest."[105]

To be sure, this situation improved somewhat between 1952 and 1954, when the temporary childcare center was replaced by three permanent facilities, supplemented by a weekly nursery where parents would leave their children from Monday morning to Friday afternoon. Together, this amounted to slightly fewer than three hundred places.[106] To put this in perspective, 2,208 births were registered in Nowa Huta in 1955.[107] Even though some parents preferred to leave their children behind in the hostels, rather than send them to daycare,[108] demand continued to outstrip supply. A correspondent for *Budujemy Socjalizm* noted that many women were forced to bring their small children to work;[109] the case of a model worker who had resigned from a training course for engine drivers because she had no childcare was cited by the party executive to demonstrate how women's vocational advancement was being stymied by the childcare shortage.[110] As one Women's League activist noted, the problem was especially acute for women with multiple children. Many such women wanted to work but could not do so without childcare: "Women demand that we give them help," the activist added, "but the Women's League alone is not in a position to do anything."[111]

The distressing prospect of children at risk of life-threatening illness or left unattended so their parents could work was a potent symbol of the gap between socialism's welfarist vision and its Stalinist reality. Similarly, despite Stalinism's "symbolic celebration" of the nuclear family, as Goven puts it, "in practice . . . many families were disintegrating" under the combined impact of industrialization, housing shortages, or political repression.[112] Alongside stories of women's empowerment and success in Nowa Huta, then, there were surely other, untold stories of psychic and physical hardship connected with the gendered experiences of child-bearing and child-rearing in difficult times. As Katherine Jolluck has shown in her study of memoirs by Polish women deported to the Soviet Union in World War II, some specifically gendered types of suffering, especially those connected with women's bodies, are less likely to be given voice in collective memory than others.[113] Publicly, anyway, the strains on family life in Nowa Huta were increasingly blamed not on the lack of adequate childcare or the imbalanced division of labor in the home, but on the gender-homogenizing effects of Stalinism.

Return of the *Baba*

In 1951, an instructor from the Women's Division of the Party Central Committee in Warsaw noted that the "girls" in Nowa Huta's hostels seemed to display a lack of seriousness and common sense, wasting their meager pocket money on cosmetics (perms, scent, antifreckle cream) or on their boyfriends. The girls were, in short, boy-crazy: "The advances of boys are their only pursuit or interest" and "outside of work they interest themselves almost completely in sexual matters." Needless to say, this came at the expense of political consciousness. For example, "Some [female] members of ZMP knew about Korea only that it was 'overseas somewhere,' of Truman that he was a 'warmonger'. . . . In the room of a girl who had been living [in Nowa Huta] for more than a year already, we came across curlpapers made out of *How the Steel Was Tempered* [a Soviet socialist realist novel], which had been given out at a ZMP meeting. The book had not been read because, as the girl explained, her 'friends said it was some kind of democratic book that there was no point at all reading, that there was nothing [interesting] in it' (i.e., it's not a love story)." And yet the instructor refused to condemn young women like these; even the one mentioned above, she noted, was "not stupid". Rather, young women needed more guidance and better ways to spend their free time, and the author of the report blamed local activists for failing to provide the girls with alternatives to their silly preoccupations.[114]

The report went on, however, to raise more troubling issues. It noted, for example, "a constant state of anxiety among girls freshly arrived in Nowa Huta," some of whom were afraid to set foot outside the hostels for weeks after their arrival. SP *junacy* "accosted women in the most vulgar fashion" at work, on the street, and in the cafeterias, and launched raids on the women's hostels. When, during one such raid, the women had poured water on the young men's heads from the hostel's upstairs windows, they had responded by breaking windows and beating up some of the women inhabitants. The fact that neither the hostel administration nor the MO had intervened on the women's behalf, the inspector wrote, illustrated the "defenselessness of girls living in the hostels." Indeed, the MO itself constituted another threat, whose members felt entitled to enter any woman's room on nighttime "inspections" which, according to rumor, "did not always conclude with looking around the beds and exiting in the company of the hotel administrator." The result of this situation ("if the inhabitants of the hostel are to be believed") was several cases of suicide by pregnant women and the discovery of newborns' corpses in the surrounding lime- and sand-pits.[115]

The report shows its author seemingly torn between a vision of Nowa Huta's young women as equally capable (with guidance) of becoming contributing, politically enlightened worker-citizens, and one of Nowa Huta as an essentially masculine terrain where women were, by their very presence, morally and physically endangered. Increasingly, commentators would point to what they saw as the unnatural transgression of sexual and spatial boundaries in the new town, raising fears of widespread moral contamination, particularly of young women.

Not surprisingly, this theme was especially present in discussions of Nowa Huta's workers' hostels, where the blurring of sexualized boundaries occurred in the most literal and obvious sense: although men were strictly forbidden in women's hostels and vice-versa, these rules were routinely disregarded, and inspectors anxiously reported even the most seemingly innocent violations to authorities. In one inspector's report from 1951, for instance, the fact that men were found sitting in the dark in conversation with the female residents (the lighting in one half of the building was broken) was associated with a variety of other transgressions, including a "wild" couple in which the wife was eight months pregnant, sharing a room with two other women, and two women with children living in an adjoining room, one of them "without a legal husband" and alleged to "conduct herself extremely immorally, which has a great influence on the other occupants." Hostel residents, moreover, were found to show a "particular lack of interest" in the Red Corner, and though many belonged to the Communist youth league, this was "on paper only." The inspector also reported the testimony of cleaning lady Adela G., who "forcefully emphasized the immoral conduct of many of the women occupants and said that all women should undergo 'Action V'"—that is, testing for venereal disease.[116]

At meetings of Nowa Huta's party executive, much credence was given to such reports, though rarely witnessed firsthand. Stories were exchanged of men breaking into women's hostels through the cellar windows and sneaking into the rooms at night, of employees from the Housing Office having relations with women in the hostels, and of hostel supervisors allowing men in at night in exchange for vodka.[117] Some hostel supervisors had allegedly been beaten by husbands whom they had tried to prevent from spending the night with their wives, visits during which "the most intimate cohabitation occur[ed] before the eyes of children and roommates." Such sexual commingling not only exposed single women to moral contamination, but even threatened established marriages: officials wrote that men in the hostels "often forget their family obligations, stop sending money, find a girlfriend, become dissipated." The women's hostels were also reportedly home to many "Alphonses" (or pimps), who took advantage of women by (falsely) promising to marry them; the executive discussed the case of one such woman who could not even name the man who had lived with her in the hostel, made her pregnant, and abandoned her. The cumulative result of such activity, according to the district council, was that 1,600 people in Nowa Huta suffered from sexually transmitted disease.[118]

In contrast to their readiness to best one another with tales of sexual disorder in the hostels, officials pointedly avoided direct discussion of two topics—rape and abortion—that were doubly taboo in Poland during the Stalinist period: first, no doubt, because of the discomfort they provoked; but second, because such problems were supposed to have ended under socialism.[119] A rare document from 1951 or 1952 describes what seems to have been a case of rape or attempted rape by a militia officer who, during a night patrol, entered a women's block, threatened the inhabitants with his revolver, and "got into bed with them." The last phrase, however, was at some stage crossed out and replaced by the more ambiguous "assaulted."[120]

Prostitution was easier to discuss if only because it was a legal category, but this did not always lead to greater clarity: according to MO statistics in 1955, for instance, 10 percent of female hostel dwellers in Nowa Huta were "prostitutes or half prostitutes."[121] Even if the police had been in a position accurately to assess levels of prostitution in Nowa Huta's fluid hostel population (which is doubtful), the inclusion of such an elastic and ill-defined category as "half-prostitute" made the attempt fairly meaningless. On the other hand, when the UB noted just one known case of an abandoned newborn and one of infanticide in Nowa Huta that same year, it did not seem to placate party members' fears of an epidemic of sexual promiscuity and unwanted children.[122]

Not all contemporaries shared authorities' concern about rumors concerning the hostels. Elf, a youth brigade member and hostel dweller in the 1950s, for instance, blamed them on "frequent [male] visitors to the [women's] block, who outdid themselves" in bragging about their amorous exploits.[123] Another skeptic was the journalist Barbara Seidler, who in 1957–59 wrote articles for the journal *Nowa Kultura* aimed at puncturing what she saw as unfounded rumors about the new town, among them its supposedly high levels of prostitution, venereal disease, and abandoned children. Writing that "a great cry [had been] raised in Poland over illegitimate children [and infanticides] in Nowa Huta" in 1954, Seidler described how local authorities had responded by building a home for foundlings in the new town. Three years later, however, only twenty of the seventy children living in the orphanage had been born in Nowa Huta, and children had had to be brought from elsewhere to fill the beds.[124] Seidler also cited records of the Civil Office showing that registered illegitimate births in Nowa Huta had peaked at 16 percent in 1954, then declined sharply to one quarter of one percent in 1959. Even assuming that many illegitimate births remained unregistered, this statistic seemed to confirm Seidler's larger argument that phenomena like out-of-wedlock births, venereal disease, and prostitution were no higher in Nowa Huta than in comparable communities—especially rapidly industrializing areas with a disproportionately young, male population.[125]

Thus, the crystallization of a sense of moral crisis around Nowa Huta's hostels—and more particularly, around their female inhabitants—can be seen as reflecting more general anxieties about the rapid social changes taking place in Poland at the time—changes that Nowa Huta, of course, symbolized. In Poland's "first socialist city," rumors of prostitution and infanticide raised the specter of a nation unable to regenerate itself, weakened first by war and then by the Stalinist assault against Polish culture and traditions. As Małgorzata Fidelis has shown, fears about the sexual behavior of women workers were a common response to Stalinist industrialization programs throughout the country. For many Poles, attempts to redraw gender divisions in the workplace had gone against biology and women's essential nature, resulting in sexual and moral chaos.[126]

Studying British youth counter-cultures in 1972, the sociologist Stanley Cohen coined the phrase "moral panic" to describe how "a condition, episode, person or group of persons" is "defined as a threat to societal values and interests . . . and presented in a stylized and stereotypical fashion by the mass media. . . . Sometimes the panic passes over and is forgotten," Cohen noted, while "at other times it has more serious and long-lasting repercussions and might produce . . . changes . . . in legal and social policy or even in the way the society conceives itself."[127] The panic that identified Nowa Huta as a site of sexual and moral contamination, as we shall see, fell into this second category; it would both contribute to the "Thaw" that preceded Stalinism's downfall and, indirectly, help shape the gendered discourse of post-totalitarian Polish communism.

That said, even if the loosening of traditional sexual morals in Nowa Huta was probably exaggerated, we should entertain the possibility that at least some women welcomed the comparative sexual freedom that life in the new town offered. Inspectors in Nowa Huta took a dim view of hostel managers like one (a party member, moreover) who allegedly asked, "Why should I bother a girl from the hostel if she wants to take several men a day? Let her do as she likes, it's a biological need. . . . We welcome every birth."[128] Such liberal views seem to have been largely out of step with popular sentiment. Officials worried, for instance, about appointing to the executive a woman living out of wedlock with the father of her children: "While we have nothing against Com. K[. . .]," one explained, "we must take account of public opinion—people see these things differently than we do"[129] And yet, for single mothers who found refuge in Nowa Huta, the claim that "every birth was welcome" could not have been unwelcome. Common sense suggests that for many young women in Nowa Huta, as well as for men, sexual experimentation held its attractions—even if admitting it was culturally unacceptable.

When the "Great Leader" died on March 5, 1953, Poland came one step closer to shaking off its Stalinist yoke. One of many small changes following Stalin's death was the dissolution later that year of the all-female casting brigade mentioned at the beginning of this chapter. The move was ordered by the women's union to achieve compliance with a ministerial resolution of August 1953 calling for stricter observance of existing health regulations on work by women and youth.[130] As Małgorzata Fidelis has shown, this policy forced skilled women to leave their jobs all over Poland in industries ranging from mining to transport; their newly gained professions were supposedly harmful to female reproductive biology. As in Nowa Huta, though, many did not give up these well-paying jobs without protest. As one Women's League activist reported, "Women did not want, at any costs, to give up the tasks they had so far performed. They cried, they protested, they wrote complaints."[131]

As Goven argues, masculine opposition to Stalinism's redeployment of gender in the workplace "became one of the few sites of successful resistance to state policy during the period."[132] Nowa Huta, meant to have led the way toward women's equality with men at work, now exhibited the reverse trend: by the late 1950s, the district had one of the lowest rates of female employment in urban Poland,[133] a situation that led women desperate for jobs to line up overnight in front of the employment office at the Lenin Steelworks.[134] With few exceptions, the steelworks, Nowa Huta's largest employer by far from the mid-1950s onward, was and would remain largely off-limits to women after Stalinism's brief experiment. The next time that women would make a visible appearance there, in fact, would be during the pro-Solidarity sit-in strikes of the 1980s—not as workers, but as the wives, mothers, and daughters of strikers, expressing support at the factory gates and bearing food and clean clothes for their menfolk inside. By the 1980s, such visual evidence of the strict gendering of labor and protest in Nowa Huta was something that few, if any, observers thought to note or question.[135]

The about-face on women's entry into new occupations was integral to the quickening pace of Polish de-Stalinization after 1953. The shift was officially framed as a return to a traditionally Polish understanding of women's essential role as a mother and a rejection of the "foreign" idea that women should perform the same work as men. As Fidelis argues, the widespread implementation of protective labor legislation after 1953 contributed to a more general thaw-era discourse of returning to national traditions and ending supposed perversions brought about by excessive Soviet influence.[136] By presenting themselves as defenders of traditional Polish family values and sexual mores, Communists dissociated themselves from unpopular elements of the Stalinist project and laid claim to the mantle of Polish patriotism. In this way, as Fidelis argues, "gender politics were a powerful instrument in negotiating the political and national legitimacy of communist regimes."[137]

The new approach to gender was firmly entrenched after 1956 when Władysław Gomułka swept back into power, pledging a return to a "Polish road to communism" from which the country had allegedly strayed under Stalinism. In keeping with a broader retreat from social experimentation and conspicuous intervention in the private sphere, "post-totalitarian" communism was characterized by the abandonment of plans to reshape gender roles in the workplace, a renewed understanding of the social sphere as the appropriate realm of female activity, and a return to traditional "family values." As Padraic Kenney writes, "Stability meant evocation of tradition—nation and family in particular" and an emphasis on the single-earner household as the fundamental social unit.[138] This shift in gender policy and rhetoric was accompanied, meanwhile, by strident and exclusionary nationalism, reflected, for example, in the compulsory settlement and police surveillance of Roma and in the vicious anti-Jewish campaign of 1968.

Did Stalinism emancipate women and Roma? Despite the doors that remained closed—or those that opened briefly, only to close again—Stalinism painted new vistas for some, including those who sought emancipation and self-fulfillment in Nowa Huta's raw and indeterminate landscape. The opposition provoked by women's entry into heavy industry in Poland's "first socialist city" attests to the significance of the experiment; Stalinism's attempt to rescript familiar dichotomies was harder to contain and channel than Polish Communists could have imagined. In this way, gender and ethnicity formed complex facets of the social revolution attempted in and represented by the new town. Like any revolution, it both attracted and repelled, above all for the freedom—not least of a sexual nature—that it seemed to promise. As we shall see in the next chapter, anxieties about both sexuality and "nihilistic freedom" followed the progress of this revolution into the arenas of Nowa Huta's youth counter-cultures and generational politics.

5

The Enlightenment of Kasza

On September 16, 1951, police officers in Nowa Huta shot and killed Ryszard W. He was an unlikely victim of Stalinist repression: no dissident or underground revolutionary, no worker-activist murdered amid strikes or protests, Ryszard W. was a *junak*, a member of one of the volunteer youth brigades building Poland's "first socialist city." Friends and family excepted, his death went largely unnoticed. But the story of Ryszard W. takes us to the heart of debates that raged both within and beyond party circles after Stalin's death about the direction Poland had taken under Stalinism.

In particular, both supporters and critics focused on the system's balance sheet on a question dear to the Polish intelligentsia's hearts: the "cultural enlightenment" of the masses, above all of those whom Stalinist industrialization had brought out of the villages to the cities and construction sites of socialism. Such rural migrants were to have been offered literacy classes and further education, exposed to culture and the arts, and guided away from any relics of the superstition and mental backwardness they may have brought from the village. But the reality, critics argued, had been different. They increasingly held up Nowa Huta as a highly charged symbol of the failure of the regime's cultural enlightenment project, pointing to epidemics of "hooliganism," promiscuity, and youthful deviance that had afflicted those like Ryszard W. and contributed to the tragic outcome on September 16.

Junacy like Ryszard W. were a mystery to authorities. Although reports by SP commanders from the early 1950s generally expressed satisfaction with young volunteers' performance during work hours (the success of youth in completing the Six-Year Plan, according to one, was "salt in the eyes" of the class enemy), they often complained that after hours the young men ran wild. They went about in public with their belts undone, unshaved and dirty, and could be found drinking in restaurants and creating a ruckus on the streets of

Kraków. Despite strict orders to the contrary, they were frequently discovered in women workers' quarters in Nowa Huta, "behaving immorally" or getting into fights, usually while drunk.[1] On Sundays and holidays, some *junacy* were a public nuisance, pushing "civilian" workers off crowded buses and intimidating others as they traveled in groups. In 1951–52, seventeen brigade members had been arrested for "hooliganism," yet when large groups of *junacy* gathered, the police could not easily manage or disperse them.[2] "Allegedly it's impossible to control [the *junacy*], as they constitute a force in themselves," reported a party commission in 1956. "An informant explained to us: 'What can five militia officers do, when two hundred *junacy* gather in front of a women's hostel?'"[3]

Jacek Kuroń, who as a youth activist in the 1950s witnessed campaigns against young "hooligans" in Warsaw, remembered that Polish police officers were relatively ineffective at crowd control; unlike later on, they had neither sticks nor dogs with which to enforce order, "only guns."[4] The many reports of open confrontations between *junacy* and police officers in Nowa Huta suggest that, as in Warsaw, young people felt they could push their luck, counting on officers not to use firearms against them even when attacked. The events in Nowa Huta of September 16, 1951 turned out to be a tragic exception that proved the rule. According to an investigation by the UB, at about 8:30 that evening eight officers comprising members of the regular police force, or Citizens' Militia (MO), and the UB had attempted to disperse a crowd of about a hundred *junacy* gathered in front of a women's hostel. The young men, engaged in one of their periodic dorm raids, began hurling insults at the officers; a youth was arrested when he allegedly attempted to throw a brick at an officer. The arrest further incensed the *junacy*, who tried (unsuccessfully) to break their colleague free and then streamed toward UB headquarters, demanding his release.

As the *junacy* approached UB headquarters, a group of officers grabbed their rifles and ran outside. And yet the shooting did not begin right away. According to the report, a tense stand-off escalated when a UB agent entered the crowd and acted "most aggressively" toward one of the young men. When the officer tried to arrest the *junak*, the crowd freed him and seized the agent in revenge. After a short struggle, however, the man broke free and rejoined the officers guarding the entrance. It was at that point, according to the report, that *junacy* began throwing stones and an unidentified officer opened fire, followed by others. Ryszard W. was shot while fleeing and died from his wounds several days later in the hospital.[5]

There was no justice for Ryszard W. The authorities engaged in a hasty cover-up, officially closing the case in May 1953 without prosecuting any of the officers;[6] meanwhile, internal party references to the "incident," even of the most discreet sort, soon disappeared. In a sense, however, Ryszard W.—and the specter of Nowa Huta's unruly youth more generally—would return in coming years to haunt those in power, and not only because some SP brigades were seized by rumors of murdered seasonal brigade members buried in the rye fields near their tents.[7] With the "thaw" that gradually loosened constraints on free speech after Stalin's death in 1953, a perception that the socialization process in Nowa Huta had failed—already widespread within party circles—would erupt into the public forum. A sharp critique of this failure by intellectuals and reformers, above all as voiced in the scandalous "Poem for Adults" by Adam Ważyk, would play no small part in the growing crisis of the Stalinist regime.

The power of this critique lay in a complex interplay of ideology and culture and in the long history of the entanglement of Communists and intellectuals in Eastern Europe. "It is not enough today to fight for good work," declared the youth activist Józef Tejchma in 1955. "It is necessary simultaneously to struggle for good people, for their high ideological, moral, and cultural level."[8] In a society where the intelligentsia had long felt the burden of moral leadership but where the divide between urban, educated society and the "backward," rural masses was profound, this meant more than mere ideological indoctrination. It implied a civilizing mission—one that might, moreover, begin at a very basic level, such as teaching people who had never encountered internal plumbing the difference between a washbasin and a flush toilet.[9]

In communist rhetoric, this project was sometimes couched in terms of creating a "new man." This new person was to be born on two fronts: work and leisure. At work, the struggle for higher productivity would forge a new socialist identity among former peasants, binding them to socialism's collective goals. Nowa Huta, encompassing the worlds of both work and leisure, was an ideal laboratory for this experiment. By directing how Nowa Huta's workers spent their leisure time, the Stalinist regime hoped to complete the process of socialization begun at the workplace, hastening their rapid transformation into new men. Party, planners, and cultural activists hoped that the appropriate structuring of space and time devoted to leisure in the new town would equip inhabitants for their leading role in the new order.

In the end, however, the geography of leisure in Nowa Huta became far more complex than anyone had anticipated. Residents, it turned out, sought out their own spaces as much in the interstices as in the planned web of leisure facilities. And while many rural migrants aspired to put their peasant past and its rustic ways behind them, many too exhibited behaviors that were neither typically peasantlike nor particularly "cultured." Youth, in particular, behaved in ways that appeared nothing short of philistine to their would-be civilizers. Unexpectedly, the campaign for culture turned out to involve not just the delivery of cultural goods under difficult circumstances, but also an active struggle against an autonomous subculture flourishing outside the bounds of formal cultural life and supervised leisure in Nowa Huta. This was as much a generational struggle, moreover, as one along more familiar social or political lines.

Just as the behavior of a Ryszard W. had caught them unawares, neither Stalinists nor reformers knew what to make of emerging working-class youth subcultures in Nowa Huta—with their own fashions, styles of dress, musical tastes, and manner of self-presentation, similar to those of other youth subcultures in postwar Europe. Taking it for granted that delinquent behavior and cultural tastes went hand-in-hand, commentators bemoaned, for example, that young people had to be dragged to the theater practically by force; "it suffices, however, to have a jazz orchestra for a moment," wrote one frustrated official, "for a tremendous gathering of youth to form instantly."[10] While Western commentators spoke of "nonconformist" youth, the "work-shy," or "narcissists,"[11] Polish contemporaries drew on the Soviet discourse of "hooliganism" and invented a new term, *bikiniarstwo*, to describe outlandish styles of dress, dance, and behavior modeled on American styles. These *bikiniarze* and their counterparts elsewhere in the Soviet Bloc were reminiscent of the "teddy boys" of Britain, *blousons noirs* of France, *teppisti* of Italy, *Schlurfe* of Austria, or *Halbstarken* of West Germany—with their blue jeans and motorbikes, Brando-esque scowls, Elvis hairstyles, and penchant for jiving in the aisles of movie theaters and concert halls—who provoked intense public scrutiny and debate among "respectable" adults throughout Europe and America.[12]

While not unique to Nowa Huta, such forms of youthful deviance came under especially intense scrutiny in the new town, which was viewed by many Poles as a barometer of the success or failure of the larger Stalinist project of social transformation. Yet while Nowa Huta's subcultures were dubbed reactionary by some, others both within and outside the regime saw that the reality was more complex—noting, for example, that some of the best, most committed workers and builders of socialism were, at the same time, the most notorious hooligans on their time off from work. This left authorities to struggle with something new and unfamiliar in generational and cultural politics, a struggle in which Ryszard W. had been, literally, caught in the crossfire.

Cultural Enlightenment

In Leninist eyes, leisure was to be much more than the cessation of work. Besides sleep (or "passive rest"[13]), leisure hours would allow the good socialist time for purposeful self-improvement (under the tutelage, of course, of the party). The Leninist model of cultural enlightenment was undeniably an element of the regime's project of political indoctrination. And yet cultural enlightenment was also an end in itself—"socialization 'through culture' but also 'for culture.'"[14] As Anne White points out, this program grew out of deeply rooted Central and East European traditions about the role of the intelligentsia and the nature of culture itself.[15] Like *Kultur* in German, in Slavic languages the word *kultura* is used to designate both what would be termed "high culture" in English and something more abstract and ineffable—the personal attributes of a cultured person. *Kultura* was reflected in the way one spoke, ate, dressed, made love, and used the toilet. It was also reflected, of course, in one's taste in music, literature, or theater.[16] East European *intelligenty* placed a high premium on *kultura* and, since the nineteenth century, had considered it part of their mission to educate and uplift the downtrodden peasant masses by imbuing them with it.[17] Doing so was considered an essential step toward national revitalization. The Communists who came to power first in Russia and then throughout Eastern Europe bore the strong imprint of this tradition. As Sheila Fitzpatrick has suggested in her analysis of power struggles between Bolsheviks and the Russian intelligentsia, the two may have "had more in common than either cared to admit"—among other things, both "shared an idea of culture as something that (like revolution) an enlightened minority brought to the masses in order to uplift them."[18]

Not surprisingly, many Polish *intelligenty* were attracted to the Communist cultural platform of 1943, which stressed goals shared across a broad political spectrum: rebuilding schools and cultural institutions, mandatory schooling to age sixteen, free high school and university study, and state support for science, literature, and the arts.[19] It was not until 1949 that cultural affairs were "Stalinized" by resolutions of the fifth plenum of the PZPR Central Committee and Central Council of Trade Unions, respectively, and the aims of cultural work were explicitly politicized, the goals of cultural enlightenment defined as "indoctrination and encouraging the fulfilment of productivity quotas."[20] But by then, many non-Stalinists were already committed to working with the new order.

For some of these fellow travelers, it was precisely the vision of Nowa Huta as a grand experiment in civilizing the masses—a project in cultural enlightenment on a scale previously not attempted outside the Soviet Union—that attracted them to the new town in particular, and, in some cases, to socialism more broadly. Józef Tejchma, who began as an activist within the Populist "Wici" youth movement, stayed on within the forcibly unified League of

Polish Youth after Stalinization in 1948. Tejchma later claimed that he was attracted by the ZMP's "broadly democratic" rhetoric and programs such as the battle against illiteracy. Tejchma remembered with special satisfaction the ways in which ZMP activities promoted the "democratization of the countryside"—as when young people from all parts of Poland helped peasants bring in the harvest or traveled across the country to tour heritage sites—in effect, "nationalizing" the masses. In Nowa Huta, Tejchma argued, these aspects of the youth movement prevailed over the crudely doctrinaire elements of the Stalinist program: "practical life," he claimed, "was always stronger than ideology and propaganda."[21]

Unfortunately, practical life also threw obstacles in the way of achieving this broad vision of cultural enlightenment. Although Nowa Huta's master plan called for an impressive range of facilities—theaters, houses of culture, libraries, cinemas, parks, sports fields, and stadiums—Warsaw was not always ready to pay for them. Investment in the city's cultural infrastructure trickled down so slowly, in fact, that by mid-decade many of these plans had been scaled back or eliminated. Throughout the early to mid-1950s, cultural workers in Nowa Huta complained bitterly about having to operate in temporary and unsuitable locations, criticizing Miastoprojekt and the National Commission for Economic Planning for failing to allocate funds for the timely construction of cultural facilities.[22] It was not the only realm in which the state's investment priorities revealed deep tensions in the Stalinist project. But the idea that the regime wanted culture in the country's flagship city on the cheap was one that would prove particularly problematic.

By default, the burden of cultural enlightenment work in Nowa Huta's first half-decade fell to those institutions that were least expensive to build and operate. These were overwhelmingly the so-called *świetlice* (or sometimes, "red corners"), multipurpose common rooms located in the workers' hostels. The intimacy of these spaces was envisioned as key in promoting culture among Nowa Huta's masses: "Without much fatigue and even in house slippers, the worker can go down to the Red Corner and join in cultural and educational life," noted one cultural instructor.[23] *Świetlice* were spaces for both planned and unplanned leisure. They were intended as places where a worker could find quiet relaxation after hours—pick up a book or newspaper, or enjoy a board game like The Oder and the Vistula or Don't Get Irritated, Man! with friends—as well as take part in literacy classes, chess clubs, lectures on current events, slide shows, out-loud readings of books and newspapers, instruction in the latest anthems and mass songs, Radio University circles, Russian language courses, book clubs, editorial clubs for the "wall newspaper," amateur music, dance, or drama troupes, and arts and crafts.[24]

The larger *świetlice* could also serve as performance space for visiting artists, such as the 1950 visit by a group of Francophone African performers to the *świetlica* in Czyżyny. According to the local newspaper *We Are Building Socialism*, the show "raised among the spectators great enthusiasm and long, loud bravos. [The workers'] interest in original African art [and] culture was great. . . . The cry given in Polish by the leader of the Black group Keit Fodeb— 'LONG LIVE PEACE'—repeated three times by the members of the group, generated unprecedented enthusiasm among the audience." The performance closed, according to the report, with Africans and Poles chanting in unison, "STALIN-PEACE."[25] Such an event would clearly have satisfied one union official who called the "fundamental assignment" of the *świetlice* to mold "the Marxist-Leninist worldview" of users and expose them to "the achievements of national and general human culture."[26] More generally, red corners and *świetlice* were to serve as antechambers to the high culture represented by the People's Theater and House of Culture, as well as gateways to further education.[27]

The earliest *świetlice* were simple affairs equipped with handmade benches and tables (built by their users), and sometimes, a radio or bookcase. By 1952, there was a total of fifty-six red corners in the workers' hostels. However, all but fifteen were deemed by inspectors to be poorly equipped: many lacked radios, games, or books.[28] Levels of activity varied widely from one to the next. For example, the *świetlica* at KGR 10 in Łęg managed to nurture a drama and "living word" (dramatic recitation) group, as well as chess and ballet sections with paid instructors; 123 workers participated in five circles of "Radio University," a nationally broadcast continuing education course, and 13 members had graduated from the program. Nonetheless, the *świetlica* was missing furniture, and its library of two hundred books was considered inadequate for its 120 users. The *świetlica* in Bieńczyce (attached to SPB C-2), on the other hand, was practically moribund, except for a few ZMP members who held meetings there; the forty books once owned by the library had, rather unfortunately, dwindled to nine. The same report noted—in an observation echoed widely in discussions of culture in Nowa Huta—that the most successful *świetlice* were used mainly by white-collar workers.[29] Several were hardly used at all; some were used as storerooms.[30]

Responsibility for cultural life in the *świetlice* or red corners was shared among a range of groups and institutions. Users, of course, were expected to take an active part, and where the *świetlica* was attached to a workplace, its activities were additionally to be supported by a culture and education committee

A winner of the Great Book Lottery of 1954 in front of the state bookstore. He has won the selected works of Gogol. Irena Jarosińska, KARTA Center Foundation, Warsaw.

of the relevant union.[31] Politically active students and cultural figures from Kraków were also expected to do their bit. During her studies at the Jagiellonian University, the ZMP member Anna Siatkowska and a group of other students pledged to "organize cultural life" in Nowa Huta's red corners. They travelled to different workers' hostels with a program of Bulgarian, Czech, and Polish songs and anti-fascist poetry.[32] Not everyone shared Siatkowska's enthusiasm for this kind of work, however; complaints were heard about actors from Kraków's Słowacki Theater who, when they "condescended" to appear in Nowa Huta, left immediately after their performances and showed no interest in developing local talent.[33]

Nowa Huta was likewise a site of literary pilgrimage for established authors, and not just locals; most came, did some readings, and left, although some Kraków-based writers—such as the charismatic author and Sejm deputy Adam Polewka—had a more sustained presence.[34] One young worker at HiL, seeking to form a Club of Spontaneous Creativity at the House of Culture, was assigned "professional help" in the form of the young Kraków-based poets Jan Zych and Tadeusz Nowak and the literary critic Jacek Kajtoch. While the worker originally feared exposing his poetic efforts to ridicule, the professionals were unpretentious and encouraging. Unfortunately, their visits ceased after two meetings, and eventually the club folded.[35]

With volunteer support from Kraków's artists and writers erratic at best, it was ultimately up to paid staff to organize daily cultural activities in the *świetlice*. *Świetlica* directors—whose wages were about half that of a well-paid manual worker[36]—did not have an easy task. On the one hand, they had to satisfy their superiors that the *świetlice* had fulfilled their weekly, monthly, or yearly plans; on the other, they had to attract users by providing lively and appealing programming. And yet an excess of innovation (for example, incentivizing workers to attend political lectures by scheduling them together with the handing out of pay envelopes) could lead to charges of "individualism" or dismissal.[37] No wonder, then, that, in a single week in September 1954, seven *świetlica* directorships changed hands.[38]

The occasional successes of cultural programming in Nowa Huta's *świetlice* thus seem all the more remarkable. One of the more robust institutions seems to have been the Inter-Union Worker's Club (MKR), which opened its doors in 1951 with an impressive three-day New Year's party for the children of Nowa Huta, complete with an orchestra, storytelling, movies, colored hats, and gifts. The event was designed to be educational as well as entertaining. When children were greeted under the tree by Grandfather Frost (rather than St. Nicholas), he "emphasized that we can play carefree because the Soviet Union looks after us [while] . . . at this moment children in Korea are being slaughtered and killed." Meanwhile, the walls were hung with slogans like "When the whole nation to Nowa Huta says 'yea,' they [the class enemy] with asinine resistance bray" (accompanied by "appropriate decoration").[39] According to organizers, the party was a big success: "The kids were enchanted with the party, so much so that when Grandfather Frost said it was time to go home, they made such a racket that they didn't want to go. . . . The parents were very pleased, and in conversations they expressed surprise that we could do all this for the children." Organizers noted that the party, which was attended by 1,545 children, had served as excellent propaganda for the center,[40] measuring their success by the fact that the clergy of nearby Mogiła had allegedly forbade congregants to attend the MKR, threatening to expel parents who took their children to Sunday events there.[41]

The Idiocy of Urban Life

In May 1953, the Council of the Ministry of Culture and Art called a special meeting to discuss problems affecting the development of culture in Nowa Huta. Held in Nowa Huta in the leaky barracks used by an amateur theatrical troupe, the meeting focused on inadequate coordination among unions, firms, and other bodies responsible for cultural programming, and led to the appointment of a special government plenipotentiary to ensure better communication and organization. Some months later, however, it was decided that this measure had not "passed the exam" because the plenipotentiary was based in Warsaw and too far removed from daily life in the new town. A subsequent special conference at the District House of Culture, therefore, called together a coordinating collective of activists from the major organizations involved in cultural work in Nowa Huta, responsible to the presidium of the District National Council. But the committee became bogged down in red tape (and apparent indifference) after only a couple of months, according to a party report of September 1954, which charged the collective with being unable to coordinate the work of its own members, let alone cultural life in Nowa Huta. To give it credit, the collective did lodge an appeal with the ministry to hasten the building of Nowa Huta's theater, cinemas, and Palace of Culture. But the National Commission for Economic Planning (PKPG) had struck both the palaces of culture and youth from 1955 budget proposals submitted by the Office of Urban Construction, whose plans for cultural institutions in Nowa Huta, while approved by the local party executive, were "not respected" in Warsaw by Miastoprojekt and PKPG. In short, the committee argued, there was little they or any other local body could accomplish without help—especially of the financial variety—from Warsaw.[42]

Perhaps inevitably, activists tended to single out Nowa Huta's *świetlice*—the weakest and most vulnerable link in the cultural chain—for their most stinging criticism. According to a union council report, the *świetlice* were "dirty, cold, and unaesthetic,"[43] while the district party executive determined in 1954 that many *świetlice* had failed to fulfill even 50 percent of their plans.[44] Striking a new note, however, increasingly cultural programming was also described as "boring"—a thinly veiled critique of its didacticism and overly political content, and a sign of the subtle change in party-circle discourse since Stalin's death and the onset of the thaw. From 1953, for instance, ZMP leadership in

Nowa Huta committed its members to a campaign, under the slogan "We are driving boredom from our *świetlice*," which consisted of a traveling talent show and a young people's club in which youth, according to activists, were urged to feel themselves the club's "owners."[45] In the meantime, however, district party officials dodged the problem of the content of cultural enlightenment work, promoting instead its increasing professionalization and centralization, moving activity away from the hostels and into more formal cultural venues.[46]

An example of this shift toward citywide institutions was the creation of the Ensemble for Song and Dance (ZPiT). ZPiT fulfilled another proposal discussed at the May 1953 meeting, namely, the creation of a model artistic ensemble worthy of representing Nowa Huta to the outside world. ZPiT was "owned" by HiL, its performers drawn from its workforce and on its pay-rolls; after an abortive first attempt (the original troupe had to be disbanded, apparently, because of poor management and lack of discipline among the performers), ZPiT took off to become one of the district's best-known cultural calling cards. Leaving nothing to chance, the Kraków party committee excused troupe members not only from work for a month prior to the premiere to allow for rehearsals, but also from all political meetings and activities. For the troupe's widely acclaimed first concert in January 1955, the program consisted of both contemporary pieces and folk songs from the Kraków/Nowa Huta region—presenting the ironic spectacle of young performers, themselves mostly of rural origin, wearing "peasant" costumes manufactured in Warsaw by the state costuming agency.[47]

On the basis of achievements such as ZPiT, by March 1955 the Culture and Education Committee of the District National Council presidium reported that key cultural institutions in Nowa Huta were operating effectively. Although the District House of Culture (sponsored by the builders' union) was based in a temporary building that was too small, it had completed 130 percent of its 1954 yearly plan, winning first place in a national competition among houses of culture.[48] The International Press and Books Club was one of the most successful cultural institutions in town; it offered regular appearances by literary figures, book signings, and weekly reviews of international events. Two libraries and a music center, though like the Press and Books Club in temporary quarters, were also said to be functioning well.[49]

Perhaps the most lasting and significant of Nowa Huta's cultural institutions, the People's Theater, also opened in 1955. Nowa Huta's theater scene had progressed rapidly from early, amateur efforts often plagued by logistical and ideological difficulties (one group's rehearsals of *Romance from Vaudeville*, for instance, had been cancelled when it emerged that the play was "forbidden"),[50] to the formation of the semi-amateur theater Nurt in 1952 by employees of one of Nowa Huta's construction firms. Sponsored by the build-ers' union, Nurt (meaning "current" or "stream") occupied a four-hundred–seat barracks that, despite a leaky roof and difficult access across unlit, unpaved terrain, regularly ran to a full house. The theater staged seven productions between 1953 and 1955, winning second prize in the All-Polish Festival of Amateur Theater in 1953 for its production of *Julius and Ethel*.[51] Audience members, many unfamiliar with theatergoing protocol and dressed in their muddy work clothes, reputedly "showed their sympathy or disapproval for the characters" during performances by shouting encouragement or abuse at the actors onstage. Nonetheless, according to the actress Aleksandra Mianowska, it was a "gracious, good public."[52]

Nowa Huta was originally meant to have two theaters: a Great Theater on Central Square, and a 422-seat Chamber Theater on Mayakovsky Street. Plans for the Great Theater, however, were abandoned along with other sweeping changes in the general plan. Work had begun on the latter in 1954 according to a design by Jan Dąbrowski and Janusz Ingarden; this smaller building became home to the People's Theater by a decree of the Ministry of Culture and Art in March 1955. Krystyna Skuszanka, the former artistic director of the Opole Theater, was brought to Nowa Huta as head of the new company; under her were seasoned professionals like the director Jerzy Kra-sowski and the stage designer Józef Szajna. The members of Nurt, meanwhile, were rather unceremoniously cast aside: only one actor and stage manager, respectively, were co-opted from the old troupe, and Nurt's barracks were dis-mantled shortly thereafter.[53] On December 3, 1955, the theater opened with a gala performance of Wojciech Bogusławski's 1794 "folk opera" *Krakoviaks and Highlanders*, adapted by Leon Schiller in 1946—an appropriate choice, given its dramatization of a dispute between peasants from the mountainous Podhale region and inhabitants of Mogiła, one of the villages that had been annexed to Nowa Huta.

The theater's trademark iconoclasm, however, became apparent only in the three productions that premiered in 1956—Carlo Gozzi's *Princess Turandot*, John Steinbeck's *Of Mice and Men*, and Shakespeare's *Measure for Measure* (designed by Tadeusz Kantor). In visual terms, the abstractly stylized spectacle created by Szajna was a shocking contrast with Nurt's period costumes and wallpapered interiors. According to Skuszanka, she and her colleagues took as their inspiration the "romantic politics of theater": "We want to throw out descriptiveness and decorativeness, to look for those means of theatrical ex-pression that would order the primary and metaphorical function of drama."[54] The critics split along political lines: the progressive journal *Życie Literackie* published favorable reviews, while the government mouthpiece *Trybuna Ludu* attacked both the productions generally, and the theater's artistic director personally.[55] The People's Theater was part of a struggle over art and politics in the thaw that resounded far beyond Nowa Huta, or even Poland, garnering international repute.[56] Locally, however, it gained the reputation of being frequented more by visitors from Kraków than from Nowa Huta itself.

Culture at the Margins

The increased professionalism of cultural offerings in Nowa Huta affected the day-to-day leisure patterns of its inhabitants unevenly. Research by the Housing Institute in 1954 ascertained that skilled workers made the most use of Nowa Huta's cultural facilities. Unskilled workers, on the other hand—short of cash and childcare—tended to spend their free time at home, while white-collar workers preferred to entertain themselves in Kraków.[57] If anything, the declining emphasis on cultural programming in *świetlice* diminished the potential impact of cultural activities on the population that was, by official estimates, most in need of them—the unskilled, young, mostly single workers inhabiting the hostels. From their own point of view, hostel dwellers still needed a comfortable, welcoming space where they could socialize and be entertained on a day-to-day basis, and the *świetlice* were not serving this purpose. Thus, as one ZMP activist noted in 1955, "generally speaking, young people occupy themselves rather outside the *świetlica*."[58]

For one thing, hostel residents often sought out indoor spaces that were cozier and more intimate—and less subject to surveillance—than the *świetlice*. Elf, for instance, writes that while stationed with the youth brigade in Czyżyny, he and his fellow volunteers used to spend their afternoons after work in the bathrooms, both while it was warmer there and while it was out of eyeshot of brigade supervisors. "Here one could give rein to the imagination," telling ghost stories and speaking about how one might sneak across the border—presumably to the West.[59] More commonly, hostel dwellers relaxed in the shared bedrooms, despite lectures on the "hygiene of communal living" that insisted such spaces should be reserved for passive repose (i.e., sleep), not, like the *świetlice*, active leisure.[60]

One obvious reason for the unpopularity of *świetlice* was that, like hostels more generally, they were off-limits to members of the opposite sex. Of course, such rules were routinely broken. In March 1951, an inspection of a women's barracks at PPRK Nr 2 (Prądnik Czerwony) at 7:30 p.m. turned up four men listening to the radio in the *świetlica*, while in an adjoining room "were found men (youth), who sat on the beds in their work clothes. On the bunks, girls lay in their clothes because, as they said, the presence of the men kept them from undressing. The men as well as the women stated that it had been announced at a meeting that men were free to be in women's rooms until 9 p.m. Foreman Borowiec, who was found in the women's barracks, stated with great indignation that no one could forbid him to be in the same room as women, since as a foreman he had the right."[61] In warmer months, improvised outdoors spaces provided alternatives to the crowded hostel rooms; one of the most popular hangouts for mixed crowds of young, single workers was the paved area outside the post office in Settlement D.[62] Open-air parties and dances there are fondly remembered by many older residents as a highlight of those years.[63]

Commercial establishments, somewhat misleadingly called "restaurants," were another alternative to the supervised common rooms. These state-run venues, sporting names like Lotus or The Little Fish, gained a reputation as the backdrop for dissipated, "Dantesque scenes"[64] such as the one described by the writer and town resident Bohdan Drozdowski: "Some [customers] are submerged in drunkenness . . ., some in sadness, still others in homesickness, while naturally the gay ones call the tune. They sing their village songs [as] swear words rise above the din every few seconds. They are carefully dressed, in suede shoes, expensive suits, watches, long hair, and whiskers. The great paws of these boys give away their workingman's strength. . . . Not one of the half-pints of vodka is full. The bills often don't add up, but who checks them? In Nowa Huta they earn well, and don't have anything to do with their money." An orchestra, a Czech dancer with great legs dubiously named Stella Vesela (Happy Stella), the *czardasz*, and the tango all enlivened the scene.[65] Notoriously, the unlit terrain surrounding the restaurant Giant, where some couples retreated after leaving the bar, was the prowl of petty thieves. Anyone who fell asleep (or, just as likely, passed out) in the open air after a night's revelries risked waking up stripped to his socks and relieved of his valuables.[66]

The stabilization of cultural life in Nowa Huta, it seemed, had still not reached its goal. According to a central ZMP report, the cultural interests of Nowa Huta's youth were "often narrow and primitive": young people took no interest in the theater, literature, or museums.[67] Although libraries in Nowa Huta reported that Polish and foreign classics were among the most borrowed books, inspectors also found sentimental and pulp fiction circulating through the hostels, with titles like *Leper, Gehenna*, and *I Was an Ugly Girl*. (Their presence indicated possible contamination by "decadent" Kraków, since they had allegedly been "brought from Kraków by intellectual workers and young intelligentsia.")[68] Such incidents were indications, the above report continued, of widespread "cultural passivity among individuals for whom thoughts of tomorrow have still not been awoken," those "who live from one day to the next, shut themselves off from collective life, and limit themselves solely to attending to the bare necessities of life. Our research on the attitude of youth who have been under the strong influence of the church shows that the old clerical principle of education, 'pray and work,' has been transformed into the principle, 'pray and work, but work only as much as is necessary to maintain a livelihood.'" In other words, old mentalities—the "primitive" and "passive" attitude of the peasant—had joined with new, urban desires (e.g., a "lust" for dancing), creating a particular kind of youthful alienation.[69] Cultural activists therefore found themselves engaged on a new front, combating not only the ignorance and superstition that newcomers brought with them from the village but also the habits they quickly picked up, unprotected by the influences of family or tradition, in the new town. These ranged from drunkenness, swearing, and fighting, on the one hand, to tastes for "American" fashion, music, and dance, on the other—in contemporary parlance, "hooliganism" and "bikini-ism" [*bikiniarstwo*], respectively.

Hooliganism

Use of the term "hooliganism" was already widespread in late Imperial Russia, where it was applied to young, urban working-class men who openly defied upper-class norms of behavior and decorum.[70] In the Soviet Union, hooliganism was a legal offense, defined in a 1922 statute as "mischief, linked with explicit disrespect toward the functioning of society."[71] In Communist Poland, hooliganism was punishable by up to six years' imprisonment.

In practice, officials in Nowa Huta used the term to connote a connection between youthful delinquency (almost always of a drunken variety) and ideological "enemy activity": as one functionary put it, hooliganism meant speaking vulgarly to someone in authority, having a "leaning toward alcohol," or all of the above (e.g., being drunk at an official function).[72] Local law enforcement officials complained with thinly veiled frustration about the difficulties of fighting such a vaguely defined crime. Nowa Huta's district prosecutor, for instance, noted in 1953 that "the idea of hooliganism is very often incorrectly interpreted, as a result of which an honest worker can drink one glass of vodka and people then make out he's a hooligan." He went on to suggest that too many people were being arrested and that hooliganism as such was actually on the decline: "If it came to hooliganism of a political character, lately such cases had not been noted."[73] ZMP officials from Warsaw, however, countered by accusing both the militia and the prosecutor's office in Nowa Huta of "serious liberality" in their struggle with young miscreants.[74]

Central authorities may have hoped that Nowa Huta's administrative bodies would be more aggressive in fighting hooliganism, but ironically, the very elasticity of the offense created difficulties for its prosecution. In 1953, for instance, the city council's Office of Administrative Punishment was responsible for adjudicating a staggering 8,231 cases of "hooliganism, drunkenness, etc." referred by the police and hotel administration. The office responsible for handling the cases, with a staff of two, managed ultimately to process only 40 percent of all files: by the time a case could be dealt with, the defendant had often changed his address and disappeared.[75] A citizens' court (its judges consisting of thirteen workers, seven housewives, five peasants, and fifteen intellectual workers), called into being by the city administration in February 1955, also dealt primarily with cases of "brawling and drunkenness," but with little more success. Most of the defendants were between the ages of nineteen and twenty-six and lived in the workers' hostels or the village of Mogiła, and almost all were manual workers. While 508,040 złoty in fines were given out in 1955, the court was toothless. It had difficulty enforcing punishments, and recidivism was common, as in the case of Kazimierz K., who reportedly was sentenced more than ten times with no improvement in his behavior.[76]

Finally, campaigns to shame hooligans in public backfired. The police complained that no one wanted to testify against accused hooligans in court[77] and a campaign of mock public trials "failed the exam," according to officials, because ZMP and other organizations could not (or would not) mobilize their membership to participate.[78] Moreover, the defendants in such spectacles had a habit of turning the public theater to their advantage. Zofia Kulinowska instituted a mock court at the Czyżyny *świetlica*, as directed by her superiors, to punish misdemeanors like drinking and swearing. One young man was charged with having hidden ten bottles of vodka under his bed. He replied in a tone of "complete amazement": "Your Excellency, if you lived in a barracks like this and held office in the mud and the cold, then your Excellency herself would drink with me!" Another defended his use of vulgarity in an argument with a female bus driver, explaining that of course he "couldn't speak to her in French, because she wouldn't have understood me." Kulinowska noted that, far from having a deterrent effect, the punishments the court meted out (week-long "imprisonment" in the hostel) "were greeted as a kind of holiday—[the accused] played cards, drank, slept."[79]

What the struggle with hooliganism, of course, masked was the serious social problem of alcoholism and excessive drinking.[80] Authorities fought a losing battle throughout the early 1950s to prevent the sale of illegal spirits in Nowa Huta, which were copiously consumed not only after hours but also throughout the working day. In a 1951 case against a local peasant charged with selling home-brewed spirits and vodka to workers from his cottage in Bieńczyce, witness Jan G. described how he and his workmates often made a collection for vodka, sending someone over to the peasant's cottage with the money. A storeroom supervisor confirmed that he was often sent to the peasant's hut to purchase alcohol for coworkers, including once by a police officer; others complained that the "larger part" of workers at the site routinely drank.[81] Overconsumption of alcohol, on and off the job, was a major health threat: in just one week in summer 1950, for instance, there were three fatal traffic accidents in Nowa Huta, all apparently involving drunken drivers or pedestrians.[82] Given the already dangerous nature of much of the work in Nowa Huta, there can be no doubt that alcohol contributed to high workplace accident rates throughout the 1950s.

The party politicized drinking by refusing to treat alcoholism as a public health problem, instead equating alcoholics with "parasites and egoists, people neglecting work through their drunkenness."[83] Shortly before his fall from favor (resulting partly from his own drinking problem), the celebrated worker-hero Piotr Ożański opined in the local paper: "Drunkenness in Nowa Huta is enemy work. All of us here are working together and breaking records in production, only so that our great Huta will grow faster, and drunks slow down the tempo of our work. That's why there's no place among us for drunks and other kinds of adventurers."[84]

In fact, untangling the relationship between alcohol and ideology in Nowa Huta was not an easy matter. Stefan B., a twenty-year-old bricklayer who had earlier been involved in a knifing at Giant, allegedly hit a ZMP member while drunk at the organization's electoral congress and "wanted to throw himself at the leader of the ZMP district office Szparniak." When hauled before a committee of district party officials, Stefan B. promised to stop drinking, upon which his party candidacy was reinstated.[85] The "notorious drunkard" Tadeusz G., on the other hand—a party member since 1948—was not met with such lenience: accepting "the charges laid against him, he explained that he couldn't stop himself from drinking vodka and that he would go right on drinking."[86] His party membership was rescinded. With tongue only somewhat in cheek, the author-*bikiniarz* Leopold Tyrmand once argued that "drunkenness . . . was a kind of humanism" under the perversions of communism—a rejection of the party's puritan ideals of discipline and self-denial, of the totality of its demands over mind and body.[87] Seemingly, the party could tolerate physical attacks more readily than the rejection of personal control implied in Tadeusz G.'s retort.

Neither party membership nor Stakhanovite medals, of course, offered a vaccine against alcoholism or hooliganism. Hooliganism within the ranks of youth organizations like ZMP and SP was a particular concern for authorities, especially because it was often charged that cadres themselves had corrupted the youth in their charge with drink. Party members like Comrade S., for example, were accused of joining ZMP excursions to the countryside "in order to drink vodka, in this way demoralizing our youth."[88] SP cadres were charged with spreading the "bacterium" of vulgarity within brigades, such as one brigade leader who humiliated a new recruit who did not know how to wear a necktie: "The company chief ordered him to tie it on his——, and then ordered him to go in front of the company and shout where he was supposed to put his tie."[89] During an inspection of the 51st ZMP Brigade, the sister of one *junak* had been discovered hiding half-dressed in a storeroom; allegedly, she had been "provoked [by commanders] to stay in the brigade and to drink wine" with them.[90] Needless to say, this was hardly the "caring guardianship" of youth the regime had proclaimed as its role.

Similar incidents within ZMP ranks were hotly discussed among regional youth leaders around the country, but this was deviance, however widespread, of an uncoordinated and individual nature.[91] The collective misbehavior of large crowds of *junacy* in Nowa Huta was of another order of concern. In October 1951, for example, the Central Committee in Warsaw learned of an attack by *junacy* on a women's hostel (perhaps the same one in which Ryszard W. participated) in which youth had rioted, breaking windows and beating and kicking inhabitants after some women had poured water on them from an upper story. All this apparently "occurred under the windows of the room of the hotel manager, who out of fear for his own safety stayed quiet."[92] Such defiance seemed to suggest not only that the paternalist state had failed to provide its wards with caring guidance, but also that it had lost its authority with them (if it had ever, indeed, had it to begin with). Meanwhile, *junacy* seemed to take special pleasure in testing their mettle against the representatives of state power, as multiple references in party documents to "scuffles" between brigade members and the police suggest.[93]

But the regime could not afford to declare all *junacy* hooligans; nor were the political valences of such attacks at all clear. The same was true of attacks by *junacy* against civilian workers. According to one former *junak*, groups of young volunteers would roam about Nowa Huta after hours and if they "didn't like the look of someone," they would challenge the person with a kind of riddle:

> "What don't you like, the system or SP?" It was dangerous to answer "the system," but worse still "SP." Then you'd have to reckon with returning home via a detour through the hospital with a dozen broken ribs.[94]

The remarkable ambiguity of this question, coupled with the random violence that accompanied it, can only complicate our view of the young hooligans' understanding of themselves and their relations to authority. According to Jacek Kuroń, hooligans in Warsaw during the same period were rebelling against "denunciation [by spies] and the absurdity of life in the workers' hostels."[95] But it is not so easy to gloss over the challenge posed by *junacy* in the above anecdote. They presented themselves as defenders of "the system" and were willing to fight in its name (fighting that was, paradoxically, condemned by the system), but group allegiance (in this case, to SP) evidently took first place. It was classic ganglike behavior: capricious, territorial, and fiercely solidaristic. And yet, unlike most Western delinquents, *junacy* situated themselves in a context coded in explicitly political terms—although what they imagined these to mean is far from clear.

Bikiniarstwo

Official campaigns in Nowa Huta against *bikiniarstwo*, a youthful subculture formed from a pastiche of supposedly American dress styles and behavior, paralleled and overlapped those against hooliganism. Fashion was central to *bikiniarstwo*: Jacek Kuroń, who first encountered *bikiniarze* as a ZMP activist in his Warsaw high school, described their essential "narrow, short trousers, under which showed striped socks, shoes with crepe rubber or other thick soles. Add to this a very colorful, hand-painted silk tie—best of all with a view of the Bikini atoll," and of course the long, combed-back hairstyle, or "swallow." Engineer Tadeusz Binek remembered Nowa Huta's *bikiniarze* in similar terms. While working on the upper story of a construction site in 1953, Binek heard a commotion at street level: "A single youth walked along between the tracks of the crane—a *bikiniarz*. Hair combed to the top of his head, a light-colored jacket with wide, quilted sleeves, narrow trousers halfway down his calves, and garishly colored socks with horizontal stripes and loafers on thick pigskin soles. The classic dress of a classic *bikiniarz*, as if taken from *Szpilki* [a satirical journal]." The noise Binek had heard, he writes, was "booming, lively, honest laughter" from other workers on the construction site.[96]

The styles of dress and behavior associated with *bikiniarstwo* may have originated among working-class youth, or perhaps it was well-off youth with access to Western goods who were later imitated by peers in Warsaw's tougher districts.[97] According to Kuroń, *bikiniarstwo* was already "a significant counterculture" in Warsaw in the late 1940s; under the influence of *bikiniarze* at his high school, for example, American music was often played on the loudspeaker system. Eventually, though, ZMP activists at his school put a stop to this and, at the urging of the organization's Warsaw leadership, began beating up their *bikiniarz* classmates.[98] Variations on the *bikiniarz* existed throughout the Soviet bloc—the Czech *pasek*, the Romanian *casa Johnny*, the Hungarian *jampec*, and the East German *Halbstarker*, for example—and bore a strong resemblance to West European teddy boys, *teppisti*, and so on. Like their counterparts elsewhere, *bikiniarze* drew inspiration from American music (jazz broadcasts from Voice of America were extremely popular) and film (as late as 1948, more Hollywood than Soviet movies were screened in Polish theaters).[99] Gift parcels from the West—the contents of which often ended up on the black market—supplied *bikiniarze* with many of their fashion props, including the slightly retro Jazz Age hand-me-downs in aid packets of used clothing.[100] The images of mushroom clouds (the first atomic tests in the Bikini atoll occurred in 1946) and scantily clad women that, according to urban legend, the *bikiniarze* carefully hand-painted on their flashy silk ties appealed, no doubt, for their combination of the explosive, exotic, and erotic.

Although the "classic *bikiniarz*," as Binek put it, may have stood out among the drably dressed workers on the construction site, in many ways he was typical of his peer group in Nowa Huta—the only difference being that others were dressed for work, and he for play. Reminiscences from the 1950s stress that clothes were a matter of great concern for both sexes; the first purchase many young men made after getting their first paycheck was a suit, shirt, and shoes. Like the *bikiniarze*, their tastes tended toward the flamboyant (rich, bright colors).[101] As sociologist Renata Siemieńska noted, such urban clothing served as a marker of assimilation within Nowa Huta and, on visits home, visually signaled young workers' successes in the new town. Not for nothing did youth brigade recruits often burn their civvies upon issuance of their uniforms, symbolically marking the break with their old lives.[102]

Authorities in Nowa Huta were keen to argue that the *bikiniarz* was an isolated figure—an object of derision, as Binek's anecdote suggested, among other workers. But often this was contradicted by their own admissions that the "struggle against *bikiniarstwo*" had to involve a wide swathe of Nowa Huta's youth. ZMP activists, for instance, launched a series of antibikiniist social evenings, at which criticism of "inappropriate behavior" and the "public unmasking of individuals steeped in *bikiniarstwo*" was accompanied by Ping-Pong and folk dancing. They claimed success in creating "a uniform opinion among the majority of youth against mannered elements, who left the party or holed themselves up in corners without the usual disputes and arguments." In particular, they noted an increasing tendency, especially among girls, to oppose "bikiniist" dances and to turn down drunken dance partners.[103] Similarly, after

Young men await entry to the 7th Festival of Soviet Film, 1954. Note the "bikini-ist" hairstyles and fashions. Irena Jarosińska, KARTA Center Foundation, Warsaw.

"widespread" *bikiniarstwo* had been found within ZPiT, the troupe's director was "satisfied that our work [against *bikiniarstwo*] was to considerable effect, both among the troupe and the individuals involved. . . . The least manifestation of such behavior today offends all members, all of whom have taken up the slogans declared by the self-government and direction of struggle with dandyism and hooliganism."[104]

These and similar formulations ("the usual disputes and arguments"; "today offends all members") suggest that the term *bikiniarstwo* artificially circumscribed what authorities in fact recognized as a widespread tendency not limited to a few outlandishly dressed individuals. It was not just the intense popularity of jazz that made *bikiniarze* representative of a broader generational phenomenon. For cultural organizers in Nowa Huta, the *bikiniarz* typified the general lack of interest in high culture among the majority of Nowa Huta's residents: "The ideology of boycotting books, theater, events, is represented by the leading active *bikiniarze* in Nowa Huta. We have determined through discussions with them that they show a complete cultural abnegation," theorized the report-giver, "even though on the other hand they don't lack a certain mental shrewdness."[105]

Rebellion and Revulsion

"I believe in rebellion as the highest value of youth. I believe in rebellion as the highest form of hatred of terror, oppression, and injustice, and I believe, moreover, that there is no rebellion without a cause—even if it is in the world's interest, [despite the fact that it] loves its rebels, to kill them."[106] The writer Marek Hłasko (sometimes dubbed the "James Dean" of Polish literature) argued that youthful rebellion was inherently political. But if so, in what sense? As poet Agnieszka Osiecka commented with reference to her fellow writer Leopold Tyrmand's outrageously colorful socks (Tyrmand was considered something of a *bikiniarz*): "[They] were a challenge and an appeal, they were a charter of human rights. These socks spoke for the right to be different, or even to be silly. They declared: 'This is me, this is me. I don't want to be one of many; it's enough to be one of two.'"[107] Some have argued that *bikiniarze* were "taking a stand against an increasingly totalitarian system," their explicit admiration of American popular culture at the height of the cold war a direct challenge to Communist hegemony.[108] But just as it would be wrong to equate the worldviews of Warsaw-based intellectuals like Hłasko or Tyrmand too strongly with those of the young people studied in this chapter, placing them on one side or another of cold war rivalries would contradict the socks' plea for individuality: "I don't want to be one of many; it's enough to be one of two."

For those most directly implicated in the Stalinist social revolution, of course, any failure of the cultural enlightenment project in Nowa Huta was "ideological" in the deepest and most obvious sense. As one union activist wrote following a hostel inspection, "It pains us to see how these workers, who work hard twelve hours a day, go about drunk on the building site in their free time after work. It pains us to see that the newly built *świetlica* echoes emptily; it pains us to see, walking through workers' quarters, how drunken workers lie fully clothed and in dirty, muddy shoes in bed. . . . Who is at fault here . . . ?

We know, comrades, that the capitalist system came to an end here, that in the new system, work should proceed along completely different tracks, but it must with regret be said that in very many parts of [Nowa Huta] the style and form of work remain just as they were under capitalism."[109] In a Stalinist frame of reference, the failure of the regime's cultural enlightenment program—above all in Nowa Huta—was a political failure, and its repercussions would be felt after 1953. Those intellectuals, especially, who had initially supported what they saw as the Communist regime's "civilizing mission" would increasingly come to criticize its flawed and perverted execution. In their eyes, the greatest philistines were no longer the backward peasants, but rather the party leaders; the Stalinists themselves were the enemies of culture.

Hłasko and Tyrmand were unusual among Polish intellectuals in identifying with the young, working-class rebels with whom they peopled their novels of the mid-1950s, and whom they romanticized as champions of individualism in an oppressively conformist system. A more common reaction to youthful working-class culture among educated Poles at the time was distaste or even revulsion. The centrality of emotions such as disapproval and disgust in thaw-era discussions of Nowa Huta indicated the importance of a new generational politics in the postwar order.

Until the publication of his "Poem for Adults" in *Nowa Kultura* on August 21, 1955, Adam Ważyk was known as a party hardliner. (He allegedly once told a fellow writer, "I like you well enough as a person, but if you write one more word against Stalin, I will shoot you with my own hand.")[110] This fact lent additional shock value to the poem, which quickly became a cause célèbre; although authorities tried to seize all copies and fired the journal's editorial staff, hand-typed carbon copies of the poem were distributed widely, read aloud in factories, and sold on the black market.[111] In it, Ważyk appeared to have undergone a total conversion: rejecting Stalinist doublespeak ("I don't believe . . . that a lion is a lamb"), he admitted to having swallowed socialism's promised "oceans of lemonade," only to vomit out sea water. For Poles of the Left, as Jacek Kuroń later recalled, the poem's impact rivaled that of Khrushchev's secret speech in Moscow the following year: "It was a poem that scratched at wounds, that spoke things that at the time we did not want or have the courage to name."[112]

One of the wounds to be scratched by the "Poem for Adults" was Nowa Huta, the unmistakable subject of the poem's fourth section—a Nowa Huta where grandiose propagandistic claims of a worker's paradise were turned on their head. Ważyk depicted the builders of this "great Eldorado" as no conscious, enlightened proletariat, but a "half-aroused, half-demented" mass: "Thrust suddenly from the medieval gloom," torn from their superstitious and ignorant rural ways, they had only sunk deeper into depravity among the "sheds, barracks, and hostels" of Nowa Huta. "Going out from boredom in the December evenings," boys flew "like cats over walls" into the women's hostels, "holy convents" that vibrated "with the sound of spawning." As a result, the Vistula, he wrote, flowed with the corpses of unwanted children. At the end of the section, Ważyk reached a crescendo of lament for the human costs of Stalinist hubris:

> Great migration, building industry,
> unknown to Poland but known to the ages,
> milked on a void of great words, living
> wild, from day to day and *pace* the preachers—
> in coal smoke, in slow torment,
> from this the working class is smelted.
> A great deal of refuse. And to date only *kasza*.[113]

Ważyk played on the claim that industrialization under socialism would be more humane than its capitalist variant; on the contrary, he wrote, Stalinist industrialization had cast aside its human by-products as waste, "kasha," groats.

Reading closely, we can see how unerringly Ważyk's poem captured Stalinist authorities' ongoing obsessions vis-à-vis Nowa Huta's youth: alienation, demoralization, boredom, promiscuity. On the other hand, Ważyk's lurid imagery raised the emotional register to one of horror—a horror seemingly prompted almost as much by the town's populace, however, as by the regime's indifference. Such a negative depiction of "inhuman Poland" drew strong criticism, not surprisingly, in Nowa Huta itself. At a discussion at the International Press and Books Club on November 18, for example, one man declared: "I'm just a worker who was socially advanced, but I understand enough about the 'Poem for Adults' to know that it's a vulgar libel."[114] Writing about Nowohucians' responses to the poem in an article for the official youth magazine *Sztandar Młodych*, Ryszard Kapuściński argued that residents of the new town "acknowledged the truth of many of the poem's images" and were glad someone was taking notice of their problems. But they could not recognize themselves in Ważyk's portrait of a "rabble," "inhuman Poland," "kasha." "We are simply people," one young man protested.

Kapuściński—whose essay "This, Too, Is the Truth About Nowa Huta" caused only slightly less of a sensation than Ważyk's poem—had been sent to Nowa Huta on party orders to counteract the poem's damaging effects on public opinion. Kapuściński, at the age of twenty-three, already had impeccable credentials. As a student of history at Warsaw University, he had once been chided by ZMP colleagues for his excessive political zeal. Kapuściński began to write for *Sztandar Młodych* in 1950 at the age of eighteen; later that year, he accompanied the well-known poet Wiktor Woroszylski on a tour of readings in Nowa Huta—a sign of the esteem he already enjoyed with editors and political authorities. Kapuściński published several reports on this visit, written in what he would later call the "numb talk" of the day: "Enthusiasm in the hall is great. The welcoming speech of Com. Szczygieł is interrupted with heated clapping and cries. The words 'Nowa Huta—Peace—Stalin—Bierut—ZMP' are chanted ceaselessly."[115]

After 1953, a change in tone—a gradual shedding of the clichéd language of Stalinism, a tentative but critical probing of problems associated with the system—had entered into publications like *Sztandar Młodych*, whose idealistic young staff wanted to purify socialism of perversions, as they saw it, introduced under Stalinism. Kapuściński's initial response to the thaw, however, was measured. For this reason, the text that he produced after returning from assignment in Nowa Huta in 1955 came as a surprise for the journal's editor Irena Tarłowska: its searing, angry critique of official indifference ("bureaucratism in Nowa Huta achieves barbaric dimensions") would never, she argued, pass the censors; there was no point even trying. But Kapuściński's colleagues at *Sztandar Młodych* demanded its publication, and Tarłowska agreed after Kapuściński promised to organize matters with an old school chum working in the censor's office. When "This, Too, Is the Truth About Nowa Huta" appeared, both chum and Tarłowska lost their jobs.[116]

Kapuściński, fearing arrest, returned to Nowa Huta and lay low in one of the very workers' hostels he had described in his article. Meanwhile, reformers within the party pushed for creation of a special commission to investigate conditions in the new town. Kapuściński's biographer Artur Domosławski summarizes the rapid and unexpected series of events that came next:

> The Commission arrives on site and sees . . . the same things that Kapuściński saw. The "Commissioners" seek contact with the reporter, but the ZMP activists from Nowa Huta who have given him shelter say that they won't give up their friend without guarantees from the Party that no harm will come to him. The Party gives not only guarantees, but even official recognition: The Golden Cross of Service. Editor Tarłowska and the friendly censor return to work. Soon after, *Trybuna Ludu*, the organ of the Central Committee, describes the pathologies rampant in Nowa Huta. The newspaper singles out the local Party organization for blame. The management of the *kombinat* is replaced, and the local Party authorities hand in their resignation.

October (that is, the political upheavals bringing an end to Stalinism through-out Poland in October 1956) had come to Nowa Huta in November 1955.[117]

In his essay, Kapuściński had presented himself as the critical voice of a younger, hipper generation. Forgoing Ważyk's oracular utterances, he used colloquial language and wrote about going among the youth of Nowa Huta and speaking with them as an equal. But occasionally, Kapuściński's genera-tional solidarity showed signs of strain. This was especially true when the topic turned to sex. "Listen," Kapuściński wrote: "Not long ago, one fourteen-year-old infected eight boys [with venereal disease]. When we spoke with her, she described her activities with such vulgarity that one had to keep oneself from vomiting. She's not the only one. Not all are so young, but there are quite a few." Kapuściński also could not hide his alienation from the young couples who had sex out of doors because Nowa Huta lacked married housing; their cynicism contrasted too sharply with his idealism, their vulgarity with his po-etic strivings. In the end, Nowa Huta made him, like Ważyk, feel sick.[118]

Stalinism's promised social revolution had been a two-edged sword for the East Central European intelligentsia. On the one hand, it offered its members a leading role by making culture an essential component of this revolution. For those both at the center (e.g., luminaries like Ważyk) and at the grassroots (cultural workers like Kulinowska or Siatkowska), this came along with mate-rial resources and job opportunities on an unprecedented scale. This point is driven home by reciting the names of just some of the Polish literary figures whose careers were advanced thanks to living in or writing about the new town in the 1950s: Marian Brandys, Ryszard Kapuściński, Tadeusz Konwicki, Sławomir Mrożek, Wisława Szymborska.[119] At the same time—not only in rhetoric but also in practice—Stalinism was about creating a new social class to supplant traditional elites. When members of this class threatened to reject the tutelage of their betters, it caused varying degrees of unease for the intel-ligentsia. In his own response to what he saw in Nowa Huta, Kapuściński revealed that for many intellectuals, the pull of social class still competed with generational solidarities and political commitments. Jacek Kuroń put it an-other way: under socialism, "everyone was liberated—from culture."[120]

In postwar Europe, Kasper Maase argues, cultural democratization went hand-in-hand with political democratization. Studying West German reac-tions to so-called *Halbstarke* youth, Maase (who points out that clean-cut Ger-man students were mobilized to beat up *Halbstarken,* much like the "healthy" Communist youth who fought with Warsaw's *bikiniarze*) links the culture wars of 1950s Germany to working-class claims for equal recognition in Ger-man society. Noting that "the treatment of popular culture as illegitimate was essential to the defense of bourgeois hegemony in Europe," Maase argues that in Germany, bourgeois conceptions of cultural value—in effect, *kultura*—had long been used to bolster the exclusion of "common people" from civil society on the basis of their "low" and "vulgar" proclivities. Maase sees the behavior of the *Halbstarken*, with their "self-exaggeration of features of working-class culture" and provocative inclusion of the most vulgar aspects of "the American way of life and entertainment," as a symbolic confrontation with these exclusionary and undemocratic features of German cultural politics.[121]

This raises important comparative questions for Poland. The cultural enlightenment project had been premised on the intelligentsia's profound sense of superiority over the common people, or *lud*, a sentiment that did not diminish with the creation of People's Democracy. As sociologist Hanna Świda-Ziemba wrote about attitudes within her own Warsaw circles in the 1950s, "Common people were 'dumb' [literally, 'dark'], lacking consciousness (also in the sense of national consciousness). . . . Belonging to the intelligentsia—a superior, much wiser, and better mannered stratum—imposed an obligation; an obligation to treat the common people well but in the first place to educate them and to raise their level of consciousness, patriotic, educational, and hygienic."[122] However benign, such paternalism was profoundly undemocratic. And it could take on a less benign aspect: Świda-Ziemba pointed out that the Polish word *cham* could be used alternately for "peasant" and for someone who is crude, ignorant, and disgusting. While it was no longer acceptable to express aristocratic disdain for the common folk in People's Poland, the image of the *cham* hangs over the "Poem for Adults" in its descriptions of "half-aroused, half-demented Poland." Nowa Huta's new working class seemed to many to have rejected the cultural hegemony of the Polish intelligentsia. As Maase points out, European elites of the 1950s responded with particular violence to signs of such rejection associated with the working-class body[123]—evident in Kapuściński and Ważyk's physical sensations of disgust at Nowa Huta's supposedly sexually degenerated youth.

Ironically, the vast majority of Nowa Huta's inhabitants never challenged the intelligentsia's cultural hegemony directly; indeed, many (if not most) were nowhere near as resistant to the attractions of high culture as hand-wringing authorities claimed. As time went on, mass literacy and cheap imprints would make Polish classics by authors like Mickiewicz and Sienkiewicz popular as never before; access to secondary and tertiary education for the children of Nowa Huta's first generation would further erase differences in tastes and habits across the social divide.[124] Meanwhile, by the 1960s, intelligentsia youth met their working-class peers halfway: Warsaw's elite youth would be hot for jazz, and Zbigniew Cybulski, the "Polish James Dean," would star in stylish Polish films shown at art houses worldwide.[125]

In her study of punk youth in Hollywood, Susan Ruddick suggests that "certain spaces and neighbourhoods by virtue of their transitional, indeterminate nature, their lack of fixity of meaning, become more fruitful ground for the production of new identities than others."[126] Nowa Huta constituted such a terrain. The space between the official ideal of the new town and the reality of its chaotic and haphazard growth provided a vibrant backdrop for those who sought to make themselves into "new men" after their own fashion, marking the distance both from their rural roots and from what their bosses and party chiefs wanted them to be. As Dick Hebdige wrote of British punks in the 1980s,

> The politics of youth culture is a politics of metaphor: it deals in the currency of signs and is, thus, always ambiguous. For the subcultural *milieu* has been constructed underneath the authorised discourses, in the face of the multiple disciplines of the family, the school, and the workplace. Subculture forms up in the space between surveillance and the evasion of surveillance, it translates the fact of being under scrutiny into the pleasure of being watched. It is a hiding in the light.[127]

Hooligans and *bikiniarze* dwelt in the gray zone between the light shone by Stalinist disciplinary institutions in Nowa Huta—the *świetlice* and hostels, the youth organizations, the local party and police, and, distantly but not insignificantly, the central organs of power in Warsaw—and the shadows of Nowa Huta's half-finished buildings and muddy byways, its chaotic and often ungovernable terrain. Their view of themselves and the world around them remains partly hidden in that half-shadow.

6

Spaces of Solidarity, 1956–89

In 1957 and 1959, two articles about the new town of Nowa Huta appeared in the influential Polish journal *Nowa Kultura*. Entitled "Nowa Huta—The Facts" and "Nowa Huta—The Facts, Two Year Later," the reports were—as their titles were clearly meant to suggest—an effort to present a dispassionate view of Poland's erstwhile "first socialist city." Here was neither the heroic "city of tomorrow" found in Stalinist propaganda nor the nightmare of social dislocation and sexual promiscuity revealed in Adam Ważyk's "Poem for Adults" (which coincidentally had appeared in the same journal two years earlier), or in the writing of other critics who had allegedly lost all "sense of perspective." Instead, Barbara Seidler argued, Nowa Huta should be seen above all as a place that was becoming "normal." By the late 1950s, she wrote, life on the once-chaotic building site had stabilized. Its dominant motif was no longer drunken workers, but rather freshly washed baby diapers, draped across every available bush and balcony to dry in the sun.[1]

Twenty years later, Seidler returned to Nowa Huta and assessed the changes that had taken place in the two decades since those articles had been published. Invited to speak to a group of schoolchildren, she marveled that the "sons and daughters of those who came from poor villages" looked no different from their peers in central Warsaw: "I tried to tell them about those times, of their fathers and mine. They listened politely, but afterward a young chit, with a big bow entwined in her flaxen braid, said emphatically: 'We thought that you would be telling us about what really happened, so why are you telling us that they used to raise pigs in their apartments?'" Describing how the "facts" she had written about some twenty-odd years ago "now seemed like fiction" to a younger generation, Seidler argued that the process of Nowa Huta's *becoming* normal, evident in 1957 to 1959, was now complete. Nowa Huta was, finally, an ordinary town—one where the experiences of "yesterday's heroes" (today's grandfathers) were incomprehensible to their own grandchildren.[2] As one respondent had predicted to sociologists in the early 1960s, "Our children won't believe us when we tell them how it used to be. They're already accustomed to [life in] the city, to comfort."[3]

But normalization did not mean stasis. Nowa Huta's landscape certainly continued to change: the mud, cranes, and barracks were gone, and the central districts, designed and built in the 1940s and 1950s, seemed old-fashioned compared to the sprawling pre-fab high-rises of the 1960s and 1970s that now ringed the district's core. As for the new town's political landscape, de-Stalinization had brought significant changes to Nowa Huta's street names, among other things: Polish–Soviet Friendship Street was now simply Friendship Street, while Avenue of the Six-Year Plan had been renamed Rose Avenue. New toponyms such as these symbolically projected the "normalcy" of the post-totalitarian order, a seeming depoliticization of everyday life welcomed by many residents. As one reader of *Budujemy Socjalizm* put it in a letter to the newspaper, "I am waiting impatiently and am already imagining going for a walk and not being menaced by signs saying 'Avenue of the Six-Year Plan.'"[4]

And yet the dynamics of normalization were uneven. For example, the former Model Workers' Avenue, in some ways the most important thoroughfare in Nowa Huta (connecting Central Square with the Lenin Steelworks), had been renamed Lenin Avenue, even though residents had protested in letters to the newspaper that "Lenin wasn't a Pole and doesn't have anything in common with Poland." Stalinist mass mobilization, represented by the figure of the model worker, may have been a thing of the past, but apparently obeisance to the Soviet Union was not. As if to drive this point home, Rose Avenue, a favorite among residents with its flowers, fountain, and park benches, was selected in 1973 as the site for a new sculpture, a colossal, multi-ton, full-figure portrait of Vladimir Ilyich himself.[5] According to urban legend, two handwritten signs appeared around town at the time of the statue's unveiling, both with a similar message. One, at the Grunwald Monument in downtown Kraków, was addressed to the imposing figure of the equestrian warrior-king Władysław Jagiełło. It observed: "You have a horse / You're really something. / That one at the Huta's / A country bumpkin." Simultaneously, someone left an old bicycle and an old pair of rubber boots (possibly a souvenir of Nowa Huta's early, muddy days) near the new Lenin monument. "Take the bike, take the boots," it rhymed in Polish. "And get the fuck out of Nowa Huta!"[6]

The same year Seidler insisted on Nowa Huta's normalcy, unknown culprits attempted to dynamite the Lenin monument (although they succeeded only in destroying part of his left leg). A year later, the independent Solidarity trade union was founded, and during the martial law crackdown that followed,

Lenin's statue became a focal point for popular demonstrations and street battles. At one "happening" in June 1989, participants, armed with a mop and a bucket of paint, exclaimed, "Let's give Lenin a makeover!"[7] Perhaps, the "chit" with the flaxen braid who had once challenged Seidler was among them. How normal a city did Nowa Huta seem to her?

This chapter argues that the generation that turned Nowa Huta into one of the most important and militant seats of Solidarity in the 1980s had learned crucial lessons from the new town's past, forging some of its most powerful political weapons out of selective memories of its parents' and grandparents' experiences. At the same time, as Seidler rightly emphasized, the world this generation inhabited was the product of Stalinist forced industrialization and the ideological and economic logic of state socialism that Nowa Huta embodied. The war, its aftermath, and experiences of industrialization and urbanization had constituted a rupture with the past, a point of no return.

Nowa Huta's embrace of Solidarity in the 1980s, therefore, cannot simply be seen (as in some political and academic narratives) as a shedding or rejection of the Stalinist experience, a kind of prodigal son's return to enduring, changeless national and religious traditions.[8] Rather, as each generation in Nowa Huta succeeded the next, discourses and repertories of contention evolved and changed; at the same time, each successive episode of protest also built on the lessons of those before. This chapter, then, suggests some of the continuities traceable from Stalinism to Solidarity between 1956 and 1989. Even as Nowa Huta underwent significant change, the legacies of "building socialism" had an indelible, enduring role in shaping inhabitants' relationships to work and the built environment. These in turn shaped their relationships to protest and the state.

October 1956

Normalization in Nowa Huta began, as elsewhere in Poland, with the upheavals of October 1956. In February of that year, Khrushchev's secret speech in Moscow had criticized Stalinist "distortions" and the "cult of personality." In Poland, news of the "secret" speech circulated widely and prompted soul-searching debate over the country's future.[9] In the midst of this ferment, in June 1956 protesters demanding "bread and freedom" were shot down by riot police in Poznań, sparking a wave of unrest that culminated in October 1956. On October 21, Władysław Gomułka, who had been released from prison earlier that year, was reelected First Party Secretary with support from reform-minded Communists. Successfully facing down threats of a Soviet intervention, the new coalition made an exhilarating, if short-lived, show of autonomy, bringing the Stalinist era to a close.[10]

The mood in Nowa Huta in 1956 seems to have been in step with developments throughout the country. After February, according to party reports, young people were greatly absorbed by current events and discussed them avidly.[11] A change in atmosphere could also be felt in party ideological training courses: "At the present moment we observe what has been missing in our political life for several years, above all independence of thought, a critical approach, openness of discussion. Participants in political schooling no longer accept the lecturer's statements uncritically but rather pose a series of additional questions, engage in polemic, and often disagree with the explanations of the lecturer." Party officials, meanwhile, hastened to contradict rumors that "people have ceased to believe in what's said at party schools."[12]

After Poznań, the party became more shrill. "We're on the defensive," declared one member of the Nowa Huta executive, as he reported that 170 workers from HiL—including party members—had signed a petition in solidarity with protesters in Poznań.[13] The UB busily noted "enemy activity" such as pro-Poznań graffiti around HiL and an appeal scribbled in chalk on the side of a railway car: "Gentlemen let's strike because otherwise we're in trouble."[14] When, in July, the Central Party Committee's Seventh Plenum echoed Khrushchev's criticism of Stalinist methods, party officials warned that "rumors have it that our heads will roll."[15] Following the outbreak of revolution in Hungary, Comrade Wiśniewski warned of "comments to the effect that we should hack the Communists to pieces, just like in Hungary. . . . People speak openly and very emphatically about these matters." The party executive discussed the possibility of arming workers' militias in preparation for an unspecified worst-case scenario.[16]

During the protests of September and October, workers around the country demanded lower norms, higher wages, better working conditions, the removal of "socialist work discipline," and more say in management decisions.[17] At several firms (including Nowa Huta's Miastoprojekt), bosses were summarily dismissed by their employees and removed from the premises in wheelbarrows.[18] At HiL in September, young workers vandalized the common room at the steel division, ripping down decorations, dumping piles of propaganda booklets on the floor, and removing and defacing portraits of party leaders from the walls; at the agglomerator division in October, four young people went from office to office, removing from their frames portraits of Konstantin Rokossowski—a Soviet marshal imposed on the Polish army, and a particularly hated symbol of Soviet dominance. They then rehung the frames, empty, on the walls.[19] On October 18, at a ZMP meeting at HiL attended by some 500 people, the first provincial party secretary Brodziński was repeatedly interrupted by a woman who called him a liar for denying a schism in party leadership. According to secret police informers, there were about 120 people present at the meeting from "outside Nowa Huta," including journalists and students from Kraków. The meeting concluded with the adoption of a set of resolutions that, according to the report, "bore a provocational character."[20]

On October 23, three workers at ZPB took over the loudspeaker at their division and made anti-Soviet statements. On October 24, a mass meeting of workers at the agglomerator passed a resolution demanding that Cardinal Stefan Wyszyński, imprisoned since 1953, be freed. The UB noted jokes such as the following, overheard at HiL: Members of the Party Central Committee in Warsaw no longer greeted each other by saying "hello," but with "Praise the Lord!"—just in case.[21] While the security services were keen to suggest that such provocation was the work of students and intelligentsia from Kraków, in reality, the relationship between protesters in Kraków and Nowa Huta was a two-way street. When protestors in Kraków demanded the ouster of the provincial party executive, for instance, workers at HiL provided critical muscle by threatening to march on the meeting hall, a threat that was enough to secure the old guard's submission.[22] The citizens of the new town showed themselves no less capable than those of old Kraków of asserting their political voice.

What message was this voice articulating as Nowa Huta's protesters joined the chorus of the Polish October? Archival documents from the period rarely comment on the content of resolutions, petitions, or other collectively voiced grievances or demands.[23] Still, Nowa Huta seems to have conformed to Paweł Machcewicz's analysis that the "dominant motifs" of October were, "on the one hand, the conviction of [the system's] economic inefficiency and the impoverishment of the population to which it led, and on the other, [the conviction] of its national and ideological foreignness."[24] Certainly, Nowa Huta's workers were particularly well situated to perceive the connections between economic inefficiencies and Soviet domination. For example, in a report from October 24 by the police informer "Jasiek," workers at the steel foundry mentioned several installations in their division that exemplified the outflow of money to the Soviets for shoddy or unnecessary goods—a never-used converter furnace, a set of deficient Soviet cranes. Such workers hoped that Gomułka's return to power would mean better management, rising standards of living, and an end to the Soviet Union's exploitation of Poland.[25] Many could not help feeling exhilarated by the possibility of change. As one woman explained before a mass meeting on October 22, for the first time she felt like singing the "Internationale": "Now a person has zest for life."[26]

A "Little Stabilization"

Within a few years it became clear that much of the October program would not be fulfilled. There would be no end to Moscow's dominance over Polish affairs, no guarantees of civil and religious freedoms, and no far-reaching economic reforms. For the next thirty-odd years, successive Polish governments would prove unable to extract the Polish economy from the rut into which it had fallen as it lurched from crisis to crisis. And yet, the period after October is often referred to in Poland as the "little stabilization"—a period characterized by the normalization of daily life, diminution of political pressures, curtailment of the secret services, and gradual improvement of living standards. In the countryside, the collectivization of agriculture was halted; restrictions were lifted on certain categories of private enterprise; and between 1955 and 1960, the production of consumer goods rose 63 percent.[27] In Nowa Huta, the city born under Stalinism and meant to embody a socialist future, this stabilization was especially striking. No longer living on a muddy construction site, but rather in a real city with sidewalks and street lamps, Nowa Huta's residents were well placed to appreciate the benefits of decent housing, good wages, and free healthcare and education. In a sense, Nowa Huta's promise had been realized.

Stabilization in Nowa Huta could also be felt in the population's changing demographics, which were no longer predominantly young, male, and single. Indeed, Nowa Huta's birth rate now outstripped the national average. These changes were associated with increased public order, as the drinking, fighting, and ganglike behavior that had attracted national attention during the thaw subsided. Seidler, in fact, criticized the draconian measures that authorities, skittish about a possible resurgence of such problems, had instituted: these had led to seven thousand cases before the city council's misdemeanor court in the space of a year, most for minor infractions, and to the fining of women for allowing men into their rooms in the hostels—usually their own husbands. Such "puritanism," she suggested, was a response to the "alarms raised by Kraków and Warsaw" in preceding years.[28]

Seidler's depiction of this orderly, broody, puritan Nowa Huta—such a contrast to the anarchic, sexually lawless frontier town portrayed in the media and party reports in the early to mid-1950s—had its echoes in forms of domesticity and consumption. According to researchers from the Warsaw-based

Housing Institute, the first families who settled in Nowa Huta's apartment blocks in the early 1950s had lived "peasant-style": they filled the rooms to bursting with antique bedsteads, wardrobes, and glass cabinets, decorating the walls with rugs, religious pictures, and other supposedly unhygienic and unaesthetic relics of village life. Rather than having separate bedrooms for parents and children, working-class families in two-room apartments had tended to sleep together in one room, reserving the other for formal entertaining.[29] The teacher Leopold Sułkowski confirmed that many new residents "kept house like mountainfolk," conducting most everyday activities in the kitchen.[30] Those unaccustomed to modern conveniences were said to store coal in the bathtub,[31] dispose of trash out the window,[32] or breed rabbits in their apartments.[33]

By the late 1950s, however, "furnishing [one's] new apartment as elegantly as possible became the realization of ambitions that were repressed under previously poor housing conditions." Such ambitions could, at last, be realized with the expansion of domestic consumption in Poland in the post-Stalinist period. Seidler wrote that Nowa Huta's residents favored a "traditional, bourgeois" style ("everything must be solid, expensive"); amateur artists, selling kitschy landscapes or religious scenes, were making brisk sidewalk sales, and it was frequently said of a married woman that she was "working for the furniture."[34] Lest we underestimate the power and appeal of such purchases, Sułkowski remembered that when his family bought a washing machine, his wife broke down and wept.[35] The appetite for new categories of durables was also strong; by 1961, Nowa Huta had more televisions per capita than Kraków.[36]

The writers and poets who had descended on Nowa Huta to sing its praises in the 1950s were now replaced by sociologists, for whom Nowa Huta was the perfect laboratory for studying the preceding decade's demographic upheavals.[37] Asking how quickly and how well rural migrants had adapted to urban life, most studies found that by the early 1970s, the lifestyles and mentalities of Nowa Huta's inhabitants had diverged significantly from those of their rural brethren. Upward mobility was a universal theme: in 1963 one sociologist noted that skilled workers almost universally aspired for their children to gain a university degree. "In the field of cultural demands and style of life," Moskal observed, such families "approached the model of professional families."[38] Social origins were becoming less important as a determinant of status and lifestyle. One resident from an educated background tellingly recalled these changes as a process not only of modernization but also of "refinement" or "improvement"—using a word that literally translates as "ennoblement."[39] Nowa Huta's workers had become a "labor aristocracy" in more than one sense of the word.

In conversations with sociologists in the 1960s, respondents from Nowa Huta expressed both satisfaction and ambivalence about changes that had taken place in the new town since the 1950s. "Life is more peaceful, stable, while at the beginning it seemed temporary," one resident told Władysław Kwaśniewicz in 1964, while others approvingly noted the disappearance of hooliganism and fighting. However, a number of respondents expressed disapproval of the perceived materialism of their neighbors and the social differentiation that had come along with rising standards of living. "People who had nothing in the village and here attained a certain position," said one, "have no regard for those who, like themselves not so long ago, have nothing."[40] The period's emphasis on consumption and upward mobility notwithstanding, comments like these suggest that social egalitarianism remained a strong value among many members of Nowa Huta's new working class.[41]

Most Nowohucians who remember this "little stabilization" recall good times. For Elżbieta Borysławska, the darkness of life at home (while released from prison in 1956, her father had come home emotionally scarred) was offset by visits to the special children's park, where a certain Miss Bilińska was always in residence to organize activities and games, powdered orangeade and "Bambino" ice cream, and wandering among the pocket gardens that tenants had planted around the apartment blocks, where she and her friends spent hours picking flowers.[42]

Likewise, Marianna Zając had been deeply affected by Stalinism: her family's land and home in Czyżyny had been expropriated when Nowa Huta was built, and until 1956 her husband had been persecuted as a veteran of the Home Army. Yet Zając greatly enjoyed her work at the childcare center of the Monopol cigarette factory, a round-the-clock facility where parents dropped children off on Mondays and picked them up at the end of the week. Zając's reminiscences, composed after the collapse of communism, dwelt on the benefits of the welfare regime in Nowa Huta: she approvingly noted how well appointed the childcare center was and mentioned other ways in which the firm looked after its employees (regular holidays at the firm's own vacation home in Zakopane, for instance). Nowa Huta's public amenities were also well maintained, such as the man-made lake with its outdoor cafes, pedal boats, and free concerts in summer. "My husband earned little," Zając told an interviewer in 2005, "but I can honestly say that we lived better then than young people today, with all their luxuries."[43]

Although the new town was still, on the whole, no more loved by its neighbors in Kraków than it had been in the 1950s, Nowa Huta now had its draws for residents of the older city: the People's Theater, the House of Books and the Press, and the well-stocked, high-ceilinged retail outlets on Central

Children in Central Square, 1958. Wiktor Pental, Imago Mundi Foundation Collection.

Square and Rose Avenue. Nowa Huta's abundance of green space was another attraction. Well into the period, the interpenetration of city and country—of planned and unplanned—remained a distinctive feature of Nowa Huta's landscape. Farmers occasionally pastured their cows in the open spaces between the newer settlements, and along the margins of Twentieth-Anniversary Settlement, "microscopic farmsteads had managed to grow up, surrounded by fences and hedges and outfitted with small wooden houses and sheds, rabbit hutches, even an apiary with several beehives."[44] Every summer, Waldemar Cichy's parents sent him from Kraków to stay with his aunt in Nowa Huta, the way other children were sent to relatives in the village, and he enjoyed playing ball in the wide streets and swimming in the Dłubnia River.

Nonetheless, differences between the two urban centers still loomed large. The young Cichy always felt, for instance, that Nowa Huta had a distinctive smell, which he associated with the powerful odor that filled the trams after the work shift at the steelworks ended—a "Nowa Huta stench" of men's sweat.[45] Nowa Huta's identity as a proletarian city, called into being to humiliate bourgeois Kraków, still defined the new town for many. Both snobbery and political mistrust, therefore, often marked the gulf that persisted between the two communities, bourgeois and working-class, old and new.

A City Without God?

A story used to circulate within Communist circles in Kraków concerning Premier Bolesław Bierut's reaction to planners' first sketches for Nowa Huta. After looking them over for a minute, he allegedly burst out, "Comrades, you forgot something here!" Puzzled, his listeners fell silent. "You overlooked a church," the great leader insisted. "Where will the church be?" Bierut asked his stunned interlocutors about the social background of the projected population. About 80 percent, they answered, would be peasant-workers. "Well, then," he allegedly replied, "they won't be Communists, they'll be believers, so a church is all the more essential."[46]

The story, no doubt apocryphal, was told to Fr. Józef Gorzelany long after Bierut's death and may have expressed wishful thinking; if Bierut *had* prevailed on planners to build a church in Nowa Huta, the party could have saved itself a lot of trouble. In particular, it could have avoided the disastrous events in Nowa Huta of April 1960, often referred to as Nowa Huta's "struggle for the cross." This two-day uprising, in which crowds of thousands were pacified by armed riot forces, was sparked when authorities reversed a 1956 decision to allow residents to build a church in the new town. Its repercussions would be broad and deep: In the short term, the "struggle for the cross" led to the coalescence of popular support for the church and a formidable alliance between church leaders, including Karol Wojtyła (the future Pope John Paul II), and the town's inhabitants. In the long run, it provided a powerful new vocabulary and institutional base, one that played an important role in Solidarity's reach and efficacy in Nowa Huta in the 1980s.

In Nowa Huta, as elsewhere in Poland, church attendance was never forbidden even at the height of Stalinism, although it was frowned upon among party members. Activists did occasionally attempt, however, to discourage religious observance—for example, by encouraging workers (fairly unsuccessfully, it seems) to engage in extra labor commitments on Sundays or by offering

One of Nowa Huta's outlying panel-built high-rise settlements of the 1960s to 1980s. Around seventy religious statues, chapels, and roadside crosses are located on Nowa Huta's territory, most pre-dating the creation of the new town. This one is a figure of Mary. Piotr Dylik, KARTA Center Foundation, Warsaw.

over five hundred ZMP brigade members who had not returned home for the holidays an educational Christmas Day outing to Auschwitz in 1950. On Pentecost the following spring, secret police closely monitored workplace absenteeism; one-quarter to one-half of employees were absent at some workplaces.[47] ZMP brigade member Edmund Chmieliński insisted in his memoirs that *junacy* respected one anothers' views on religion. While he himself "believed only in the idea of socialism, others believed in God, and they too built socialism. [None] of us was persecuted, we had the right to freedom."[48]

Not only workers but also cadres in the new town were said to be quite religious. The secret police, for example, noted "a number of individuals occupying responsible positions in the economy and the government apparatus"—including party members, a functionary of the citizens' militia, a member of the District National Council, and a "social activist"—who were regular visitors to the monastery in Mogiła or sent their children there for religious instruction.[49] Many party members were also known churchgoers.[50] Perhaps partly for this reason, when local activists exerted pressure against religious traditions and clergy influence, they were simultaneously careful not to appear overtly antireligious. In 1955, for instance, party officials noted that priests frequently visited patients in hospital; after a discreet word to the hospital direction from the head of the party organization at Nowa Huta's health services department, such visits decreased, but they did not stop altogether. In the villages annexed to Nowa Huta, where religious feeling was at its strongest, officials noted with apparent relief that no one complained after religious images were moved from the fronts of classrooms to the back walls during spring cleaning.[51]

In 1952, one Bieńczyce resident allegedly asked a visiting party agitator whether citizens would be allowed to build a church in their town. To this question, "he got a positive answer," noted a party report—"which to a certain degree was not in keeping with the foundations of [Nowa Huta], and this was not explained by the speaker."[52] The need for a church in Nowa Huta, however, was obvious to most observers, especially as the new town's population continued to swell. On a visit to Poland in 1955, journalist S.L. Shneiderman described a constant stream of people to and from the church of St. Bartholomew in Mogiła for the Feast of the Epiphany: "The narrow road . . . [was] crowded with men, women and children in two rows. One going toward the church, the other leaving it. In the crowd were hundreds of young couples pushing baby carriages or leading small children by the hand." There, the picturesque wooden church was stuffed to bursting: "In the huge courtyard of the church, . . . several hundred people were waiting their turn to enter and attend Mass. In the meantime they were busily buying packets of incense, holy pictures, crucifixes and rosaries, all of them carrying the stamp of Częstochowa. The church was filled to capacity and, as one group of worshipers left, another group would pack the nave and a new Mass would commence. As I left the church courtyard the road was still crowded with people streaming toward the village."[53] In 1957, Seidler wrote without hesitation, "Nowohucians are religious. On Sunday in the hostels, the older [workers] drive the young ones off to church. From all settlements, people stream to Bieńczyce, Czyżyny, and Mogiła. But it is obvious that these three nearby churches don't satisfy Nowohucians' needs."[54]

In the wake of political changes in October 1956, Nowa Huta was among several hundred Polish communities to seek permission to build new churches and chapels.[55] Before the month was out, a twelve-person delegation from Nowa Huta had travelled to Warsaw to meet with Gomułka, who granted permission for a church to be built with parishioners' own funds and labor. In February 1957, planners allocated a parcel of land at the corner of Marx Avenue and Mayakovsky Street for the future sanctuary.[56] Permit in hand, a citizens' committee began to raise funds for the future church and organize an architectural competition for its design. Zbigniew Salawa's design prevailed over some four hundred other entries. Its most distinctive feature was a crucifix-topped, 83-meter tower that would have risen higher than the smokestacks of HiL.[57] On March 17, 1957, members of the citizens' committee joyously consecrated the site of the future church with a simple wooden cross.

A mere three years later—on February 8, 1960—Nowa Huta's Association for Building the Church was dissolved by official decree and its assets seized. Similar measures, meanwhile, were undertaken in other communities across the country, reflecting a wider retreat from the more liberal policies of the thaw era.[58] Publicly, Gomułka argued that, instead of churches, Poland needed more "apartments, schools, and hospitals"; meanwhile, the party intensified its struggles against church influence.[59] In Nowa Huta, however, local authorities were posed with a dilemma. Residents had defiantly left the cross standing at the corner of Marx and Mayakovsky Streets, an unwelcome reminder of their unfulfilled demands. Moreover, Gomułka would shortly be paying a state visit to Nowa Huta for annual Day of the Steelworker celebrations. Local authorities pressed church officials to see to the cross's removal. Instead, during mass on Sunday, April 24, local priests warned parishioners that the cross was under threat. Early in the morning of April 26, an anonymous handwritten sign appeared at the construction site: "Defend the cross."[60]

On April 27, between seven and eight-thirty in the morning, a work crew arrived at the site with orders from provincial party officials in Kraków to remove the cross. The authorities do not seem to have anticipated trouble.[61] Few men were on the streets, as the morning shift had begun. Very quickly, however, a crowd of women and children formed around the workers at the cross. Some women started to cry; others upbraided the men. "Władek, what are you doing?" one woman remembered asking, suggesting that the workers were from Nowa Huta. Such gendered forms of protest as tears and motherly scolding, however, were not the only strategies employed in this early encounter: some onlookers started throwing stones at the workers, who quickly retreated.[62]

More and more people now arrived, placing candles and flowers at the cross and singing hymns. One woman copied out the section of the Polish Constitution guaranteeing religious freedom from her son's school textbook, writing above it, "We demand our Constitutional rights," and nailed the slogan to the cross's arms. By now, the crowd, mainly women and children, numbered between three hundred and a thousand. Some cops (again local boys, "ours") sauntered by and suggested that the women disperse, that there could be "unpleasantness." The sinister appearance of "photojournalists" snapping pictures of the crowd (later used by secret police to identify participants) suggested trouble to come, but still more protesters gathered—now in front of the District National Council as well—shouting, "We want the church!"[63]

At 2 p.m., the first shift let out at HiL, and men streamed into the streets, heading for the cross. Now the protests took on a sharper edge. At 2:30, two members of the militia were attacked and chased. A portion of the crowd moved from the cross to the DRN headquarters, where stones were thrown at the police in their cars. Militia agents repeatedly exited their cars and shot into the air in order to disperse the crowd, but each time, the crowd moved back in. During one such maneuver, the militia seized five men, who turned on the agent guarding them and beat him up. By 4 p.m., an estimated three thousand protesters had gathered in front of the DRN and another two thousand at the cross.[64]

It was not until 4:40 p.m., more than eight hours after the first crowds had gathered, that the militia used its batons for crowd control, attempting to drive away the now four-thousand-strong crowd in front of the DRN offices. Protesters responded by throwing stones. At 5:20 an unknown civilian (possibly a party official from the steelworks) was beaten by the crowd. The militia retreated from the DRN. A little before 7:00, protesters vandalized a bulldozer, telephone booth, and police box. Only at this point did the provincial command of the MO seek permission from the Ministry of the Interior to mobilize the armored riot-control force (ZOMO), allowing for the use of water cannons and tear gas. Meanwhile, a pastry shop and a furrier's were vandalized, and a food shop and kiosk were set on fire. When members of the militia attempted to intervene, the crowd destroyed two of their vehicles.[65]

A little after 8:00, the militia, attacking the crowd in Central Square with batons, succeeded in driving protesters out of the square and back toward the cross.[66] As darkness fell, the sounds of protest and battle—singing, shouting, and the percussive noise of firearms—created an eerie soundscape. The confrontation between police and protesters now went in waves: when the militia attacked, people would scatter, hiding in stairwells or on roofs; when the coast was clear, they returned to the streets. The police beat protesters indiscriminately with their sticks, both on the streets and, when captured, in police wagons; meanwhile, several officers were beaten or injured by improvised missiles (bricks, stones, pieces of metal, or fragments of building facades) thrown by protestors or dropped from apartment balconies, and one was badly burned by a homemade Molotov cocktail. A little after 9:00, a large group attacked the militia near the DRN, throwing rocks at the building and at a few escaping councilors. At 9:30, there was an electrical blackout; when the lights went on again a quarter of an hour later, the crowd stormed the DRN, breaking windows up to the fourth floor and setting fire to a militia jeep. At 10:15, two hundred people entered the building and vandalized the interior. The building and a nearby kiosk were set on fire.[67]

At the cross, meanwhile, protesters held their positions and erected barricades blocking access to the militia. This was probably the high point of protester control. Within an hour, the tide had turned; the militia had taken apart the barricades, dispersed the crowd at the construction site, and occupied government buildings. Protesters continued to throw rocks, orangeade bottles, and Molotov cocktails, but were no match for the militia, who were now in a position of safety behind walls and armed with guns. Significantly, when the second shift let out at the steelworks at 10 p.m., the workforce dispersed instead of joining the protest. Around midnight, police reinforcements arrived, and thereafter government forces turned their attention to reprisals and arrests.[68]

No sooner had the blood dried than both party and church officials sought to put their own spin on the uprising. Of key importance was the way it had evolved from the (relatively) peaceful protest of women and children, with its strong religious overtones, to the violent *zadyma*, or street battle, between (mainly) young men and the police, with its attendant vandalism. Privately, authorities distinguished between the protests' earlier "fanatical-religious" and later "hooligan" character.[69] Publicly, the events were portrayed as a breakdown in law and order *tout court*: appearing in Nowa Huta not long afterward, Gomułka emphasized the "hooligan excesses," whose perpetrators had been "correctly condemned" by the healthy workforce of the Lenin Steelworks.[70]

For church officials, on the other hand, it was essential to downplay the riots' lawlessness. According to the secret service, "the clergy was surprised by the turn of events and in connection with the incident is keeping quiet, being fully aware that the sudden appearance of a 'hooligan ally' does not reflect well on it."[71] Teachers of catechism classes allegedly expelled children who had thrown stones, and an abbot criticized vandalism.[72] Church officials like Karol Wojtyła, recently appointed to the curial clergy of the Kraków archdiocese, exhorted the people of Nowa Huta to stay calm, reminding them that the cross remained standing, at least for now. Meanwhile, Wojtyła pursued negotiations with authorities over the possibility of allowing a church to be built in a different location. In 1965 authorities allocated a parcel of land for a church in Bieńcyzce, just beyond the boundaries of the "old" Huta in an area of rapid residential expansion; ultimately, permission was also granted for the construction of a second church in Mistrzejowice. Wojtyła would be present at the consecration of both sanctuaries. That of the Church of the Mother of God and Queen of Poland, commonly known because of its boat-like shape as Arka Pana ("Ark of our Lord"), in Bieńcyzce in May 1977 was attended by a jubilant crowd of seventy thousand. By the time he presided over the consecration of the Church of St. Maksymilian Maria Kolbe in Mistrzejowice, Wojtyła was already pope.[73]

By refocusing people's energies on church building in the aftermath of April 1960, the Catholic hierarchy stressed an apolitical interpretation of the protests. In other words, these had been about Nowohucians' deep attachment to the cross as a Christian symbol and their demands for a church of their own, nothing more, nothing less. According to members of the secret service, this was also the version of events heard on the street in the days following the protests. The mood was "peaceful," they reported, and "already local people see everything that happened with different eyes. Today, *no one thirsts for a street demonstration of a political character* [my italics], but rather, one hears about defending the cross and demanding the building of a church, if not in that location then in another."[74]

There were both tactical and psychological advantages to downplaying the protests' political dimensions and presenting them in a purely religious light. It cast the regime in the role of ruthless aggressor against the faithful, and disowned the more violent aspects of the riot with their diffuse and ambiguous expressions of anger. It gave the protestors a powerful ally in the church, as well as common ground with those in the party hierarchy who shared, however quietly, the protesters' Catholic faith. Finally, perhaps most importantly, it snatched victory from the jaws of defeat. Unknown numbers had died, thousands had been beaten and arrested, and nothing, in the bigger political picture, had changed. But the cross remained standing, making, in this version of the story, the people of Nowa Huta—not the government—the victors.

This particular outcome would be critical for later generations as well: the cross's continued triumphal presence at the corner of Marx and Mayakovsky would provide important lessons in the "repertoire of symbolic action," as Maryjane Osa puts it, in which religious symbols would contribute to "an expressive master frame that emphasized identity and solidarity." In the 1970s and 1980s, activists would draw on this master frame in their search for a viable opposition discourse.[75] The historian Jarosław Szarek, for instance, has shown how a small group of opposition intellectuals based in Nowa Huta created and propagated a usable myth of the "struggle for the cross" for its twentieth anniversary in 1980. The Christian Association of Working People was founded on the nineteenth anniversary of the protests; in 1980, with the assistance of politically engaged clergy, it organized a march to commemorate the twentieth anniversary of April 1960. The route of the thousand-strong march began at Arka Pana and ended at the cross. For Szarek, this constitutes a pivotal moment in the evolution of protest in Nowa Huta; thereafter, one could always find candles burning at the foot of the cross, which became a key point on an alternative, oppositional map of Nowa Huta. Moreover, the association's underground newsletter, *Nowa Huta's Cross*, and the publishing house of the same name propagated knowledge of the 1960 events beyond Nowa Huta itself, inserting it into broader national narratives of protest and resistance.[76]

The association repoliticized the way in which people saw the 1960 protests, but did so within an ideological framework that subsumed secular legal and democratic rights to Catholic spiritual values and a religiously grounded national identity. Yet in 1960 protesters had sent mixed messages. They sang hymns, but also the "Internationale." They linked their demands for a church to democratic principles such as freedom of religion, with specific reference to the Constitution of the Polish People's Republic.[77] They did not articulate a dichotomous opposition between Catholicism (or Polishness) and communism or between socialism and civil rights. Indeed, two years after the protest, church officials were still worrying about a perceived lack of piety among Nowa Huta's inhabitants; Fr. Stanisław Czartoryski spoke of the difficulty of "catching up" in Nowa Huta, where allegedly "paganism" dominated and "secular life took precedence over religion."[78] It would take some time before the alliance between the church and Nowa Huta's population would be fully cemented.

Although hundreds of communities had been denied permission to build churches thanks to Gomułka's about-face in the late 1950s, Nowa Huta was one of only two localities where this led to open conflict.[79] In a letter to the authorities, Wojtyła suggested that it was not just residents' religious sensibilities that had been offended by the cross's removal, but also the "writing off" of their "effort" (using a Polish word, *wysiłek*, that connoted physical exertion).[80] Nowa Huta's wooden cross, representing the church residents planned to build, was a potent symbol: it associated religious faith with the pride of manual labor and communal ownership. Up until that point, all plans for the city had emanated from experts and politicians. The church would have been the first structure in Nowa Huta initiated, planned, and supervised entirely by the people themselves. Far from negating Nowa Huta's unique origins as a city by and for the workers, then, the church was to be an act of completion, or *oswojenie* (domestication)—of making Nowa Huta truly one's own.

Were there other legacies of the new town's origins that contributed to the ferocity of the response in April 1960? Surely some members of the crowd would have remembered how, not so long ago, gangs of rowdy youth-brigade workers had engaged in scuffles with police, emboldened by their numerical advantage and the authorities' poor control of Nowa Huta's frontierlike terrain. Some former brigade members were, no doubt, among the crowds of April 27; in this way, the "struggle for the cross" can be seen as a thread linking Nowa Huta's chaotic and lawless early days with the street riots of the martial law period in the 1980s, a subject that will be explored shortly. Social memories of Stalinism embedded knowledge of the limits of social control; later, memories of April 1960 would help transmit this awareness to a new generation.

Crisis and Dissent at HiL, 1957–79

In August 1980, the "Solidarity" Independent Trade Union was legalized by agreement between the government and striking workers on the Baltic Coast. Chapters of Solidarity immediately began forming in Nowa Huta, and by September 1980, 90 percent of the workers at HiL had joined (99 percent in some divisions). By December, a total of 34,085 out of 38,376 HiL employees were Solidarity members, making it the largest workplace chapter in the country.[81] Throughout the 1980s, Nowa Huta served as Solidarity's nerve center in southern Poland, one of five regions (jointly with Kraków) consistently represented in the organization's national leadership structures.[82] When General Wojciech Jaruzelski declared martial law in December 1981, workers defiantly occupied HiL in response; after the *kombinat*'s "pacification" by an invasion of armored tanks, Nowa Huta continued to be a key center of underground activity, noted for the militancy of both its leadership and rank and file. Nowa Huta also witnessed some of the largest street battles between police and pro-Solidarity demonstrators during the martial law period.[83] Although Nowa Huta's Solidarity structures emerged much weakened following the amnesty of 1986, a wildcat strike at HiL on April 26, 1988 helped to precipitate the so-called Round Table negotiations and, ultimately, the first largely free elections in postwar Poland. To everyone's surprise, when the results came in on April 4, 1989, Solidarity had swept the table; with 89 percent, Nowa Huta's Mieczysław Gil, a Solidarity candidate, tallied the highest vote in Poland.[84]

The depth and breadth of Nowa Huta's support for Solidarity took many outside the district by surprise. After so many years of propaganda about the new town's "healthy" working-class, many Poles had simply absorbed the image of a regime-loyal, quiescent population.[85] During the creation of Solidarity's regional structure in 1980, activists from Nowa Huta felt the mistrust of certain of their Kraków colleagues, some of whom allegedly accused the

A steelworker at HiL, 1966. Henryk Makarewicz, Imago Mundi Foundation Collection.

new town's workers of being "pinko" [*skomunizowana*].[86] Prior to that, in the 1970s, as the progressive Catholic journalist Halina Bortnowska remembered, very few Kraków oppositionists bothered to find out what was happening in Nowa Huta, including the "struggle for the cross" and the church's increasing involvement in grassroots activism there. "On Wiślna St." (where the editorial offices of the liberal Catholic journals *Tygodnik Powszechny* and *Znak* were located) "no one was interested in Nowa Huta" in the late 1970s. When colleagues heard she lived there, they expressed their sympathy.[87] For oppositionists such as these, the events of 1980 in Nowa Huta came like a bolt from the blue.

Like much propaganda, the official depiction of Nowa Huta's quiescence prior to 1980 had been premised on falsehood. During the nationwide youth protests of March 1968, for instance, school dormitories in Nowa Huta had had to be put under virtual lockdown to prevent secondary and technical school students from joining their protesting peers in Kraków.[88] As the historians Filip Musiał and Zdzisław Zblewski have also shown, after official price increases in December 1970 provoked nationwide protests, key figures in HiL management and party structures—including the general director and the first secretary of the factory committee—were replaced "under pressure from the workforce."[89] If labor conflict in Nowa Huta did not erupt out into the open before 1980, it may have been because authorities, fearful of the negative propaganda that a strike at socialism's flagship enterprise would engender, did whatever they could to prevent such a scenario.[90] Ultimately, we know little about the nature and extent of labor conflict in Nowa Huta in the Gomułka and Gierek eras. Suggestive though fragmentary evidence of a narrowly averted strike at HiL in March and April 1957, however, seems to support Roman Laba's thesis that Solidarity's roots can be traced further back in time than usually thought.[91] Secret police records from this period describe a workforce at HiL on the verge of a multidivision strike; at issue was an abortive bid for negotiations with Warsaw over pay issues. The strike was averted, finally, only by an emergency visit from the minister for steel and the provincial party secretary. Significantly, key forms of worker organization—in particular, the sit-down strike, identified by some scholars as an "organizational breakthrough" of strikers on the Baltic Coast in 1980—were already known to workers at HiL in 1957. Nowa Huta's new workers, although first-generation proletarians, were no laggards in developing new traditions and forms of protest, supporting the argument that these were engendered precisely by the experience of work in a "workers' state."[92]

Similarly, Musiał and Zblewski show that, even though Nowa Huta did not strike in 1970, discourse on the ground was already complex and multivalent at least a decade before the founding of Solidarity. Among popular demands noted by secret police in 1970 were dismissal of the Central Committee and punishment of those responsible for the massacres of striking workers on the Baltic Coast, amnesty for the strikers and assistance for the victims' families, and punishment of those responsible for the invasion of Czechoslovakia. Specific proposals for reform included demands for a viable, legal political opposition party, for the expansion of the Sejm's powers (including a suggestion that a majority of the representatives be from parties other than the PZPR), and for a loosening of censorship.[93] In other words, like workers on the Baltic Coast, those in Nowa Huta did not require the input of intellectuals (which came only in the mid- to late 1970s) to link political and economic demands or envision far-reaching programs of systemic reform.[94]

The emergence of an independent workers' movement in Nowa Huta in 1980, then, was not the sudden development that it seemed to many outsiders at the time. There was an "accumulation of experience" from protests in 1956, 1967, 1968, and 1970, and "each successive crisis tended to improve the chances of the one following."[95] For *Polityka's* reporter in Nowa Huta in 1957, the near-strike of that year constituted a "story without an epilogue."[96]

In retrospect, however, the obvious epilogue was Solidarity—the culmination of workers' pursuit of fairness, transparency, and reform.

The 1980s: Spaces of Struggle

The story of Solidarity in Nowa Huta resembles similar stories around Poland. It begins with the moment when people realized that they could speak their minds without fear and that "they"—the overbearing bosses and officials—were on the defensive. It reflects the exhilarating sense of freedom and "public happiness," as Hannah Arendt described it, that characterizes a revolution.[97] As happens anywhere, however, local factors were crucial in shaping the specific patterning of events and timbre of participants' experience. Nowa Huta's particular past—its legacy of Stalinist industrialization, urbanization, and mobilization—contributed to an explosive mix: from HiL's size and economic significance to the city's spatial configuration, from memories and myths of the town's origins to its unique symbolic geography, Nowa Huta's economic, cultural, and physical infrastructure offered a rich substrate for new contentious repertoires and discourses.

Solidarity's strength in Nowa Huta was, not least, a reflection of the *huta's* sheer size and importance in the top-heavy state socialist economy. HiL was an unmatched concentration of resources and skills, one that Solidarity activists put to excellent use. For instance, activists could relatively easily "facilitate" (*załatwiać*) the matériel of opposition (transmitters, paper, carbons, reproduction machines) from HiL's many storerooms and offices—so much so, that they were able to distribute surplus to less well-resourced Solidarity branches elsewhere.[98] And just as, in normal times, workers had often done their own work "on the side" at their factory or workplace, much illegal printing in Nowa Huta was performed on site using HiL equipment (sometimes while managers looked the other way).[99] By this means, HiL-based publications such as *The Steelworker* and *Wartime Observer* attained runs of fifteen thousand without putting a strain on Solidarity's resources. Even the first samizdat published in Nowa Huta during martial law, a holiday card from Solidarity to the people of Nowa Huta, emanated from HiL's printing presses.[100]

The steelworks' integration of production on such a large scale also created a communication network exceeding the size of most interfactory strike committees. Since almost everyone in Nowa Huta had family members or acquaintances working at the *kombinat*, HiL served as an information clearinghouse for the entire community. This advantage became especially clear during martial law, when samizdat became a lifeline for activists and their supporters.

Throughout the period, HiL's distribution network was never disrupted. Illegal publications, so-called *bibuły,* were delivered to the central storeroom and divided into packets, which were then picked up by workers from across the *huta* in the course of ordinary visits to the storeroom for supplies. These couriers then dropped the materials off at designated points in their own divisions. Their movements, consistent with the production routine, aroused no suspicion and minimized contact among those involved.[101] Even cleaners at HiL contributed to the information flow, retrieving secret party telexes from office waste and passing them to activists.[102] Technicians from the *kombinat* helped set up and maintain an underground radio network for all of southern Poland.[103] In this way, Nowa Huta became the information nerve center for an entire region.

Nowa Huta's urban geography also offered a range of strategic advantages. One was the spatial integration of the city and the factory: a national Solidarity organizer noted approvingly that "in Nowa Huta, you've got twenty thousand workers in the center of town the moment the first shift ends." In Warsaw, by contrast, workers had to "show slightly more initiative" to find their way to a demonstration.[104] The configuration of Nowa Huta's public spaces also facilitated street protests of unprecedented duration and intensity: its wide avenues and squares had been purpose-built for mass demonstrations, but the decentralized layout of its residential neighborhoods, with their internal courtyards and multiple entry stairs, offered escape routes and hiding places (often in helpful strangers' apartments) for demonstrators chased by police, whose riot-control vehicles were too wide to enter the housing courtyards. In Kraków, by contrast, the police had easily surrounded and cut off the first and last real street demonstration of the martial law period in the town's Main Market Square, ending in a debacle for protesters. Around the same time, during the first major protest in Nowa Huta, on June 13, 1982, a five-thousand-strong crowd had "attacked the police with a ferocity heretofore not encountered in Kraków." Solidarity's regional leaders quickly agreed that future demonstrations would be held in Nowa Huta rather than in Kraków.[105]

Nowa Huta's *zadymy* (or "smokescreens") followed a regular pattern. Typically, a peaceful march, often begun after mass at Arka Pana, would be charged by riot police using sticks, water cannons, and tear gas. Protesters would then escape and regroup, engaging in a cat-and-mouse game pitting thousands of demonstrators (at this stage, primarily young people in their teens and twenties) against armed riot police. For protesters, the objective (besides evading beatings or arrest) was to break through police lines and reach landmarks such as Arka, Central Square, the cross, or Lenin's statue. If they reached the latter, they might douse it with benzene and paint, "necklace" it with a tire, and set it alight.[106] Other goals were to obstruct the movement of security forces, usually by means of improvised barricades, and to do as much damage as possible to security equipment and personnel. Protesters fought with Molotov cocktails, milk bottles, or paving stones (sometimes dropped on policemen from upper-story apartments). They attempted to entrap and set fire to police vehicles, and if they managed to capture stranded officers or secret police agents, they chased or beat them. Hundreds of officers were injured, but ultimately, of course, it was the police themselves—with their armored vehicles, tear gas, water cannons, riot gear, and rubber truncheons—who inflicted the greatest damage. Some seemed to take pleasure in doing so: "Don't think that we're ZOMO-Kraków or ZOMO-Katowice," one group of officers shouted at a young man after beating him viciously. "We're ZOMO-Łódź—remember it, and fuck off!"[107]

Nowa Huta's riots illuminate another distinctive feature of the new town's public spaces, specifically, the heightened political signification of its landscape. From Stalinist times, Nowa Huta had been, to borrow a phrase from the sociologist Jan Kubik, a "symbol of power," a place where every element of the urban ensemble had been intended by the regime to communicate a particular vision of order and authority.[108] At the same time, Nowa Huta had also always inspired an informal, folk geography that cut against the grain of official discourse—for example, in the use of ironic place names, such as "Mexico" or "Taiwan" for hostel barracks in the 1950s and 1960s or "Square of St. Vladimir of the Severed Foot" for Rose Avenue in the 1980s (a reference to the Lenin monument after its encounter with dynamite).[109] In the Solidarity period, protesters marked out a new, oppositional geography with their movements through space. The routes of marches and street fighters' targets linked sites associated with Nowa Huta's origins (the steelworks, Central Square, Lenin) to more recent landmarks (Arka, the cross). This oppositional geography was, like the oppositional economy of organizing Solidarity at HiL, parasitic on an official one, drawing its power from Nowa Huta's Stalinist past.

Arka Pana—the church that symbolized the delayed success of the popular campaign begun in 1956, if not before—drew its power of association from this juxtaposition between the prescribed and the proscribed, between "their" spaces and "ours." Resembling a vast ship in motion, its design was a retort to the *kombinat*. Matching it in scale, the church offered feminine, curvaceous lines in place of the soaring vertical tower in Salawa's unbuilt design. Just like HiL's concentration of power and resources, moreover, Arka's size offered logistical as well as symbolic value, since six thousand faithful could be called on from the altar to join in demonstrations after mass, and crowds of protesters could shelter inside from attacks by police.

Cover of an underground opposition magazine published by students in Kraków to commemorate May Day 1983. The panels depict protests in Nowa Huta, the storming of protesters by riot police, and the use of tear gas. Piotr Dylik, KARTA Center Foundation, Warsaw.

The building's symbolism was deepened by extensive participation of the lay community in every aspect of its planning and building. Parishioners organized materials and donated labor; every man, woman, and child in Nowa Huta was asked to contribute a pebble for the building's facade.[110] Just as the party had once mobilized the workers, so now the church mobilized the faithful. Arka thus resonated with multiple associations: It represented the strength of faith and tradition, but also the triumph of participatory struggle and solidaristic cooperation. It implicitly echoed and challenged not only Stalinist labor mobilization campaigns but also the new town's original ideals of popular ownership and collective effort.

Two Lenins

The end of communism brought the restructuring of HiL and its renaming for the prominent Polish-born engineer Tadeusz Sendzimir (Huta im. T. Sendzimira). It also brought the seemingly inevitable pain of closings and layoffs.

> The last marten furnace in Huta Sendzimira went out the day before yesterday. Despite the dust, fumes, and heat prevailing in the hall, the steelworkers parted with their place of work with tears in their eyes. The platform, on which in past years party leaders had observed each furnace as it was started up for the first time, was empty now. The last smelting of steel took place without flowers or cheers. Only in the pouring vat . . . had one of the smelters stuffed a spray of linden. So that it would be more ceremonial. A scattering of people came to bid farewell to the unit—for years a symbol of Polish steelworking. . . . In a few months the hall will be empty. Slag, dust, and bricks . . . will go to the waste heap, the gantry to other firms, the steel constructions to scrap.[111]

Another chapter of history was over, and it was now possible to look back on Nowa Huta's Stalinist beginnings with different eyes. Interviewing young people in Nowa Huta in 1991, the journalist Dorota Gut often encountered nostalgia, and even a touch of envy: "I envy the [pioneers'] enthusiasm and belief in the future," said one informant, "the belief that they were doing something for themselves and the country." For some of the older people Gut interviewed, however, the legacy of the builders—understood as a shared commitment to struggling for a higher cause—linked the younger generation with themselves. "The intelligentsia fights through petitions," they told her, but in Nowa Huta "the fighting was in the streets, for real. Without those young people from the Huta . . . there would have been no struggle."[112] Nowa Huta as a city of action—of hard-won effort and self-sacrifice—had secured its enduring place in the national struggle, even if the successful fight for democracy had consigned an earlier generation's efforts to the scrap heap.

Stalinism created the framework in which the subsequent social history of Communist Poland played out. The centrality of workers to the Polish protest movement was a direct legacy of Stalinist forced industrialization: Solidarity was not born in the traditional centers of Polish industry (Łódź, Silesia, or Warsaw), but rather on the Baltic Coast—where new workers, one generation removed from the village, created their own distinctive forms of worker culture in the years after World War II. Some of the most militant centers of protest in the 1980s (for example, Gdańsk, Szczecin, or Wrocław) were also, in a sense, new towns: German cities before World War II, they had been almost entirely repopulated in the late 1940s to 1950s by a demographic similar to Nowa Huta's. Having the most to gain from Stalinist industrialization, many had responded enthusiastically to the Stalinist emphasis on active citizenship through labor. Thus, Stalinist political culture reinforced desires for civic inclusion, while the structures and rhythms of urban and factory life offered new social solidarities and mechanisms for self-organization.

Post-totalitarianism, rather than bringing October's hopes to fruition, merely shifted the struggle onto new turf. As new repertoires of contention emerged in response to changing political realities, the rhetoric of "building socialism" was gradually replaced by new tropes. In Nowa Huta, however, the consciousness of their town's onetime importance as a symbol of a better future, and of their own achievements in raising its walls, remained in the minds of its inhabitants. In February 1971, the following rhyme appeared in Nowa Huta, written on a factory wall in Łęg:

> Comrades, Lenin is weeping
> You have distorted his ideas
> This is the party's fault
> The idea was something else.[113]

In 1989, when news came that Gdańsk's Lenin Shipyards had joined HiL on strike, the word on the street was that "what one Lenin had begun, two Lenins would finish." When the Leninist political project finally collapsed, however, steelworkers parted from their jobs "with tears in their eyes" but without ceremony or protest; the plant closing had the character of a small, discreet funeral. The time for shouting was over.

Conclusion

During Nowa Huta's sixtieth anniversary celebrations in June 2009, bright yellow posters depicting what seemed to be two interlinked wreaths—on closer inspection, a toothed machine gear and an *obwarzanek*, a sort of round pretzel—appeared around town, announcing an open-air spectacle to be held on Nowa Huta's Rose Avenue. As the event's website declared, the multimedia concert would end with a wedding: "Whose? Nowa Huta and Kraków's, naturally!" To music performed by a symphony orchestra, machines, tools, and electronic instruments, the two cities "would stand side-by-side on stage, . . . confirming their unbreakable bond in culture, music, tradition, and numerous legends." Get ready, concluded the announcement, for "total madness!"[1]

The event cleverly echoed a performance that had taken place in Nowa Huta over a half-century earlier. In 1951, as cultural activist Maria Rokoszkowa recalled, "they sent me ten boys . . . and said I should do something for May Day." Rokoszkowa built up a successful amateur theater troupe, the Living Word Ensemble, which performed in common rooms and red corners across the building site. Often performances were adaptations of Polish literary classics—Mickiewicz, Sienkiewicz—in a pastiche of spoken word and song, but "The Marriage of Nowa Huta with Old Kraków" was Rokoszkowa's signature piece. In it, Nowa Huta professed her love for Old Kraków ("for your proud walls, and because every one of your monuments is a lesson in culture"), who in turn replied: "I love you, Nowa Huta, because you teach work and raise your walls ever higher while teaching socialist culture, because you are as Polish as an ode of Mickiewicz, because you take your example from Komsomolsk and set an example for all youth, because Bierut's words inspired your youth, dearest Nowa Huta."[2] In 2009 concert organizers' implicit reference to this ideological artifact raised a dilemma: where, between irony, condemnation, and nostalgia, was the appropriate register for commemorating the town's Stalinist past?

This question hung over many of the discussions leading up to the sixtieth-anniversary celebrations, reflecting ongoing tensions between Rokoszkowa's erstwhile newlyweds. In 2008 representatives of Poland's far-right Law and Justice Party in the Kraków city council had argued that any official commemoration of Nowa Huta's founding would be tantamount to pro-Communist propaganda, while some local Catholic clergy had threatened to boycott celebrations of the "model Soviet city without God." The first budget put forward by Kraków's mayor contained no funding for the commemorations, but under pressure from a cross-party group of city delegates, the final budget allocated modest funds to the events.[3]

To a certain extent, these controversies were lost amid larger debates over another historic anniversary that fell in the same month as Nowa Huta's celebrations. Twenty years earlier, Solidarity had swept to power in Poland's first free elections since World War II. So while opening ceremonies for a conference on Nowa Huta were getting underway at Kraków's city hall in June 2009, one political faction was celebrating Solidarity's victory at Wawel Castle nearby, another in Gdańsk. Poland's two main political tendencies had been unable to agree on a common program for the commemorations, or, by extension, on a shared understanding of the recent past. Meanwhile, anarchists marched through the streets outside city hall, adding (as one conference participant half-jokingly put it) to the overall "semantic and epistemological chaos."

For Nowohucians, the more than twenty years since 1989 have certainly brought their share of semantic and epistemological chaos. Certainly Nowa Huta's path to a market economy has been anything but smooth. The Lenin Steelworks became first the Sendzimir Steelworks and then, following its takeover by the multinational steel giant ArcelorMittal in 2004, the ArcelorMittal Poland Kraków Unit. After nearly collapsing in the first shocks of transition, the *kombinat* was dramatically restructured in the 1990s, most of its units closed or spun off as subsidiary firms. Its workforce, once 34,000, had dropped to 4,400 by 2010, although Nowa Huta's unemployment rates were still lower than in some comparable Polish centers of former state industry.[4] The roughly 700 hectares of land within the old plant's perimeters had become one of the largest brownfields in Europe, a graveyard for hundreds of objects in various states of disrepair. The spectacle of the plant's first buildings, erected with so much effort, falling into ruin had lent an eerie melancholy to the *kombinat*'s postindustrial landscape.

Transition brought other forms of degradation. Although the urban fabric of Kraków's old town was looking steadily smarter throughout the 1990s and 2000s, benefiting from infrastructural investments and tourism, many of Nowa Huta's public spaces fell into disrepair. Local shops and co-ops closed, the friendly cursive of their neon signs having long ago stopped glowing. Bookstores became banks or cell-phone outlets, and symbolically, the 1953 landmark Świt (Daybreak) Cinema was transformed into a bazaar, its socialist realist façade ignominiously covered with vendors' signs for used clothes and motor parts.[5]

But as the first shocks of transition subsided, something else happened, too: Nowa Huta's old districts began to seem interesting, unique, even charming. Contrasted now not only to the dreary, substandard, pre-fab housing of the 1960s and 1970s, but also to the chaotic, unregulated sprawl that had covered so much of the urban landscape since 1989, Nowa Huta's "plannedness" looked better and better. Just as formerly working-class American neighborhoods like New York's SoHo and Williamsburg gained "cultural distinction" over time, the atmosphere of Nowa Huta came to possess an aura of authenticity: as Sharon Zukin puts it, when "every new building looked like the same big glass box," suddenly, the "old redbrick buildings" gained renewed appreciation.[6] Nowa Huta became a bohemian destination, attracting young people from Kraków like filmmaker Bogumił Godfrejów, who (echoing some of the district's original migrants) claimed he "fell in love with Nowa Huta." Godfrejów took part in underground "happenings" in the early 2000s—like one at the 1950s-era Stylowa Café, with guests dressed in period costume and tickets printed to look like ration cards for meat and sweets.[7] A group of friends renting out studio space in Świt's basement started organizing events there after hours; soon, word got around that "at Świt there was something cool, half-legal, unregistered, unregimented . . . fresh!" Eventually, they rented the small screening room, bought a film projector, and restored the screen, using the space for projects and events ranging from independent film, music, and theater, to a skate team that practiced in the corridors and a line of made-in-Nowa Huta clothing. This came to an end in 2007, when a thief stole the projector, clothes, and cash.[8]

Such developments reflect what the geographer Judith Otto called the "grassroots . . . re-imaging [of] Nowa Huta," a range of initiatives by and for local residents that fruitfully drew on the district's heritage in creative and unexpected ways, and that constituted, in her view, "possibilities for resistance against a predominantly negative discourse formed and promoted by elites outside the district." Some of these initiatives became institutions in their own right, including the avant-garde Łaźnia Nowa theater; a local branch of the

Kraków Historical Museum; the Cyprian Norwid House of Culture in the former Sfinks Cinema; an annual outdoor film festival in Central Square; and the 1949 Club, a cafe and gallery "devoted to telling a more positive story about Nowa Huta . . . focusing on the people who built it and live there and their contributions to a sense of place."[9] Łaźnia Nowa also housed a music studio, the Slabbing Mill of Sound, which offered development and recording facilities for local musicians and fostered crossover acts like the cyberpunk group Wu-Hae (whose work incorporated socialist realist poetry about Nowa Huta by Wisława Szymborska and fragments of Adam Ważyk's "Poem for Adults").[10]

In some ways, Nowa Huta had come full circle. As in the days of the People's Theater, for instance, it was again home to one of Poland's most innovative theaters. On the other hand, many residents of Kraków continued to perceive Nowa Huta as dangerous and crime-ridden; instead of *junacy*, however, it was now the tracksuit-wearing youth of Nowa Huta's apartment blocks who were feared.[11] Nowohucians also still substantially lacked political control over their district; annexed to Kraków in 1951, Nowa Huta's fortunes remained linked to those of its larger, older neighbor. This became clear when Kraków's city council voted in 2004 to rename Central Square in honor of U.S. president Ronald Reagan over heated objections from locals. Councilor Maciej Twaróg, one of a group of local politicians who fought the change, spoke for many Nowohucians when he called the change an assault on "our Nowohucian identity." Some pointed out that Central Square had as much cultural and historical significance for Nowa Huta as the Main Market Square had for Kraków, asking how Krakovians would feel if they woke up one day to find their beloved *Rynek* renamed for a foreign leader. ("Reagan doesn't bother me," as one woman told interviewers, "but Central Square is Central Square.")[12] Ultimately, a compromise was reached allowing the square to keep its name with "Ronald Reagan" ("*im. Ronalda Reagana*") tacked on the end.[13]

The future of local institutions like Świt, too (under renovation as of going to press) hung for many years in the balance. (Apollo Film, the building's owners, promised a "film cafe" in the restored small screening room, earmarking the remainder of floor space for upmarket retail.) Issues like these have cut across political and generational lines, and it can be argued that their effect has been galvanizing: over the course of a decade, residents of Nowa Huta became ever more vocal in expressing pride in their "little fatherland" (*mała ojczyzna*) and active in searching for ways to preserve its genius loci. Ironically, after all the efforts another generation of young people expended trying to blow up Lenin's statue, some have expressed the wish that it would be restored to its former place on Rose Avenue. Other residents have suggested that Nowa Huta should finally build its unrealized city hall, to give its residents self-government at last and a "chance for public dialogue with the rulers."[14]

Utopian thinking, according to Zygmunt Bauman, hinges on a feeling of incompleteness; the better world it envisions must be "felt as still unfinished and requiring an additional effort to be brought about." In this sense, Nowa Huta is today a utopian endeavor; the early visions of the town's planners and builders, only partially realized by an ambivalent sponsoring regime, are felt by many of Nowa Huta's partisans as an ongoing challenge, and ones that will never be fulfilled "unless fostered by a deliberate collective action." That challenge has only intensified with the transition to market capitalism. Nowa Huta now fulfills all the more another of Bauman's conditions of utopia, in that it represents "a system essentially different from, if not antithetical to, the existing one." Underlying Nowa Huta's current measure of retro chic is the fact that it tangibly embodies a critique of the present social and political order.[15]

The dominant trend in scholarship on postwar East Central Europe since 1989 has been to complicate and replace a totalitarian model inherited from the cold war, and the present study, which is informed and enriched by that work, is no exception. To begin with, endogenous factors were crucial in building support for Nowa Huta. Although domestic visions for the new town repeatedly came up against the hard reality of Soviet hegemony, planners and professionals were able to carve out space for pursuing their own goals. Widespread popular support for Stalinism's promised social revolution was visible, moreover, in the enthusiasm with which mostly young, rural Poles flocked to and built the town, and sometimes participated in labor competition. Likewise, members of the intelligentsia supported Nowa Huta's project of "cultural enlightenment," as long as it seemed to produce the desired results.

The present study has also tested the limits of coercion under Stalinism. Nowa Huta in the late 1940s to the mid-1950s was an unstable and chaotic, sometimes even anarchic environment. Attempts to mobilize and restructure society are necessarily destabilizing, and the creation of Nowa Huta unleashed forces that, given the regime's limited resources and capacity, were difficult for it to channel and control. In Nowa Huta young people broke away from their parents; women, from their fathers, brothers, and husbands. Nowa Huta offered spaces of freedom: the dance floor, the street, the body. Young people and authorities in Nowa Huta battled over these spaces, and the outcome was not always favorable to the regime.

De-Stalinization was thus, among other things, an attempt to rein in some of those social forces that Stalinism had unleashed—not least, the unruly behavior of a newly created class of young workers. The moral panic surrounding Nowa Huta, culminating in the "Poem for Adults," crystallized deep anxieties about the direction Poland had taken under Stalinist leadership. Polish Stalinists attempted to defuse these critiques during the thaw—in part, by distancing themselves from Stalinism's stated aims of revolutionary social transformation, aims symbolized par excellence by Poland's "first socialist city."

The reformist counternarrative of Nowa Huta's supposedly failed social revolution, and the political crisis it provoked in 1956, demonstrate key contrasts between Polish Stalinism and its Soviet counterpart. In a study of urbanization under late Stalinism (roughly, 1945–1956) in the Soviet Union, Donald Filtzer describes many of the same structural imbalances that existed in Nowa Huta, leading to horrendous living conditions for those who, like the Poles drawn to Nowa Huta, settled in new industrial centers across the Soviet Union: "The decision to erect factories and coal mines at breakneck speed, to bring millions of peasants into the towns to build and staff them, but not to provide these workers with accommodation, infrastructure, and public services was a political decision, a reflection of the regime's essential priorities and its view of its citizens as expendable objects, valuable only for their capacity to generate the surplus from which the Soviet elite drew its privileges."[16] Soviet and Polish political culture differed in this respect, however. Unlike its Soviet counterpart, the Polish Stalinist leadership could not appear to treat the nation's human resources as "expendable objects" or human "kasha" without endangering its support among a wide range of constituencies. The reformist critique of Nowa Huta successfully took aim at this Achilles' heel, calling the regime's legitimacy fundamentally into question.

In sum, utopian visions of a new town for the masses were a luxury Polish communism could not afford: either the economic costs or the political ones would be too high. In demoting Nowa Huta to a mere industrial district of Kraków, the Communists attempted to regain some of the political and cultural capital lost in the course of Nowa Huta's inconclusive (or, as critics would have it, failed) experiment. Yet Stalinism would not have presented such challenges to stability if it had not involved aspects of genuine social revolution—extending and consolidating processes set in motion during World War II and completing the decisive breakdown of Poland's postfeudal social structure. Nowa Huta was just one product of the extraordinary demographic transformations taking place in Poland between 1939 and 1960, in which traditional urban elites decimated by war were replaced by rural migrants to the cities and factories. In the 1970s, roughly 30 percent of administrative elites, 33 percent of intelligentsia, 40 percent of middle and upper management, 50 percent of skilled workers, and 61 percent of semiskilled workers were one or two generations removed from the peasantry. Inequality, as measured for example by income, education, or physical height, decreased dramatically with urbanization and the welfare state: 72.8 percent of fourteen-to-seventeen-year-olds attended school in 1962–63, compared to 13.5 percent in 1937–38; in the same period, the income differential between nonmanual and manual workers decreased from 300 percent to 9 percent.[17] In a country where the barriers between urban elites and rural masses had historically seemed unbridgeable, these were changes with revolutionary implications for Polish culture and identity.

For many who built Nowa Huta, becoming a modern, urban person was simultaneously a form of enfranchisement. Former peasants effectively became citizens, entitled to participate in a wider world through literacy, access to media and technology, and, above all, labor. In a particularly Polish way, Nowa Huta's workers claimed the mantle of national heroism and struggle, once the sole possession of noble insurgents prepared to fight and die in battle. Nowa Huta's workers showed they, too, were willing to make every sacrifice for Poland, but through their sweat rather than their blood. Reinforced by the mobilizing rhetoric and practices of Stalinism, these new workers came to see themselves as a moral community of labor, later drawing from this identity the solidarity and sense of purpose they needed to mount a sustained challenge to the status quo.

Despite all that was unique to the state-socialist context, in both East and West postwar new towns symbolized Europe's rapidly changing social landscape: the transition from rural to urban life, the rise of the nuclear family, challenges to gender and generational roles, the triumph of mass consumption, and the hegemony of transatlantic popular culture, among other secular changes. Postwar new towns can thus be viewed as pressure points of European societies moving from rationed scarcity to expanding horizons of freedom, choice, and mobility. Nowa Huta represented in miniature the utopian impulses of a liberated continent—impulses that informed, but ultimately diverged from, those of politicians and technocrats, who committed themselves to planning prosperity in exchange for tutelary control over their citizenries. Ultimately, Nowa Huta's inhabitants turned Poland's "first socialist city" into a site of conflict and negotiation over those contradictory postwar promises. To quote E. P. Thompson, with a nod to Andrzej Wajda, it would not do to look upon their struggles with the "condescension of posterity."[18] The answers to the questions they posed remain unanswered.

Notes

Introduction

1. Quoted in Andrzej W. Tymowski, "Workers vs. Intellectuals in Solidarność," *Telos* 24, no. 4 (1991/92), 165.

2. Stan Persky and Henry Flam, eds., *The Solidarity Sourcebook* (Vancouver: New Star Books, 1982), 90–91.

3. *Man of Marble* [*Człowiek z marmuru*], dir. Andrzej Wajda with screenplay by Aleksander Ścibor-Rylski, produced by Zespół Filmowy "X," 1977.

4. For an overview of new-town building programs in postwar Europe, see Ilse Irion and Thomas Sieverts, eds., *Neue Städte: Experimentierfelder der Moderne* (Stuttgart: Deutsche Verlags-Anstalt, 1991) and Pierre Merlin, *New Towns: Regional Planning and Development* (London: Methuen, 1971). Of course, some of the most ambitious new towns in this period were outside Europe; see, e.g., James Holston, *The Modernist City: An Anthropological Critique of Brasília* (Chicago: University of Chicago Press, 1989) and Ved Prakash, *New Towns in India* (Durham: Duke University Program in Comparative Studies on Southern Asia, 1969).

5. When I first began this research in 1997–98, the secondary literature on Nowa Huta was limited to a clutch of sociological studies from the 1960s and 1970s, a few chapters and articles by architectural historians, and one set of conference papers. Since then, the situation has changed dramatically. Although there is still no other full-length monograph on Nowa Huta in Polish or English, two comparative studies deserve mention: Bartholomew Goldyn, "Cities for a New Poland: State Planning and Urban Control in the Building of Gdynia and Nowa Huta" (PhD diss., Georgetown University, 2003); and Dagmara Jajeśniak-Quast, *Stahlgiganten in der sozialistischen Transformation: Nowa Huta in Krakau, EKO in Eisenhüttenstadt, und Kunčice in Ostrava* (Wiesbaden: Harassowitz Verlag, 2010). Jajeśniak-Quast's economic history draws on a different set of core sources than this study (firm records, documents of central political and planning bodies) but echoes many of its themes and conclusions. Goldyn highlights fascinating similarities between interwar Gdynia and postwar Nowa Huta, both in the making of urban planning policy and in its unforeseen outcomes. Among edited volumes, *Nowa Huta—Miasto walki i pracy*, ed. Ryszard Terlecki, Marek Lasota, and Jarosław Szarek (Kraków: Instytut Pamięci Narodowej, 2002), contains important chapters on labor conflict and political opposition in Nowa Huta but unfortunately neglects the Stalinist period.

More scholarship has been devoted to Nowa Huta's present realities in the fields of geography, cultural heritage, and memory studies; see especially *Futuryzm miast przemysłowych: 100 lat Wolfsburga i Nowej Huty*, ed. Martin Kaltwasser, Ewa Majewska, and Kuba Szreder (Kraków: Korporacja Ha!art, 2007) and Alison Stenning's books and articles. Meanwhile, the beautifully produced exhibition catalogs of the Historical Museum of the City of Kraków (Nowa Huta branch) and a large number of websites and online publications, often supported by devoted amateurs, have contributed greatly to an awareness of Nowa Huta's distinctive heritage.

6. See, e.g., Stephen Kotkin, *Magnetic Mountain: Stalinism as a Civilization* (Berkeley: University of California Press, 1995).

7. Anders Åman, *Architecture and Ideology in Eastern Europe During the Stalin Era: An Aspect of Cold War History* (New York: Architectural History Foundation, 1992), 151, 163–64. For studies of other socialist cities, see, e.g., Ulf Brunnbauer, "'The Town of the Youth': Dimitrovgrad and Bulgarian Socialism," *Ethnologia Balkanica* 9 (2005): 91–114; Timothy Dowling, "Stalinstadt/Eisenhüttenstadt: A Model for (Socialist) Life in the German Democratic Republic, 1950–1968" (PhD diss., Tulane University, 1999); Pal Germuska, "Soviet Theories of City Planning and the Hungarian Socialist Cities" (paper given at the European University Institute, Florence, 2005); Ruth May, *Planstadt Stalinstadt* (Dortmund: Dortmunder Betrieb für Bau- und Planungsliteratur, 1999); and Mark Pittaway, "Creating and Domesticating Hungary's Socialist Industrial Landscape: From Dunapentele to Sztálinváros, 1950–1958," *Historical Archaeology* 39, no. 3 (2005): 75–93.

8. Jacek Salwiński, "Obszar historyczny Nowej Huty," in *Dziedzictwo kulturowe Nowej Huty w rozwoju obszaru strategicznego Kraków–Wschód. Materiały konferencyjne*, ed. Krakowskie Forum Rozwoju (Kraków: Krakowskie Forum Rozwoju, 1997), 18.

9. Merlin, *New Towns*, 13.

10. Anna Bikont and Joanna Szczęsna, *Lawina i kamienie: Pisarze wobec komunizmu* (Warsaw: Prószyński i S-ka, 2006), 251.

11. Among other world leaders who visited Nowa Huta were Walter Ulbricht, Konstanty Rokossowski, János Kadar, Jawaharlal Nehru, and the Shah of Iran. Jerzy Mikułowski Pomorski, *Kraków w naszej pamięci* (Kraków: Secesja, 1991), 267–68; Maciej Miezian, *Nowa Huta: Socjalistyczna w formie, fascynująca w treści* (Kraków: Wydawnictwo Bezdroża, 2004), 22.

12. Åman, *Architecture and Ideology*, 151.

13. James C. Scott, *Seeing Like a State: How Certain Schemes to Improve the Human Condition Have Failed* (New Haven: Yale University Press, 1998).

14. Henri Lefebvre, "Notes on the New Town (April 1960)," in *Introduction to Modernity: Twelve Preludes. September 1959–May 1961* (Verso, 1995), 116–20, 125–26.

15. Jane Jacobs's passionate defense of "old" cities in *The Death and Life of Great American Cities* (New York: Vintage Books, 1989) has served as an important point of reference for many of these critiques. See, for example, Holston, *Modernist City*. On the Gorbals, former residents' lively debates about these "filing cabinets for people" can be found at http://www.thejoyofconcrete.org/gorb/gorbalsdebate.htm (last viewed February 24, 2012). China, notably, has enthusiastically embraced new town development in the last decade. See Rachel Keeton, *Rising in the East: Contemporary New Towns in Asia* (Amsterdam: SUN architecture, 2011).

16. Lefebvre, *Introduction to Modernity*, 119.

17. Janusz Kurtyka, "Wstęp," in Terlecki, Lasota, and Szarek, *Nowa Huta*, 7–8.

18. See, for example, ibid., 7.

19. Jan T. Gross, "Social Consequences of War: Preliminaries to the Study of Imposition of Communist Regimes in East Central Europe," *East European Politics and Societies* 3, no. 2

(1989): 198–214; and Bradley F. Abrams, "The Second World War and the East European Revolution," *East European Politics and Societies* 16, no. 3 (2003): 623–64. See also Norman Naimark, "Revolution and Counterrevolution in Eastern Europe," in *The Crisis of Socialism in Europe,* ed. Christiane Lemke and Gary Marks (Durham: Duke University Press, 1992), 61–83.

20. Kotkin, *Magnetic Mountain,* 21–22.

21. For two synthetic attempts to bring social and cultural themes from the margins to the center of historiography on this period, see Dariusz Jarosz, *Polacy a stalinizm, 1948–1956* (Warsaw: Instytut Historii PAN, 2000), and Henryk Słabek, *O społecznej historii polski, 1945–1989* (Warsaw: Wydawnictwo "Książka i Wiedza," 2009). Likewise, the red-jacketed series from the publisher TRIO, *"W krainie PRL-u"* (In the land of the Polish People's Republic) for a number of years brought out an eclectic and popular set of monographs on the cultural and social history of the postwar period, many of which will be cited here. here.

22. Józef Tejchma, *Pożegnanie z władzą* (Warsaw: Projekt, 1996), 42; interviews with Franciszek K., Kraków, May 12, 1998, and Władysław M., Kraków, June 22 and 30, 1998.

23. Carl Joachim Friedrich and Zbigniew Brzeziński, *Totalitarian Dictatorship and Autocracy* (Cambridge: Harvard University Press, 1956).

24. Lászlo Peter, "'East of the Elbe': The Communist Takeover and the Past," in Robert B. Pynsent, *The Phoney Peace: Power and Culture in Central Europe, 1945–1949* (London: School of Slavonic and East European Studies, 2000), 37; and Padraic Kenney, "Polish Workers and the Stalinist Transformation," in *The Establishment of Communist Regimes in Eastern Europe, 1944–1949,* eds. Norman Naimark and Leonid Gibianskii (Boulder, CO: Westview Press, 1997), 139.

25. Examples include Paul Betts, *Within Walls: Private Life in the German Democratic Republic* (Oxford: Oxford University Press, 2010); Paulina Bren, *The Greengrocer and His TV: The Culture of Communism After the 1968 Prague Spring* (Ithaca: Cornell University Press, 2010); Ulf Brunnbauer, *"Die sozialistische Lebensweise": Ideologie, Gesellschaft, Familie, und Politik in Bulgarian (1944–1989)* (Vienna: Böhlau Verlag, 2007); John Connelly, *Captive University: The Sovietization of East German, Czech, and Polish Higher Education, 1945–1956* (Chapel Hill: University of North Carolina Press, 2000); Małgorzata Fidelis, *Women, Communism, and Industrialization in Postwar Poland* (Cambridge: Cambridge University Press, 2010); Mary Fulbrook, *The People's State: East German Society from Hitler to Honecker* (New Haven: Yale University Press, 2006); Konrad H. Jarausch, ed., *Dictatorship as Experience: Towards a Socio-Cultural History of the GDR* (New York: Berghahn Books, 1999); Padraic Kenney, *Rebuilding Poland: Workers and Communists, 1945–1950* (Ithaca: Cornell University Press, 1997); and Mark Pittaway, "The Workers' State: Industrial Labor and the Making of Socialist Hungary, 1944–1958," unpublished manuscript.

26. Thanks to an anonymous reviewer for this phrase.

27. Alain Touraine, *Solidarity: The Analysis of a Social Movement: Poland, 1980–1981,* trans. David Denby (Cambridge: Cambridge University Press, 1983), 15.

28. Krystyna Kersten and Jerzy Eisler, "Dyskusja nad historią PRL," *Polska 1944/45–1989: Studia i materiały* 1 (1995): 18. In a subsequent article, however, Eisler stresses continuities between the pre- and post-1956 periods. Jerzy Eisler, "Jakim państwem była PRL w latach 1956–1976?," *Pamięć i sprawiedliwość* 2, no. 10 (2006): 11–23.

29. Krystyna Kersten, "The Terror, 1949–1954," in A. Kemp-Welch, ed., *Stalinism in Poland, 1944–1956: Selected Papers from the Fifth World Congress of Central and East European Studies, Warsaw, 1995* (London: Macmillan Press, 1999), 79. Eisler also points out that even after 1956, the police state did not give up its totalitarian aims of total surveillance over society and, in fact, came far closer to achieving this goal after 1956 than before ("Jakim państwem była PRL," 16).

30. Abbott Gleason, *Totalitarianism: The Inner History of the Cold War* (New York: Oxford University Press, 1995), 176–80.

31. Jochen Hellbeck, "Everyday Ideology: Life During Stalinism," http://www.eurozine. com/articles/2010-10-05-hellbeck-ru.html (last viewed April 19, 2011).

32. On the methodological challenges of conducting research in former police-state archives, see *Die Überlieferung der Diktaturen. Beiträge zum Umgang mit Archiven der Geheimpolizeien in Polen und Deutschland nach 1989,* ed. Agnès Bensussan, Dorota Dakowska, and Nicolas Beaupré (Essen: Klartext Verlag, 2004); other useful discussion appears in Sheila Fitzpatrick and Robert Gellately, "Introduction to the Practices of Denunciation in Modern European History," *The Journal of Modern History* 68 (1996): 747–67; Moritz Föllmer, "Surveillance Reports," in *Reading Primary Sources: The Interpretation of Texts from Nineteenth- and Twentieth-Century History,* ed. Miriam Dobson and Benjamin Ziemann (London: Routledge, 2009); and the special issue *Polska 1944/45–1989: Studia i materiały* 6 (2003).

33. Gina Herrmann, *Written in Red: The Communist Memoir in Spain* (Urbana: University of Illinois Press, 2010), 5. See also Igal Halfin, *Terror in My Soul: Communist Autobiographies on Trial* (Cambridge: Harvard University Press, 2003), and Jochen Hellbeck, *Revolution on my Mind: Writing a Diary Under Stalin* (Cambridge: Harvard University Press, 2006).

34. Katherine Lebow, "The Conscience of the Skin: Interwar Polish Memoir and Social Rights," *Humanity: An Interdisciplinary Journal of Human Rights, Humanitarianism, and Development* 3, 3 (2012): 297–319.

35. I have in mind memoirs like those of "Elf" and Edmund Chmieliński, respectively.

36. Dorota Gut, "Nowa Huta w świetle publikacji z lat 50-tych i w świadomości jej mieszkańców" (MA thesis, Jagiellonian University, 1991), 68.

1. Unplanned City

1. Irving Brant, *The New Poland* (New York: Universe Publishers, 1946), 51; Jacek Purchla, *Kraków: Prowincja czy metropolia?* (Kraków: Universitas, 1996), 124–25.

2. Purchla, *Kraków,* 124–26; and Piotr Wróbel, *Historical Dictionary of Poland, 1945–1996* (Westport, CT: Greenwood Press, 1998), 260.

3. Purchla, *Kraków,* 126–30.

4. *Gazeta Krakowska,* July 22, 1949, quoted in Maria Christian, "Początki Nowej Huty w prasie i w sprawozdaniach Referatu Ochrony Wojewódzkiego Urzędu Bezpieczeństwa Publicznego w Krakowie," in *Narodziny Nowej Huty. Materiały sesji naukowej odbytej 25 kwietnia 1998 roku* (Kraków: Towarzystwo Miłośników Historii i Zabytków Krakowa, 1999), 141.

5. Greater Kraków has been listed as one of the "four ecological disaster zones" in post-World War II Poland, with higher-than-average air, soil, and water pollution. Emissions from the Lenin Steelworks have been the major source of pollution in the area, although, given prevailing wind patterns, a power plant at Skawina is probably more directly responsible for poor air quality in the city center. Other significant causes of environmental pollution in Kraków have included coal heating, transportation, emissions from other industrial centers as far away as Upper Silesia, and atmospheric conditions (inversion) unfavorable to pollution dispersion. Anita Bokwa, "Environmental Impacts of Long-Term Air Pollution Changes in Kraków, Poland," *Polish Journal of Environmental Studies* 17, no. 5 (2008), 673–75.

6. Mieczysław Gil, "Paradoks *historii—rola Nowej Huty w walce o system demokratyczny w Polsce*," in *Dziedzictwo kulturowe Nowej Huty*, 71. Cf. Jerzy Mikułowski Pomorski, "U genezy powołania nowego miasta. Między pogłoską a dedukcją," in *Narodziny Nowej Huty*, 96–97; Purchla, *Kraków*, 134.

7. Edmund Osmańczyk, *Sprawy Polaków* (Katowice: Wydawnictwo "Śląsk," 1982), 25. See also Tadeusz Binek, *Śląsk—Wojna—Kresy—Wrocław—Nowa Huta: Wspomnienia, 1930–1960* (Krakow: Oficyna Cracovia, 1997), 72.

8. *Konkurs na wspomnienia i pamiętniki budowniczych Nowej Huty: Wybór na prawach rękopisu* (Kraków: n.p., 1984), 8.

9. Anne E. Mosher, *Capital's Utopia: Vandergrift, Pennsylvania, 1855–1916* (Baltimore: Johns Hopkins University Press, 2004), 3.

10. Bikont and Szczęsna, *Lawina i kamienie*, 157.

11. Ibid.

12. See Stanislaus A. Blejwas, *Realism in Polish Politics: Warsaw Positivism and National Survival in Nineteenth-Century Poland* (New Haven: Yale Council on International and Area Studies, 1984).

13. Jerzy Jedlicki, *A Suburb of Europe: Nineteenth-Century Polish Approaches to Western Civilization* (Budapest: Central European University Press, 1999), 286.

14. Hanna Mortkowicz-Olczakowa, "O Stefanie Żeromskim. Ze wspomnień i dokumentów" (Warsaw: Państwowy Instytut Wydawniczy, 1964), 288.

15. Stefan Żeromski, *The Coming Spring* (Budapest: Central European University Press, 2007).

16. Martin Kohlrausch and Katrin Steffen, "The Limits and Merits of Internationalism: Experts, the State, and the International Community in Poland in the First Half of the Twentieth Century," *EUI Working Papers* RSCAS 41 (2009): 3–4.

17. Quoted in Marian Marek Drozdowski, "Eugeniusz Kwiatkowski a Centralny Okręg Przemysłowy," *Kwartalnik Historyczny* 94, no. 3 (1987), 78–79.

18. Goldyn, "Cities for a New Poland," 43–63.

19. Goldyn, "Cities for a New Poland," 136–37.

20. Adam Rybka, *Centralny Okręg Przemysłowy a polska awangardowa urbanistyka międzywojenna* (Rzeszów: Oficyna Wydawnicza Politechniki Rzeszowskiej, 1995), 173. In other versions of the story, Piłsudski used the *obwarzanek* as a metaphor for the cultural richness of Poland's ethnically mixed borderlands. Małgorzata Fidelis, personal communication, January 29, 2010.

21. Cf. Eugeniusz Kwiatkowski, *Dysproporcje: Rzecz o Polsce przeszłej i obecnej* (Warsaw: Czytelnik, 1989 [orig. 1932]).

22. Drozdowski, "Eugeniusz Kwiatkowski," 79.

23. Ibid., 82–85; and Rybka, *Centralny Okręg Przemysłowy*, 174–75.

24. From 1936 to 1939 a total of about 3 billion złoty of state funds were spent on public investments, of which roughly 690–750 million went to COP, completing the plan by 80 percent. Jerzy Gołębiowski, *COP: Dzieje industrializacji w rejonie bezpieczeństwa, 1922–1939* (Kraków: Wydawnictwo Naukowe Akademii Pedagogicznej, 2000), 255–66; and Rybka, *Centralny Okręg Przemysłowy*, 174.

25. Rybka, *Centralny Okręg Przemysłowy*, 313–16.

26. Wojciech Leśnikowski, "Functionalism in Polish Architecture," in *East European Modernism: Architecture in Czechoslovakia, Hungary, and Poland Between the Wars, 1919–1939*, ed. Wojciech Leśnikowski (New York: Rizzoli, 1996), 230–39.

27. Kohlrausch and Steffen, "Limits and Merits of Internationalism," 10–12.

28. Tadeusz Binek, *Służby inwestycyjne Nowej Huty* (Kraków: Klub b. pracowników służb inwestycyjnych Nowej Huty, 2009), 5.

29. *Konkurs na wspomnienia i pamiętniki budowniczych Nowej Huty*, 12–13; see also 22.

30. Mariusz Muszyński, Przemysław Sypniewski, and Krzysztof Rak, eds. *Sprawozdanie w przedmiocie strat i szkód wojennych Polski w latach 1939–1945 (Report on Poland's Wartime Losses and Damage in the Years 1939–1945)* (Warsaw: Fundacja "Polsko-Niemieckie Pojednanie," 2007), 92–100.

31. Gross, "Social Consequences of War," 213–14.

32. William Cary, *Poland Struggles Forward* (New York: Greenberg, 1949), 23–24.

33. Stanislaw Jankowski, "Warsaw: Destruction, Secret Town Planning, 1939–44, and Postwar Reconstruction," in *Rebuilding Europe's Bombed Cities*, ed. Jeffry M. Diefendorf (Basingstoke: The Macmillan Press, 1990), 77–93.

34. Mark Mazower, *Dark Continent: Europe's Twentieth Century* (New York: Alfred A. Knopf, 1999), 185–90; and Bradley F. Abrams, "The Second World War and the East European Revolution," 637.

35. Kazimierz Przybysz, ed. *Wizje Polski: Programy polityczne lat wojny i okupacji, 1939–1944* (Warsaw: Dom Wydawniczy i Handlowy "ELIPSA," 1992), 221.

36. AAN IBM 2/4, k. 4, 29.

37. Aleksander Bocheński, *Wędrówki po dziejach przemysłu polskiego, 1945–1970* (Kraków: PHILED, 1997), 26.

38. Bobrowski's memoirs quoted in Sheldon Anderson, *A Dollar to Poland Is a Dollar to Russia: U.S. Economic Policy Toward Poland, 1945–1952* (New York: Garland, 1993), 7; Bocheński, *Wędrówki po dziejach przemysłu polskiego*, 26; and Zbigniew Landau and Jerzy Tomaszewski, *The Polish Economy in the Twentieth Century* (London: Croom Helm, 1985), 196–200.

39. Janusz Kaliński, "Forsowna industrializacja Polski w latach 1949–1955," in *Narodziny Nowej Huty*, 57–59; Bocheński, *Wędrówki po dziejach przemysłu polskiego*, 26; and Landau and Tomaszewski, *Polish Economy*, 196.

40. Tadeusz Gołaszewski, *Kronika Nowej Huty od utworzenia działu projektowania Nowej Huty do pierwszego spustu surówki wielkopiecowej: Na podstawie materiałów archiwalnych Huty im. Lenina* (Kraków: n.p., 1955), 9; and Jacek Salwiński, "Decyzje o lokalizacji," 83–85. See also Kotkin, *Magnetic Mountain*, 37.

41. Anderson, *A Dollar to Poland*, 150–51.

42. Kaliński, "Forsowna industrializacja Polski," 62–63; George R. Feiwel, *Poland's Industrialization Policy: A Current Analysis: Sources of Economic Growth and Retrogression* (New York: Praeger, 1971), 236–37; and Landau and Tomaszewski, *Polish Economy*, 216–19.

43. Feiwel, *Poland's Industrialization*, 237.

44. Hilary Minc, "Sześcioletni plan rozwoju gospodarczego i budowy podstaw socjalizmu w Polsce," *Nowe Drogi* 5 no. 4 (1950): 46–49.

45. Czesław Bąbiński, "O budowie Huty im. Lenina," *Budownictwo Przemysłowe* 3, nos. 7–8 (1954): 2–3.

46. Salwiński, "Decyzje o lokalizacji," 83–87; and Gołaszewski, *Kronika Nowej Huty*, 10.

47. Zbigniew Loreth, "Pierwsze lata budowy huty w Krakowie" (Kraków: Krakowskie Forum Rozwoju, 1997), 33. HiL director Jan Anioła allegedly told Marian Brandys that the demands of production "exceeded" the knowledge and capacity of his technical and managerial staff. ZMP Zarz. Gł., Wydz. Młodzieży Rob. 451/XI-31, k. 28.

48. Salwiński, "Decyzje o lokalizacji," 86–89.

49. Ibid., 90–92.

50. Http://www.ma.krakow.pl/oddzial_Nowa_Huta/pradzieje (viewed September 26, 2010); Zbigniew Beiersdorf, "Wartości kulturowe Nowej Huty," in *Dziedzictwo kulturowe Nowej Huty,* 81–89; and Salwiński, "Obszar historyczny Nowej Huty," 18–20.

51. For technical considerations that may have played a role, see Salwiński, "Decyzje lokalizacji," 89–90. Cf. Loreth, "Pierwsze lata," 35; and Irion and Sieverts, *Neue Städte,* 247–48.

52. Pomorski, "U genezy powołania," 103–4; Jan Adamczewski, *Kraków od A do Z* (Kraków: Krajowa Agencja Wydawnicza, 1992), 136–37; Marian Brandys, "Pierwsze kroki," in *Krajobraz ogni: Antologia reportaży o Nowej Hucie,* ed. Stefan Kozicki and Zbigniew Stolarck (Warsaw: Iskry, 1971), 15–30.

53. *Dziennik Polski,* December 2, 1949, quoted in Christian, "Początki Nowej Huty," 142.

54. Gołaszewski, *Kronika Nowej Huty,* 10, 19–24, 581.

55. Waldemar Komorowski, "Urbanistyka i architektura Nowej Huty lat pięćdziesiątych: Historia i współczesność," in *Dziedzictwo kulturowe Nowej Huty,* 104.

56. Richard Stites, *Revolutionary Dreams: Utopian Vision and Experimental Life in the Russian Revolution* (New York: Oxford University Press, 1989), 238.

57. Åman, *Architecture and Ideology,* 243.

58. Leśnikowski, *East European Modernism,* 293–95; Piotr Winskowski, "Architektura polska lat 50.—Idee zbiorowe i indywidualne," in Kaltwasser et. al., *Futuryzm miast przemysłowych,* 224–25.

59. Paul Robeson visited the exhibition. See Binek, *Śląsk—Wojna—Kresy,* 86–89.

60. Ibid., 69; Renata Radłowska, "Inżynier, który wymyślił Nową Hutę," *Gazeta Krakowska,* January 31, 2008, http://krakow.gazeta.pl/krakow/1,57820,4888231.html (viewed September 22, 2010).

61. "Stanisław Juchnowicz," *Moja Nowa Huta, 1949–2009: Wystawa jubileuszowa* (Kraków: Muzeum Historyczne Miasta Krakowa, 2009), 58.

62. Leszek Sibila, "Twórcy 'miasta idealnego'—Wybrane biogramy," in *Nowa Huta—Architektura i twórcy miasta idealnego: Niezrealizowane projekty* (Kraków: Muzeum Historyczne Miasta Krakowa, 2006), 99–107; "Stanisław Juchnowicz," *Moja Nowa Huta,* 58; Radłowska, "Inżynier, który wymyślił Nową Hutę." Ptaszycki's collaborators included Adam Fołtyn, Janusz Ingarden, Marta Ingarden, Tadeusz Janowski, Stanisław Juchnowicz, Tadeusz Rembiesa, and Bolesław Skrzybalski. Komorowski, "Urbanistyka i architektura," 104.

63. "Stanisław Juchnowicz," *Moja Nowa Huta,* 56.

64. Janine Wedel, *The Private Poland* (New York: Facts on File Publications, 1986); cf. Connelly, *Captive University,* 153.

65. "Stanisław Juchnowicz," *Moja Nowa Huta,* 56, 64; and Radłowska, "Inżynier, który wymyślił Nową Hutę."

66. Radłowska, "Inżynier, który wymyślił Nową Hutę."

67. "Stanisław Juchnowicz," *Moja Nowa Huta,* 56; and Radłowska, "Inżynier, który wymyślił Nową Hutę."

68. Jan Anioła, *Huta im. Lenina* (Kraków, 1954), 141–42, quoted in Pomorski, *Kraków w naszej pamięci,* 107.

69. Andrzej Lorek, "Kompozycja przestrzenna Nowej Huty w kontekście teorii i praktyki urbanistycznej socrealizmu," *Narodziny Nowej Huty,* 127–33.

70. Åman, *Architecture and Ideology,* 152.

71. Lorek, "Kompozycja przestrzenna Nowej Huty," 127–29.

72. Judith Emily Otto, "Representing Communism: Discourses of Heritage Tourism and Economic Regeneration in Nowa Huta, Poland" (PhD diss., University of Minnesota, 2008), 94.

73. Ingrid Apolinarski and Christoph Bernhardt, "Entwicklungslogiken sozialistischer Planstädte am Beispiel von Eisenhüttenstadt und Nova Huta [*sic*]," in *Grammatik sozialistischer Architekturen: Lesarten historischer Städtebauforschung zur DDR*, ed. Holger Barth (Berlin: Dietrich Reimer Verlag, 2001), 56–57.

74. Åman, *Architecture and Ideology*, 152.

75. Otto, "Representing Communism," 4.

76. Miezian, *Nowa Huta*, 5.

77. Moshe Lewin, *The Making of the Soviet System: Essays in the Social History of Interwar Russia* (London: Methuen, 1985), 209.

78. Bąbiński, "O budowie Huty im. Lenina," 3.

79. Pomorski, *Kraków w naszej pamięci*, 264.

80. Gołaszewski, *Kronika Nowej Huty*, 710–12; Narcyz Kaźmierczak, "Pierwszy spust surówki w Nowej Hucie," July 21, 1954, Radio Kraków, sygn. 645.

81. Bocheński, *Wędrówki po dziejach przemysłu polskiego*, 177.

82. Bąbiński, "O budowie Huty im. Lenina"; Michał Rojowski, "O błędach budowy Huty im. Lenina i środkach ich usunięcia," *Budownictwo Przemysłowe* 3 nos. 7–8 (1954): 8–9.

83. Rojowski, "O błędach," 8.

84. Ibid.

85. ORZZWK p. 594 syg. 6455 n.p.

86. Kotkin, *Magnetic Mountain*, 42.

87. Minc, "Sześcioletni plan 46.

88. Minc, "Sześcioletni plan," 43–49.

89. Bocheński, *Wędrówki po dziejach przemysłu polskiego*, 178.

90. Archiwum Państwowe w Krakowie, ORZZWK p. 594, t. 6466.

91. Bocheński, *Wędrówki po dziejach przemysłu polskiego*, 176; "Tadeusz Świerzewski" in *Moja Nowa Huta*, 80–81; and ORZZWK p. 592 syg. 6426.

92. Zbigniew Landau and Wojciech Roszkowski, *Polityka gospodarcza II RP i PRL* (Warsaw: Wydawnictwo Naukowe PWN, 1995), 108.

93. AAN ZMP 451/XI-32, k. 157.

94. Minc, "Sześcioletni plan," 46–47.

95. Stanislaw Wellisz, *The Economies of the Soviet Bloc: A Study of Decision Making and Resource Allocation* (New York: McGraw-Hill, 1966), 66–70.

96. Gołaszewski, *Kronika Nowej Huty*, 68.

97. See, for example, "Wukajsiak," "Akcja 66," in *Konkurs na wspomnienia i pamiętniki budowniczych Nowej Huty: Wybór na prawach rękopisu* (Kraków: n.p., 1984), 4–7.

98. Interview with "Edward" by Alison Stenning, Nowa Huta, July 5, 2001.

99. John Michael Montias, "The Polish Iron and Steel Industry," *American Slavic and East European Review* 16, no. 3 (1957): 303.

100. Katherine Verdery, *What Was Socialism, and What Comes Next?* (Princeton: Princeton University Press, 1996), 26.

101. Author interview with Bogumił Korombel, Kraków, March 20, 1998.

102. Landau and Roszkowski, *Polityka gospodarcza*, 108–9; and Wellisz, *Economies of the Soviet Bloc*, 105.

103. Komorowski, "Urbanistyka i architektura," 105.

104. Bohdan Bukowski, in online magazine *Lodołamacz*, http://www.lodolamacz.pl/txt/numer_11/miasto.html; and Komorowski, "Urbanistyka i architektura," 105.

105. Pomorski, *Kraków w naszej pamięci*, 109.

106. *Nowa Huta—Architektura i twórcy miasta idealnego.*

107. Leszek Sibila, *Nowohucki design: Historia wnętrz i ich twórcy w latach 1949–1959* (Kraków: Muzeum Historyczne Miasta Krakowa, 2007).

108. Stanisław Juchnowicz, "Nowa Huta—z doświadczeń warsztatu projektowego," in *Nowa Huta—Architektura i twórcy miasta idealnego*, 33.

109. Gil, "Paradoks historii," 73.

110. See Grzegorz Miernik, ed. *Polacy wobec PRL: Strategie przystosowawcze* (Kielce: Kieleckie Towarzystwo Naukowe, 2003).

111. David Crowley, "Warsaw Interiors: The Public Life of Private Spaces, 1949–1965," in *Socialist Spaces: Sites of Everyday Life in the Eastern Bloc*, ed. David Crowley and Susan E. Reid (Oxford: Berg, 2002), 182.

112. Karl R. Popper, *Conjectures and Refutations: The Growth of Scientific Knowledge* (New York: Basic Books, 1965), 358.

113. Scott, *Seeing Like a State.*

114. Andreas Faludi, ed., *A Reader in Planning Theory, Urban and Regional Planning Series*, vol. 7 (Oxford: Pergamon Press, 1973), 140.

115. Radłowska, "Inżynier, który wymyślił Nową Hutę."

116. Vladimir Paperny, *Architecture in the Age of Stalin: Culture Two* (Cambridge: Cambridge University Press, 2002), 251–52.

2. New Men

1. Krystyna Kersten, *The Establishment of Communist Rule in Poland, 1943–1948* (Berkeley: University of California Press, 1991), 165.

2. Ibid., 163–64; and Norman Davies, *God's Playground: A History of Poland* (New York: Columbia University Press, 1982), 2:562.

3. Davies, *God's Playground*, 563.

4. See, for example, Richard Bessel and Dirk Schumann, eds. *Life after Death: Approaches to a Cultural and Social History of Europe During the 1940s and 1950s* (Cambridge: Cambridge University Press, 2003), and Hanna Schissler, ed., *The Miracle Years: A Cultural History of West Germany, 1949–1968* (Princeton: Princeton University Press, 2001).

5. Edmund Chmieliński, "Tu chciałem żyć i pracować," in *Robotnicze losy: Życiorysy własne robotników*, vol. 1, ed. Aurelia Szafran-Bartoszek et al. (Poznań: Wydawnictwo Naukowe UAM, 1996), 445–46.

6. Ibid.

7. Sociologists estimated that 85,000 of the roughly 211,400 who passed through Nowa Huta within the decade settled in the new town. "Sekcja Nowohucka: Posiedzenie z dnia 20 grudnia pod przewodnictwem czl. K. Dobrowolskiego," *Sprawozdania z posiedzeń komisji* (1963): 466.

8. Gut, "Nowa Huta w świetle publikacji," 68.

9. Muszyński, *Sprawozdanie w przedmiocie strat i szkód wojennych Polski*, 93; and Kersten, *The Establishment of Communist Rule*, 164–65.

10. David Lane and George Kolankiewicz, eds. *Social Groups in Polish Society* (London: Macmillan, 1973), 15–16.

11. Franciszek Adamski, "Nowa Huta na tle procesów urbanizacyjnych Polski powojennej," *Roczniki nauk społecznych* 3 (1975): 233. In 1960, over half of the city's population came originally from Kraków province (about 10 percent of those from the city of Kraków); 21 percent were from the neighboring provinces of Katowice, Rzeszów, and Kielce; 10 percent were from Wrocław province; and 13 percent were from the villages that had been subsumed by Nowa Huta. Ewa Pietsch, Antoni Stojak, and Jerzy Sulimski, "Budowa i rozwój Huty im. Lenina oraz kształtowanie się społeczeństwa Nowej Huty," in *Prace socjologiczne. Zeszyt 3, Huta im. Lenina i jej załoga*, ed. Antoni Stojak (Kraków: Uniwersytet Jagielloński, 1976), 15.

12. See, for example, Tejchma, *Pożegnanie z władzą*, 38.

13. Binek, *Śląsk—Wojna—Kresy—Wrocław—Nowa Huta*, 103. In 1954, about half of all white-collar personnel had come to Nowa Huta on a work order. Instytut Budownictwa Mieszkaniowego, "Wyniki wstępnego badania warunków bytu ludności w Nowej Hucie," *Materiały i dokumentacja* Seria B, no. 4/26/1954 (1954), 17.

14. Memoirist "X," quoted in Renata Siemieńska, *Nowe życie w nowym mieście* (Warsaw: Wiedza Powszechna, 1969), 98. Cf. Binek, *Śląsk—Wojna—Kresy—Wrocław—Nowa Huta*, 103; and APKr Radio Kraków, "Relacja Anny Siatkowskiej—Materiał," 1996, no. aud. 2661.

15. Kenney, *Rebuilding Poland*, 145.

16. Bocheński, *Wędrówki po dziejach przemysłu polskiego*, 177; and APKr Radio Kraków, "Relacja Leopolda Sułkowskiego," 1989, no. aud. 1239.

17. Dorota Gut, personal communication, Kraków, February 25, 1998.

18. "Elżbieta Borsyławska," *Moja Nowa Huta*, 128.

19. "Korzeń," in Siemieńska, *Nowe życie*, 71–72.

20. "Wodnik," in ibid., 72–73.

21. Ibid., 72.

22. Ibid., 73.

23. Olga A. Narkiewicz, *The Green Flag: Polish Populist Politics, 1867–1970* (London: Croom Helm, 1976), 101–2.

24. Jerzy Sulimski, *Kraków w procesie przemian: Współczesne przeobrażenia zbiorowości wielkomiejskiej* (Kraków: Wydawnictwo Literackie, 1976), 155.

25. Cary, *Poland Struggles Forward*, 119–20.

26. Keely Stauter-Halsted, *The Nation in the Village: The Genesis of Peasant National Identity in Austrian Poland, 1848–1914* (Ithaca: Cornell University Press, 2001), 3–10.

27. Edward S. Kerstein, *Red Star Over Poland: A Report from Behind the Iron Curtain* (Appleton, WI: C.C. Nelson, 1947), 116.

28. Cary, *Poland Struggles Forward*, 126, 130–31.

29. Henryk Słabek, "Socio-Political Aspects of the Polish Peasants (1944–1948)," *Acta Poloniae Historica* 57 (1988): 138.

30. Wróbel, *Historical Dictionary of Poland*, 167–68.

31. M.K. Dziewanowski, ed., *Poland Today as Seen By Foreign Observers* (London: The Polish Freedom Movement, 1946), 53.

32. Słabek, "Socio-Political Aspects," 137–39.

33. Ibid., 140–42.

34. Chmieliński, "Tu chciałem żyć," 445.

35. Ibid., 446–47.

36. Quoted in Anna Bikont and Joanna Szczęsna, "O Nowej to Hucie poemat," *Gazeta Wyborcza* February 26–27, 2000, 24.

37. Richard Cornell, *Youth and Communism* (NY: Walker, 1965), 5–7.

38. AAN KG POSP 953, k. 120.

39. Cary, *Poland Struggles Forward*, 102.

40. Bocheński, *Wędrówki po dziejach przemysłu polskiego*, 180.

41. Jan Hellwig, *Powszechna Organizacja Służba Polsce* (Warsaw: Iskry, 1977), 12–18.

42. Ibid.

43. APKr Radio Kraków, "Wspomnienia o budowie Nowej Huty," 1978, no. aud. 948.

44. Hellwig, *Powszechna Organizacja*, 31, 44–45.

45. Bogdan Hillebrandt, *Związek Młodzieży Polskiej* (Warsaw: Młodzieżowa Agencja Wydawnicza, 1980), 360. Marian Brandys, *Początek opowieści* (Kraków: Państwowy Instytut Wydawniczy, 1951), quoted in Hillebrandt, *Związek Młodzieży Polskiej*, 363–64.

46. "Damian," "Wpsomnienie," in *Konkurs na wspomnienia i pamiętniki budowniczych Nowej Huty*, 1.

47. Hillebrandt, *Związek Młodzieży Polskiej*, 358–62.

48. APKr Radio Kraków, "Wspomnienia o budowie Nowej Huty."

49. Hellwig, *Powszechna Organizacja*, 54.

50. Hillebrandt, *Związek Młodzieży Polskiej*, 360–61.

51. AAN ZMP 451/XI-52, k. 5.

52. AAN ZMP 451/XI-30, kk. 1–2.

53. APKr SPKr 109, k. 113.

54. AAN ZMP 451/XI-52, k. 107.

55. "Elf," "Najgorszy był jednak początek," in Kozici and Stolarek, *Krajobraz ogni*, 48.

56. APKr Radio Kraków, "Relacja Anny Siatkowskiej."

57. Chmieliński, "Tu chciałem żyć," 450.

58. AAN ZMP 451/XI-30, k. 3; APKr SPKr 109, k. 53. There were 865 desertions out of 3,809 participants in the first year-long brigades (April 1950 to March 1951). Of these, 37.6 percent returned voluntarily, 36.3 percent were forced to return, and 26.1 percent were not found. ZMP Zarz. Gł. 451/VI-40, k. 3.

59. "Elf," "Najgorszy był jednak początek," 48.

60. SPKr 109, kk. 53, 161.

61. "Elf," "Najgorszy był jednak początek," 48.

62. Chmieliński, "Tu chciałem żyć," 450.

63. ABM f69, Hipoteza Ludnościowa, k. 12 and Barbara Seidler, "Nowa Huta: Fakty," *Nowa Kultura* (July 21, 1957): 1.

64. Pietsch, Stojak, and Sulimski, "Budowa i rozwój Huty im. Lenina," 15–16.

65. The gender ratio gradually approached parity, but in 1960 Nowa Huta was still 50.43 percent male, as compared to 47.77 percent for Kraków, as a whole. Bolesław Skrzybalski, Zygmunt Pajdak, and Elżbieta Skrzybalska, "Studium demograficzne dzielnicy Nowa Huta: Stan na 1.8.1954 r." (Kraków: Miastoprojekt–Kraków, 1955), 2; and Władysław Kwiecień, "Stan i dynamika stosunków demograficznych miasta Krakowa ze szczególnym uwzględnieniem Nowej Huty w latach 1955–1960," *Zeszyty Naukowe Wyższej Szkoły Ekonomicznej w Krakowie*, no. 19 (1962): 11, 13.

66. Skrzybalski, Paidak, and Skrzybalska, "Studium demograficzne," 2.

67. ORZZWK p. 592 syg. 6427, n.p.

68. Bąbiński, "O budowie Huty im. Lenina," 4.

69. See Gut, *Nowa Huta*, 71; and "Damian," "Wpsomnienie," *Konkurs na wspomnienia*, 1.

70. Szczepan Brzeziński, "Polubiłem ten fach," *Polityka* 14, no. 27 (1970): 1.

71. Pomorski, *Kraków w naszej pamięci*, 260.

72. Chmieliński, "Tu chciałem żyć," 448–50.

73. "Elf," "Najgorszy był jednak początek," 49.

74. Chmieliński, "Tu chciałem żyć," 454.

75. Instytut Budownictwa Mieszkaniowego, "Wyniki," 36.

76. Quoted in Pomorski, *Kraków w naszej pamięci*, 259.

77. "Rozmowa Jacka Dargiewicza z Niki Wiecheć," in *Nowa_Huta: Księga uwolnionych tekstów*, ed. Łucja Piekarska-Duraj (Kraków: Małopolski Instytut Kultury, 2005), 69; and Aleksander Matejko, "Wartość użytkowa nowych mieszkań w świetle doświadczeń ich mieszkańców," *Zaludnienie i użytkowanie mieszkań w nowych osiedlach. Prace Instytutu Budownictwa Mieszkaniowego* 8, no. 23 (1959): 81.

78. Celina Kulik quoted in Bocheński, *Wędrówki po dziejach przemysłu polskiego*, 176; and Barbara Seidler, "Nowa Huta—Fakty po dwóch latach," *Nowa Kultura* (June 14, 1959): 1, 4–5.

79. Brzeziński, "Polubiłem ten fach," 7. One of Gut's respondents quoted a rhyme that translates as, "You'll know a fellow / from Nowa Huta / from his quilted jacket / and rubber boots." Gut, *Nowa Huta*, 71.

80. Tejchma, *Pożegnanie z władzą*, 42.

81. APKr Radio Kraków, "Spotkanie po latach: Stanisława Siudut," no. aud. 969.

82. APKr KP PZPR 60/IV/5, k. 423; Brzeziński, "Polubiłem ten fach," 8; cf. APKr SPKr 101, n.p.

83. "Rozmowa Ewy Dębskiej z Mateuszem Kardasem," in Piekarska-Duraj, *Nowa_Huta*, 11–15.

84. "Stanisław Juchnowicz," *Moja Nowa Huta*, 58–59.

85. Chmieliński, "Tu chciałem żyć," 452.

86. "Elf," "Najgorszy był jednak początek," 54–55.

87. APKr SPKr 158, 85; and "Józef Zięba," *Moja Nowa Huta*, 49.

88. Brzeziński, "Polubiłem ten fach," 9.

89. Pomorski, *Kraków w naszej pamięci*, 271–72.

90. Gut, *Nowa Huta*, 69.

91. Barbara Seidler, "Tamten czas, który minał," *Życie Literackie* (June 24, 1979), 5; cf. "Rozmowa Aleksandry Ziemby z Waldemarem Cichym," in Piekarska-Duraj, *Nowa_Huta*, 80.

92. Siemieńska, *Nowe życie*, 77.

93. Seidler, "Tamten czas, który minał," 5.

94. Maciej Miezian, e-mail to author, March 23, 2012.

95. Brzeziński, "Polubiłem ten fach," 7.

96. Siemieńska, *Nowe życie*, 89.

97. Pomorski, *Kraków w naszej pamięci*, 284.

98. Ibid., 284.

99. APKr ORZZWK p. 594 t. 6453, n.p.

100. AAN ZMP Zarz. Gł. 451/VI-40, k. 176.

101. ORZZWK p. 594 t. 6468, n.p.

102. Cary, *Poland Struggles Forward*, 102.

103. Zdzisław Olszewski, *Dwa lata w Nowej Hucie* (Kraków: Wydawnictwo Literackie, 1970), 26–27.

104. PDRN Komisja Zdrowia 185/9, n.p.

105. ORZZWK p. 594 t. 6453, n.p.

106. Instytut Budownictwa Mieszkaniowego, "Wyniki," 12.

107. Ibid., 11.

108. DRN 44, n.p.

109. Chmieliński, "Tu chciałem żyć," 467. See also KD PZPR 60/IV/12, 547; DRN 11, n.p.; and KD PZPR 60/IV/18, kk. 383–88.

110. Warsaw's hostels are described in Błażej Brzostek, *Robotnicy Warszawy. Konflikty codzienne (1950–1954)* (Warsaw: Wydawnictwo TRIO, 2002), 164–67.

111. "Tadeusz Świerzewski," *Moja Nowa Huta*, 7.

112. "Z Nowej Huty wieją wiatry, a w oddali widać Tatry. Chociaż tutaj wielkie nudy, to napełniam puste dudy, potem siedem pod reglami, przy was owce z baranami" (Pomorski, *Kraków w naszej pamięci*, 260–61).

113. Brzeziński, "Polubiłem ten fach," 7.

114. Pomorski, *Kraków w naszej pamięci*, 284–85.

115. Dariusz Jarosz, "Wybrane problemy kultury życia codziennego kobiet pracujących w Nowej Hucie w latach 50-tych XX wieku," in *Kobieta i kultura życia codziennego wiek XIX i XX*, ed. Anna Żarnowska and Andrzej Szwarc (Warsaw: Wydawnictwo DiG, 1997), 417.

116. Siemieńska, *Nowe życie*, 89, 102.

117. Brzeziński, "Polubiłem ten fach," 7.

118. Siemieńska, *Nowe życie*, 79. For students' complaints about living conditions in the hostels, see ORZZWK p. 594 syg. 645, n.p.

119. Brzeziński, "Polubiłem ten fach," 7.

120. "Elf," "Najgorszy był jednak początek," 48.

121. Marian B. Michalik, ed., *Kronika Krakowa* (Warsaw: Wydawnictwo "Kronika," 1996), 378.

122. Adam Andrzejewski, "Postwar Housing Development in Poland," in *City and Regional Planning in Poland*, ed. Jack C. Fisher (Ithaca: Cornell University Press, 1966), 155–57.

123. Instytut Budownictwa Mieszkaniowego, "Wyniki," 9, 19; and Matejko, "Wartość użytkowa nowych mieszkań," 71–72.

124. Irena Paczyńska, *Gospodarka mieszkaniowa a polityka państwa w warunkach przekształceń ustrojowych w Polsce w latach 1945–1950 na przykładzie Krakowa* (Kraków: Uniwersytet Jagielloński, 1994), 119–20; DRN, Skargi i zażalenia, passim.

125. DRN 11, Skargi i zażalenia, letter of October 22, 1953.

126. Figures from the end of 1953, Instytut Budownictwa Mieszkaniowego, "Wyniki," 1.

127. KD PZPR 60/IV/18, k. 371. Elsewhere, groups were formed to combat the widespread theft of light bulbs. ZMP 451/VI-40, kk. 3–4.

128. ORZZWK p. 594 t. 6453, n.p.

129. KD PZPR 60/IV/13, k. 789–90.

130. Dariusz Jarosz, "'Notatka o sytuacji w Nowej Hucie' z października 1955 roku," *Polska 1944/45–1989: Studia i Materiały* 2 (1996): 316.

131. KD PZPR 60/IV/17, k. 42; and PDRN Komisja Pracy i Zatrudnienia 185/9, n.p.

132. DRN 11, Skargi i zażalenia, letter of October 22, 1953.

133. Roman Wolski, "Zmartwienia młodych małżeństw w Nowej Hucie," *Gazeta Krakowska*, no. 88 (1954): 3. See also Eugeniusz Cygan, "Raz jeszcze w sprawie młodych małżeństw w Nowej Hucie [Listy do Redakcji]," *Gazeta Krakowska* no. 40 (1955): 8.

134. Wolski, "Zmartwienia młodych małżeństw," 3; ZMP Zarz. Gł. 451/VI-40, kk. 2, 248; and KD PZPR 60/IV/17, k. 44.

135. Jarosz, "'Notatka o sytuacji,'" 318.

136. Ibid.

137. KD PZPR 60/IV/16, k. 973a; and KD PZPR 60/IV/17, k. 44.

138. KD PZPR 60/IV/17, k. 45.

139. KP PZPR 60/IV/5, k. 419.

140. ORZZWK p. 594 syg. 6453, n.p.; and KD PZPR 60/IV/16, k. 973.

141. DRN 11, n.p.

142. PDRN 185/9 or 10.
143. KD PZPR 60/IV/10, kk. 99–100.
144. KP PZPR 60/IV/5, kk. 408–9.
145. KD PZPR 60/IV/10, kk. 99–100.
146. Brzeziński, "Polubiłem ten fach," 9–10.
147. Pomorski, *Kraków w naszej pamięci*, 264.
148. Chmieliński, "Tu chciałem żyć," 462–67.
149. Siemieńska, *Nowe życie*, 79.
150. Chmieliński, "Tu chciałem żyć," 466–67.
151. Siemieńska, *Nowe życie*, 36–37, 104.
152. Ibid., 37–38.
153. Władysław Kwaśniewicz, *Czytelnictwo prasy w Nowej Hucie: Jego podłoża i funkcje społeczno-kulturowe* (Kraków: Ośrodek Badań Prasoznawczych RSW "Prasa," 1964), 64.
154. Siemieńska, *Nowe życie*, 107.
155. Chmieliński, "Tu chciałem żyć," 465–66.
156. "Sekcja Nowohucka: Posiedzenie z dnia 26 maja 1961 pod przewodnictwem prof. K. Dobrowolskiego," *Sprawozdania z posiedzeń komisji* (1961), 165. See also "Sekcja Nowohucka: Posiedzenie z dnia 20 grudnia, 467.
157. Kwaśniewicz, *Czytelnictwo prasy*, 66.
158. Siemieńska, *Nowe życie*, 88.

3. The Poor Worker Breaks His Legs

1. Andrzej Krzysztof Wróblewski, "Bez pomników," in Kozicki and Stolarek, *Krajobraz ogni*, 427–28; Michał Mońko, "Birkut na emeryturze," *Polityka* 29, no. 17 (1985): 3; and Hubert Wilk, "Piotr Ożański—Prawda o 'Człowieku z marmuru': Przyczynek do refleksji nad losami przodowników pracy," *Polska 1944/45–1989: Studia i Materiały* 9 (2010): 35.
2. Mońko, "Birkut na emeryturze," 3; and Wróblewski, "Bez pomników," 427–28.
3. Wilk, "Piotr Ożański," 37–38.
4. Quoted in Isaac Deutscher, *Heretics and Renegades and Other Essays* (London: Hamish Hamilton, 1955), 140, 144–45.
5. Deutscher, *Heretics and Renegades*, 139–50.
6. Mark Pittaway, "The Social Limits of State Control: Time, the Industrial Wage Relation, and Social Identity in Stalinist Hungary, 1948–1953," *Journal of Historical Sociology* 12, no. 3 (1999): 287.
7. Michael Burawoy, "Piece Rates, Hungarian Style," *Socialist Review* 15, no. 1 (1985): 43–69; Pittaway, "Social Limits of State Control," 293; Kenney, "Polish Workers and the Stalinist Transformation," 153; David Ost, "Polish Labor Before and After Solidarity," *International Labor and Working-Class History* 50 (1996): 35–36.
8. Lane and Kolankiewicz, *Social Groups in Polish Society*, 18.
9. Hanna Świda-Ziemba, *Mechanizmy zniewalania społeczeństwa - Refleksje u schyłku formacji* (Warsaw: Uniwersytet Warszawski - Instytut Stosowanych Nauk Społecznych, 1990), 233; Dariusz Jarosz, "'Pastuchy,' 'okrąglaki,' 'wieśniacy,'": Miasto peerelowskie i jego chłopscy mieszkańcy." *Więź* 5, no. 583 (2007): 106–15; Błażej Brzostek, *Robotnicy Warszawy: Konflikty codzienne (1950–1954)* (Warsaw: Wydawnictwo TRIO, 2002), 162–63; and Kenney, *Rebuilding Poland*, 162.
10. Kenney, *Rebuilding Poland*, chap. 3.

11. Ibid., 238.

12. Brzostek, *Robotnicy Warszawy*, 67–74; 152; Jarosz, "'Pastuchy,'okrąglaki,'wieśniacy,'" 111–12; and Kenney, *Rebuilding Poland*, 176.

13. Hubert Wilk, *Kto wyrąbie więcej ode mnie?: Współzawodnictwo pracy robotników w Polsce w latach 1947–1955* (Warsaw: Wydawnictwo TRIO, 2011), 330.

14. Stanisław M. Zawadzki, "Zmiany w strukturze przestrzennej gospodarki narodowej w latach 1955–1955," in *Gospodarka Polski Ludowej, 1944–1955*, ed. Janusz Kaliński and Zbigniew Landau (Warsaw: Książka i Wiedza, 1978), 332.

15. In November 1950 there were about 1,800 qualified versus 17,722 unqualified manual workers, and 4,762 white-collar workers. ORZZWK p. 593 syg. 6439, n.p.

16. Pomorski, *Kraków w naszej pamięci*, 262.

17. Chmieliński, "Tu chciałem żyć," 454, 456.

18. Marcin Zaremba, "Komunizm jako system mobilizacyjny: Casus Polski," in *Komunizm: Ideologia, system, ludzie*, ed. Tomasz Szarota (Warsaw: Wydawnictwo NERITON and Instytut Historii PAN, 2001), 110–13.

19. See Jan Behrends, "Agitacja w zyciu codziennym. Kampanie w szczytowym okresie stalinizmu w Polsce i NRD (1949–1955)," in *Socjalizm w życiu powszednim. Dyktatura a społeczeństwo w NRD i PRL*, ed. Sandrine Kott, Marcin Kula, and Thomas Lindenberger (Warsaw: Wydawnictwo TRIO, 2006); and Piotr Osęka, *Rytuały stalinizmu: Oficjalne święta i uroczystości rocznicowe w Polsce, 1944–1956* (Warsaw: Wydawnictwo TRIO, 2006).

20. Hubert Wilk, "Propaganda współzawodnictwa pracy," *Polska 1944/45–1989: Studia i Materiały* 7 (2006): 156.

21. APKr ORZZWK p. 595 syg. 6483, n.p.

22. See Tejchma, *Pożegnanie z władzą*, 48.

23. Zaremba, "Komunizm jako system mobilizacyjny," 113.

24. APKr KD PZPR 60/IV/15, kk. 422–23; APKr KD PZPR 60/IV/15, k. 394.

25. KP PZPR 60/IV/5, kk. 235–44.

26. KD PZPR 60/IV/13, kk. 748–55.

27. KD PZPR 60/IV/13, k. 775.

28. IPN Kr 021/2, t. 2, k. 86; cf. ibid., k. 110–13.

29. KD PZPR 60/IV/13, kk. 748, 757, 775–76.

30. Moritz Föllmer, "Surveillance Reports," in *Reading Primary Sources: The Interpretation of Texts from Nineteenth- and Twentieth-Century History*, ed. Miriam Dobson and Benjamin Ziemann (London: Routledge, 2009), 77–78. For two Polish historians who take diametrically opposed views of what such sources reveal, see Jędrzej Chumiński, *Ruch zawodowy w Polsce w warunkach kształtującego się systemu totalitarnego, 1944–1956* (Wrocław: Wydawnictwo Akademii Ekonomicznej im. Oskara Langego, 1999), 401; and Jerzy Eisler, *Polski rok 1968* (Warsaw: Instytut Pamięci Narodowej, 2006), 9–10.

31. Miriam Dobson, "Letters," in Dobson and Ziemann, *Reading Primary Sources*, 65.

32. APKr KD PZPR 60/IV/10, kk. 47, 163; see also 60/IV/10 kk. 81, 116, 137, 164; 60/IV/11 kk. 285–86; 60/IV/13 k. 687

33. APKr KP PZPR 60/IV/4, kk. 198, 217–19, 224.

34. AAN ZMP 451/XI-30, k. 10.

35. AAN ZMP Zarz. Gł. 451/XI-32, k. 157.

36. "Elf," "Najgorszy był jednak początek," 51.

37. AAN KP PZPR 60/IV/4, kk. 349–50.

38. APKr Radio Kraków, "Relacja Leopolda Sułkowskiego."

39. Hubert Wilk, "Realia współzawodnictwa pracy w Nowej Hucie (1949–1956)," *Dzieje Najnowsze* 39, no. 2 (2007): 99, 115. Cf. Kenney, *Rebuilding Poland*, 238.

40. Lewis H. Siegelbaum, *Stakhanovism and the Politics of Productivity in the USSR, 1935–1941* (Cambridge: Cambridge University Press, 1988), 302–3.

41. Mońko, "Birkut na emeryturze," 3.

42. KD PZPR 60/IV/10, k. 155.

43. Michael Burawoy, "From Capitalism to Capitalism via Socialism: The Odyssey of a Marxist Ethnographer, 1975–1995," *International Labor and Working-Class History* 50 (Fall 1996): 84.

44. Pittaway, "Social Limits of State Control," 290.

45. APKr ORZZWK, p. 591, t. 6392, n.p.

46. APKr SPKr 102, t. 10, k. 42.

47. APKr SPKr 101, n.p.

48. APKr SPKr 100, k. 65.

49. APKr ORZZWK, p. 591, t. 6392, n.p. See also AAN ZMP 451/XI-52, k. 15.

50. APKr SPKr 100, k. 65.

51. APKr SPKr 109, k. 174.

52. ORZZWK p. 594 syg. 6471, n.p.

53. AAN ZMP 451/XI-32, k. 158.

54. IPN Kr 021/2, t. 2, k. 252.

55. KP PZPR 60/IV/5, kk. 71, 134.

56. KD PZPR 60/IV/17, kk. 40–41, 54.

57. DRN 9, Skargi i zażalenia, letter of August 31, 1954.

58. APKr DRN 44, Skargi i zażalenia, n.p.

59. Ibid., letter of December 1952.

60. Gut, "Nowa Huta w świetle publikacji," 74.

61. Ibid., 74–75. Teresa Torańska highlighted the dichotomous division in Polish popular consciousness between "us" and "them" in her book of interviews with high-ranking party officials, *Them: Stalin's Polish Puppets* (New York: HarperCollins, 1988).

62. *Man of Marble [Człowiek z marmuru]*, dir. Andrzej Wajda, screenplay by Aleksander Ścibor-Rylski, featuring Krystyna Janda and Jerzy Radziłłowicz; produced by Zespół Filmowy "X," 1977.

63. Tejchma, *Pożegnanie z władzą*, 37; http://www.wajda.pl/en/filmy/film20.html.

64. KP PZPR 60/IV/5, k. 370.

65. Wróblewski, "Bez pomników," 434, 428. *Man of Iron [Człowiek z żelaza]*, dir. Andrzej Wajda, screenplay by Aleksander Ścibor-Rylski, featuring Krystyna Janda and Jerzy Radziłłowicz; produced by Zespół Filmowy "X," 1981.

66. Chmieliński, "Tu chciałem żyć," 471–72.

67. Ibid., 471–87.

68. Burawoy, "From Capitalism to Capitalism," 86–87.

4. Women of Steel

1. Gołaszewski, *Kronika Nowej Huty*, 599–600; and ORZZWK 592, t. 6426, n.p.

2. Dariusz Jarosz, "Wzory osobowe i modele awansu społecznego kobiety wiejskiej w Polsce w prasie periodycznej z lat 1944–1955," in *Kobieta i edukacja na ziemiach polskich w XIX i XX wieku*, ed. Anna Żarnowska and Andrzej Szwarc (Warsaw: Instytut Historyczny Uniwersytetu Warszawskiego/Wydawnictwo DiG, 1995), 1:183–92. For an overview of policy toward the Roma in this period, see Andrzej Mirga, "Romowie—proces

kształtowania się podmiotowości politycznej," in *Mniejszości narodowe w Polsce. Państwo i społeczeństwo polskie a mniejszości narodowe w okresach przełomów politycznych (1944–1989)*, ed. Piotr Madajczyk (Warsaw: Instytut Studiów Politycznych PAN, 1998), 110–32.

3. Mieczysław Przedpelski, *Struktura zatrudnienia kobiet w Polsce Ludowej* (Warsaw: Państwowe Wydawnictwo Naukowe, 1975), 54.

4. Renata Siemieńska, *Płeć, zawód, polityka: Kobiety w życiu publicznym w Polsce* (Warsaw: Instytut Sociologii, Uniwersytet Warszawski/Oficyna Wydawnicza "Forum," 1990), 80–92.

5. Przedpelski, *Struktura zatrudnienia*, 112.

6. *Rocznik Statystyczny 1950* (Warsaw: Główny Urząd Statystyczny, 1951), 34.

7. Fidelis, *Women, Communism, and Industrialization in Postwar Poland*, 21–43.

8. Elizabeth A. Wood, *The Baba and the Comrade: Gender and Politics in Revolutionary Russia* (Bloomington: Indiana University Press, 1997), 2.

9. Barbara Einhorn, *Cinderella Goes to Market: Citizenship, Gender, and Women's Movements in East Central Europe* (London: Verso, 1993), 5.

10. Eric D. Weitz, "The Heroic Man and the Ever-Changing Woman: Gender and Politics in European Communism, 1917–1950," in Laura L. Frader and Sonya O. Rose, *Gender and Class in Modern Europe* (Ithaca: Cornell University Press, 1996), 328.

11. Wood, *Baba and the Comrade*, 5.

12. Jarosz, "Wzory osobowe," 184, 187–88.

13. Joanna Goven, "Gender and Modernism in a Stalinist State," *Social Politics* (Spring 2002): 8.

14. *Kobiety w walce o pokój i socjalizm* (Warsaw: Książka i Wiedza, 1951), 14.

15. Goven, "Gender and Modernism," 9.

16. Stefan Gałan, "Nowohutnickie kobiety (wypowiedź konkursowa)," *Budujemy Socjalizm* 3, no. 9 (1953): 4.

17. Brzeziński, "Polubiłem ten fach," 7.

18. KC PZPR Wydział Przemysłu Cieżkiego 237/IX-45, k. 10; Pomorski, *Kraków w naszej pamięci*, 284.

19. Aleksandra Bartosik, "Kochany Jerzy!," *Budujemy Socjalizm* 1, no. 16 (1950), 4.

20. Siemieńska, *Nowe życie w nowym mieście*, 100.

21. Letter of August 10, 1954, DRN 9.

22. DKS 254, n.p.

23. Radio Kraków, "Relacja Janiny Radwan," nr. aud. 2671.

24. Martha Lampland, "Biographies of Liberation: Testimonials to Labor in Socialist Hungary," in *Promissory Notes: Women in the Transition to Socialism*, ed. Sonia Kruks, Rayna Rapp, and Marilyn B. Young (New York: Monthly Review Press, 1989), 309.

25. Elizabeth H. Tobin and Jennifer Gibson, "The Meanings of Labor: East German Women's Work in the Transition from Nazism to Communism," *Central European History* 28, no. 3 (1995): 336–39.

26. The female population of Nowa Huta fluctuated considerably, dipping from 42.03 percent in 1950 to 31.95 percent in 1953, before rising to 46.95 percent in 1956. Jarosz, "Wybrane problemy kultury," 407. See also Skrzybalski, Pajdak, and Skrzybalska, *Studium demograficzne*, table 17.

27. ABM f69, Hipoteza Ludnościowa, k. 2.

28. Skrzybalski, Pajdak, and Skrzybalska, *Studium demograficzne*, table 22.

29. Jarosz, "Wybrane problemy kultury," 407; Bąbiński, "O budowie Huty im. Lenina," 4; and ORZZWK 594, t. 6471, n.p.

30. ORZZWK 592, t. 6426, n.p.

31. ORZZWK 305, t. 3109, n.p.; ORZZWK 594, t. 6471, n.p.; and ORZZWK 215, t. 2329, n.p.

32. *Budujemy Socjalizm* July 22, 1950, 3.

33. Ibid., August 1, 1950, 4; October 10, 1950, 1; October 17, 1950, 1; November 7, 1950, 3; and January 16, 1951, 3.

34. Ibid., August 22, 1950; ORZZWK 591, t. 6391, n.p.; ORZZWK 593, t. 6445, n.p.; and ORZZWK 593, t. 6452, n.p.

35. ORZZWK 594, t. 6471, n.p.; and KD PZPR 60/IV/12, k. 512.

36. KP PZPR 60/IV/5, k. 272.

37. KP PZPR 60/IV/5, k. 283.

38. ORZZWK 594, t. 6471, n.p.

39. ORZZWK 305, t. 3109, n.p.

40. ORZZWK 595, t. 6481, n.p.; *Rocznik statystyczny miasta Krakowa, 1945–1960* (Kraków: Wydział Statystyki Prezydium Rady Narodowej w mieście Krakowie, 1961), 16–17.

41. ORZZWK 594, t. 6465, n.p. See also ORZZWK 592, 6422, n.p., and ORZZWK 595, t. 6482, n.p.

42. Author interview with Augustyn and Krystyna G., July 8, 1998, Kraków; and "Krystyna Gil," *Moja Nowa Huta*, 69.

43. Andrzej Mirga, "Romowie w historii najnowszej Polski," in *Mniejszości narodowe w Polsce*, ed. Zbigniew Kurcz (Wrocław: Wydawnictwo Uniwersytetu Wrocławskiego, 1997), 156, 160.

44. Ibid., 156–66; Ficowski, *Cyganie Polscy*, 182–85; and Adam Bartosz, *Nie bój się Cygana* (Sejny: Pogranicze, 1994), 183–84.

45. Mironowicz, *Polityka narodościowa*, 19.

46. Ibid., 32.

47. Ibid., 31–35.

48. Marcin Zaremba, *Komunizm, legitymizacja, nacjonalizm: Nacjonalistyczna legitymizacja władzy komunistycznej w Polsce* (Warsaw: Wydawnictwo TRIO, 2001), 397.

49. "Romowie—Dyskrymynowana mniejszość: Sytuacja społeczna Romów w Polsce," http://www.etnologia.pl/wspolny-worek/teksty/romowie-dyskryminowana-mniejszosc-III.php (last viewed March 12, 2012).

50. Mironowicz, *Polityka narodościowa*, 12.

51. Adam Bartosz, "O sytuacji politycznej i społecznej Romów," *Przegląd Powszechny* 11 (1993): 285.

52. Mirga, "Romowie w historii," 162–63.

53. Ficowski, *Cyganie Polscy*, 186–93; and KD PZPR 60/IV/19, k. 628.

54. *Budujemy Socjalizm* 1, no. 1 (1950): 3.

55. Gołaszewski, *Kronika Nowej Huty*, 151; and Ficowski, *Cyganie Polscy*, 193.

56. Barbara Seidler, "Tamten czas, który minał," *Życie Literackie* 29, no. 1430 (1979): 5.

57. KD PZPR 60/IV/16, n.p.

58. Zdzisław Olszewski, *Dwa lata w Nowej Hucie* (Kraków: Wydawnictwo Literackie, 1970), 57.

59. Radio Kraków, "Spotkania po latach," interview with Stanisława Siudut, nr. aud. 969.

60. PDRN (różne komisji Rady), Og. 1–3, 1/9, n.p. See also ORZZWK 594, t. 6468, n.p.

61. Olszewski, *Dwa lata*, 57.

62. Ficowski, *Cyganie Polscy*, 190–91; and Olszewski, *Dwa lata*, 93.

63. "Krystyna Gil," *Moja Nowa Huta*, 69.

64. PDRN (różne komisji Rady), Og. 1–3, 1/9, n.p.; and KD PZPR 60/IV/18, k. 542.

65. "Krystyna Gil," *Moja Nowa Huta*, 70–71.

66. Jadwiga Depczyńska, "Cyganie w środowisku pracy (na przykładzie zbiorowości Cyganów w Nowej Hucie)," *Annales Universitatis Mariae Curie-Skłodowska* sectio H, 4, no. 11 (1970): 246–54.

67. Ficowski, *Cyganie Polscy*, 192.

68. KD PZPR 60/IV/18, k. 542; and PDRN, różne komisji Rady, Og. 1–3, 1/9, n.p.

69. KD PZPR 60/IV/19, k. 624–25.

70. KD PZPR 60/IV/19, k. 628. See also Halina Krywdzianka, "Hanka Kapias i jej mąż," *Młodzi stąd. Reportaże, 1950–1965*, ed. Anna Pawłowska and Jerzy Feliksiak (Warsaw: Iskry, 1966), 303–8.

71. "Romowie—Dyskrymynowana mniejszość."

72. Ficowski, *Cyganie Polscy*, 190.

73. "Krystyna Gil," *Moja Nowa Huta*; and "List do Romów i Romek," http://kobiety romskie.free.ngo.pl/x/index.html (viewed March 12, 2012).

74. Mirga, "Romowie w historii," 158, 168; and "The Limits of Solidarity: Roma in Poland after 1989" (Budapest: European Roma Rights Centre, 2002), http://www.errc.org/cms/upload/media/00/0A/m0000000A.pdf (viewed March 8, 2012).

75. Goven, "Gender and Modernism," 7–8.

76. Donna Harsch, "Communist Plans, Workers' Reality: Gender Relations in East German Factories in the 1950s," paper given at the Berkshire Conference on the History of Women, Rochester, NY, June 3–7, 1999, 2.

77. Ibid.

78. KP PZPR 60/IV/4, kk. 421, 424. See also KC PZPR 237/XV-15, kk. 75–77.

79. KC PZPR 237/XV-15, kk. 75–76.

80. KC PZPR 237/XV-15, k. 141.

81. DRN 11, n.p.

82. "Piórkowska," "Trzeba się więcej interesować brygadami żeńskimi," *Budujemy Socjalizm* 2, no. 36 (1951): 4. See also the plight of female bricklayers at Settlement C-2 in ORZZWK 594, t. 6471, n.p.

83. KP PZPR 60/IV/5, k. 271.

84. ORZZWK 594, t. 6462, n.p.

85. ORZZWK p. 592 syg. 6422, n.p. Cf. Barbara A. Nowak, "Serving Women and the State: The League of Women in Communist Poland" (PhD diss., The Ohio State University, 2004), 222–24.

86. KP PZPR 60/IV/4, k. 129.

87. KC PZPR Sekretariat—Wydział Kobiecy 237/V/72, kk. 2–3a. Barbara Nowak argues that, despite its subordination to Stalinist programs, the league "also exhibited signs of local initiative and included women from various backgrounds, who had reasons of their own (often not ideological) for joining." Nowak, "Serving Women and the State," 95.

88. "Wielki konkurs czystości mieszkań," *Budujemy Socjalizm* 1, no. 22 (1950): 4. Cf. ORZZWK 594, t. 6462, n.p.

89. ORZZWK p. 594 syg. 6477, n.p.; KC PZPR 237/XV-15, k. 137; ORZZWK 592, t. 6422, n.p.

90. Speech for International Women's Day (possibly 1951), ORZZWK 592, t. 6422, n.p.

91. ORZZWK 594, t. 6462, n.p.

92. KC PZPR Sekretariat—Wydział Kobiecy 237/V/72, k. 64. KC PZPR Sekretariat—Wydział Kobiecy 237/V/72, k. 64. The order is undated, but probably from 1953. See Nowak, "Serving Women and the State," 40.

93. KD PZPR 60/IV/10, k. 206.

94. KD PZPR 60/IV/19, k. 623.
95. See Nowak, "Serving Women and the State," chap. 5.
96. KD PZPR 60/IV/12, k. 474.
97. Einhorn, *Cinderella Goes to Market*, 5.
98. "Spotkania po latach."
99. ORZZWK 305, t. 3107, n.p.
100. Centralna Rada Związków Zawodowych w Polsce, *Praca kobiet w świetle obowiązujących norm prawnych, III wyadnie* (Warsaw: Wydawnictwo Związkowe CRZZ, 1951), 7 [ORZZWK 305, t. 3114, n.p.].
101. ORZZWK 592, t. 6426, n.p.
102. KC PZPR Wydz. Kobiecy 237/XV-15, k. 154; and KP PZPR 60/IV/4, k. 129.
103. KC PZPR Wydz. Kobiecy 237/XV-15, kk. 154–57.
104. "Spotkania po latach."
105. KC PZPR Wydz. Kobiecy 237/XV-15, kk. 155–58a; see also KP PZPR 60/IV/5, k. 271.
106. KC PZPR Wydz. Kobiecy 237/XV-15, kk. 109, 158a; KD PZPR 60/IV/10, kk. 122–28.
107. Kwiecień, "Stan i dynamika," 25.
108. KP PZPR 60/IV/5, k. 273; and KD PZPR 60/IV/10, kk. 122–25.
109. Jadwiga Werbowska, "Przyspieszyć budowy obiektów socjalnych," *Budujemy Socjalizm* 2, no. 34 (1951): 3.
110. KP PZPR 60/IV/5, k. 276.
111. KD PZPR 60/IV/17, k. 291.
112. Goven, "Gender and Modernism," 11.
113. Katherine R. Jolluck, "The Nation's Pain and Women's Shame," in *Gender and War in Twentieth-Century Eastern Europe*, ed. Nancy M. Wingfield and Maria Bucur (Bloomington, IN: Indiana University Press, 2006), 194.
114. KC PZPR 237/V-72, kk. 48, 50.
115. KC PZPR 237/V-72, kk. 47–50.
116. ORZZWK p. 594 t. 6469, n.p.
117. KP PZPR 60/IV/4, k. 189; and KC PZPR 237/V-72, k. 49.
118. Jarosz, "'Notatka o sytuacji," 318–19.
119. Abortion, illegal until 1956, was never mentioned in any of the documents I saw. See Magda Gawin, "Planowanie rodziny–hasła i rzeczywistość," in *Równe prawa i nierówne szanse: Kobiety w polsce miedzywojennej*, ed. Anna Żarnowska and Andrzej Szwarc (Warsaw: Instytut Historyczny Uniwersytetu Warszawskiego/Wydawnictwo DiG, 2000), 225–26.
120. KC PZPR Wydz. Przem. Ciężkiego, 237/IX–45, k. 14. Cf. ORZZWK 595, t. 6480, n.p. See also a 1955 allusion to the "creation of wild, illegal bands of youth [in Nowa Huta] for the exploitation of girls." KD PZPR 60/IV/16, k. 924.
121. Jarosz, "Wybrane problemy kultury," 414–15.
122. Ibid.
123. "Elf," "Najgorszy był jednak początek," 62.
124. Seidler, "Nowa Huta: Fakty," 2.
125. Seidler, "Nowa Huta: Fakty," and "Nowa Huta—Fakty po dwóch latach," 1, 4–5. For a more recent version of the same argument, see Jarosz, "Wybrane problemy kultury," 418.
126. Fidelis, *Women, Communism, and Industrialization*, 170–202.
127. Stanley Cohen, *Folk Devils and Moral Panics: The Creation of the Mods and Rockers* (Oxford: Martin Robertson, 1972), quoted in Garland, "On the Concept of Moral Panic," 10.

128. KC PZPR 237/V-72, k. 49. Cf. Marek Wierzbicki, *Związek Młodzieży Polskiej i jego członkowie* (Warsaw: Wydawnictwo TRIO, 2006), 337.

129. KD PZPR 60/IV/20, kk. 712–13.

130. ORZZWK 592, t. 6426, n.p.

131. Małgorzata Fidelis, "Equality through Protection: The Politics of Women's Employment in Postwar Poland, 1945–1956," *Slavic Review* 63, no. 2 (2004): 321–22; cf. Goven, "Gender and Modernism," 14; and Alena Heitlinger, *Reproduction, Medicine, and the Socialist State* (London: Macmillan, 1987), 57–58.

132. Goven, "Gender and Modernism," 17.

133. Women worked in one in eight households in Nowa Huta, compared to eight in thirteen in Łódź and one in two in comparable working-class districts in Warsaw. Matejko, "Warstość użytkowa nowych mieszkań," 62–63.

134. One demand was for local women to be given preference in hiring over men from outside Nowa Huta. KD PZPR 60/IV/19, k. 625; and KD PZPR 60/IV/18, k. 489.

135. Padraic Kenney, "The Gender of Resistance in Communist Poland," *American Historical Review* 104, no. 2 (1999): 399–425.

136. Fidelis, "Equality through Protection," 308–9.

137. Fidelis, *Women, Communism, and Industrialization*, 3.

138. Kenney, "Gender of Resistance," 401–5.

5. The Enlightenment of *Kasza*

1. APKr SPKr 100, n.p.

2. APKr SPKr 158, kk. 178–89; ZMP Zarz. Gł., Wydz. Młodzieży Rob. 451/XI-32, 159a; APKr SPKr 158, k. 85; APKr SPKr 100, k. 28; and AAN ZMP 451/XI-32, k. 160. One *junak* claimed militia officers "simply avoided" SP members. "Elf," "Najgorszy był jednak początek," 62.

3. Dariusz Jarosz, "Jak słowo stawało się ciałem," *Mowią wieki* 38, no. 10 (1996): 20.

4. Jacek Kuroń and Jacek Żakowski, *PRL dla początkujących* (Wrocław: Wydawnictwo Dolnoślaskie, 1997), 64.

5. IPN Kr III/1734, kk. 31, 34; see also KG POSP 316, k. 30.

6. IPN Kr II/1734, k. 31, 34.

7. APKr SPKr 109, kk. 196–97.

8. Józef Tejchma, *Z notatnika aktywisty ZMP* (Warsaw: Iskry, 1955), 44.

9. Author interview with Leszek Kałkowski, Kraków, Poland, March 3, 1998.

10. ZMP Zarz. Gł. 451/VI-40, k. 245.

11. Dirk Hebdige, *Hiding in the Light: On Images and Things* (London: Routledge, 1988), 30.

12. Paolo Capuzzo, "Youth Cultures and Consumption in Contemporary Europe," *Contemporary European History* 10, no. 1 (2001): 155–70.

13. APKr PDRN Komisja Zdrowia 185/9, n.p.

14. Anne White, *De-Stalinization and the House of Culture: Declining State Control over Leisure in the USSR, Poland, and Hungary, 1953–1989* (London: Routledge, 1990), 1–3.

15. White, *De-Stalinization*, 6.

16. Norbert Elias, *The Civilizing Process: The History of Manners* (New York: Urizen Books, 1978), 5.

17. Vadim Volkov, "The Concept of Kulturnost\<pr\>: Notes on the Stalinist Civilizing Process," in *Stalinism: A Reader*, ed. Sheila Fitzpatrick (London: Routledge, 2000), 210–12.

18. Sheila Fitzpatrick, *The Cultural Front: Power and Culture in Revolutionary Russia* (Ithaca: Cornell University Press, 1992), 5. See Katerina Clark's observation that "the Party itself [was] in a sense only one group of that larger class called the intelligentsia." Katerina Clark, *The Soviet Novel: History as Ritual* (Chicago: University of Chicago Press, 1981), 7.

19. Jerzy Kossak, *Rozwój kultury w Polsce Ludowej* (Warsaw: Iskry, 1974), 28.

20. Party Secretary Edward Ochab, quoted in White, *De-Stalinization*, 48.

21. Tejchma, *Pożegnanie z władzą*, 37, 41–42. Cf. Bikont and Szczęsna, "O Nowej to Hucie poemat," 24.

22. For example, APKr KD PZPR 60/IV/12, k. 594.

23. APKr KP PZPR 60/IV/5, k. 425. The idea of the *świetlica* in Poland dated to the interwar period, while the term "red corner" was Soviet. White, *De-Stalinization*, 46.

24. APKr ORZZWK p. 593 t. 6443, n.p.

25. *Budujemy Socjalizm* 1, no. 10 (1950): 3.

26. APKr ORZZWK p. 593 t. 6443, n.p.

27. Besides *świetlice* at all workers' hostels, plans foresaw four workers' clubs to be built between 1952 and 1955 and six *świetlice* just for children. There were to be a total of twenty children's *świetlice* built by 1958, or one per five thousand inhabitants. Many fewer were built. APKr ORZZWK p. 591 t. 6392, n.p.; APKr ORZZWK p. 593 t. 6441, n.p.; and APKr ABM Nowa Huta f69, n.p.

28. APKr ORZZWK p. 593 t. 6443, n.p.

29. Ibid.

30. APKr PDRN, różne komisji Rady, Og. I-3, 1/9, n.p.

31. APKr ORZZWK p. 593, t. 6443, n.p.

32. Radio Kraków, "Relacja Anny Siatkowskiej."

33. AAN ZMP Zarz. Gł., Wydz. Młodzieży Robotniczej 451/XI-31, k. 30; see also AAN ZMP Zarz. Gł., Wydz. Młodzieży Robotniczej 451/XI-32, k. 156a.

34. Radio Kraków, "Relacja Anny Siatkowskiej."

35. Pomorski, *Kraków w naszej pamięci*, 262–63.

36. APKr ORRZWK p. 593, t. 6443, n.p.

37. Radio Kraków, "Bez patosu," no. aud. 2782; and ORZZWK p. 594 syg. 6466, n.p.

38. APKr KD PZPR 60/IV/12, k. 596.

39. "Gdy cały naród budować Nową Hutę chce, oni z oślim uporem mówią nie."

40. APKr ORZZWK p. 594 t. 6477, n.p.

41. APKr ORZZWK p. 594 t. 6475, n.p.

42. APKr KD PZPR 60/IV/12, kk. 593–94.

43. APKr ORZZWK p. 594 syg. 6453, n.p.

44. APKr KD PZPR 60/IV/12, kk. 595–96.

45. AAN ZMP Zarząd Główny 451/VI-40, k. 54.

46. For example, APKr KD PZPR 60/IV/19, k. 637.

47. APKr KD PZPR 60/IV/14, kk. 272–74.

48. APKr KD PZPR 60/IV/12, k. 595.

49. PDRN Komisja Kulturalno-Oświatowa 185/9, "Działalność instytucji kulturalno-oświatowych (koordynacja ich pracy)," March 10, 1955, n.p.

50. APKr ORZZWK p. 592 t. 6425, n.p.

51. Jerzy Timoszewicz and Andrzej Władysław Kral, *Teatr Ludowy Nowa Huta, 1955–1960* (Kraków: Wydawnictwo Literackie, 1962), 4; Pomorski, *Kraków w naszej pamięci*, 293; Radio Kraków, "Relacja Leopolda Sułkowskiego"; and *Encyklopedia Nowej Huty* (Kraków: Wydawnictwo Towarzystwa Słowaków w Polsce, 2006), 81.

52. Aleksandra Mianowska, *Teatr "Nurt," Nowa Huta: Kartki ze wspomnień* (Kraków: Towarzystwo Przyjaciół Książki, n.d.), 22; and Seidler, "Tamten czas, który minął," 5.

53. Joanna Woźniak, *Trzydzieści lat Teatru Ludowego w Krakowie–Nowej Hucie* (Kraków: Krajowa Agencja Wydawnicza, 1988), 5–6; and Mianowska, *Teatr "Nurt,"* 26.

54. Woźniak, *Trzydzieści lat Teatru Ludowego*, 6.

55. Radio Kraków, "Relacja Anny Siatkowskiej."

56. Woźniak, *Trzydzieści lat Teatru Ludowego*, 8.

57. IBM 1954, 34–35.

58. APKr ORZZWK p. 262 t. 2654, n.p.

59. "Elf," "Najgorszy był jednak początek," 49–50.

60. PDRN Komisja Zdrowia 185/9, n.p.

61. ORZZWK p. 594 t. 6468, n.p.

62. Pomorski, *Kraków w naszej pamięci*, 261.

63. Author interview with Krystyna and Augustyn G., Nowa Huta, July 8, 1998.

64. "Elf," "Najgorszy był jednak początek," 62.

65. Bohdan Drozdowski, *Tylko pamięć: Reportaże, 1955–1963* (Kraków: Wydawnictwo Literackie, 1964), 30.

66. Chmieliński, "Tu chciałem żyć i pracować," 480–82.

67. AAN ZMP Zarz. Gł. 451/VI-40, k. 244–45.

68. Ibid., k. 48.

69. AAN ZMP 451/VI-40, k. 246.

70. Joan Neuberger, *Hooliganism: Crime, Culture, and Power in St. Petersburg, 1900–1914* (Berkeley: University of California Press, 1993).

71. Gorsuch, *Youth in Revolutionary Russia*, 175–76.

72. APKr KD PZPR 60/IV/14, k. 275.

73. APKr KD PZPR, 60/IV/10, kk. 19–22.

74. AAN ZMP 451/XI-32, k. 159a.

75. APKr KD PZPR, 60/IV/10, k. 21.

76. APKr KD PZPR 60/IV/18, kk. 363–66.

77. Ibid.

78. APKr KD PZPR, 60/IV/10, k. 21.

79. Radio Kraków, "Bez patosu."

80. On alcohol and alcoholism see Krzysztof Kosiński, "Z historii pijaństwa w czasach PRL. 'Peerelowskie' wzory picia alkoholu," *Polska 1944/45-1989. Studia i materiały* 7 (2006): 267–305.

81. APKr DKS 258, n.p.

82. APKr SPKr 158, k. 348.

83. APKr ORZZWK p. 593 syg. 6435.

84. "Dla pijaków nie ma u nas miejsca!," *Budujemy Socjalizm* 2, no. 5 (1951), 4.

85. APKr KD PZPR 60/IV/10, k. 183.

86. APKr KD PZPR 60/IV/10, k. 81.

87. Leopold Tyrmand, *The Rosa Luxemburg Contraceptives Cooperative: A Primer on Communist Civilization* (New York: Macmillan, 1972), 13.

88. APKr KP PZPR 60/IV/5, k. 134.

89. AAN ZMP 451/XI-52, kk. 22–23. Cf. Joanna Kochanowicz, *ZMP w terenie: Stalinowska próba modernizacji opornej rzeczywistości* (Warsaw: Wydawnictwo TRIO, 2000), 87–89.

90. APKr SPKr 109, k. 3.

91. Wierzbicki, *Związek Młodzieży Polskiej*, 337–39.
92. AAN KC PZPR 237/V-72, kk. 48–49.
93. APKr SPKr 100, kk. 28, 85.
94. "Elf," "Najgorszy był jednak początek," 62.
95. Kuroń and Żakowski, *PRL dla początkujacych*, 63–64.
96. Binek, *Śląsk—Wojna—Kresy—Wrocław—Nowa Huta*, 124.
97. See Kuroń and Żakowski, *PRL dla początkujących*, 63–64; Rodger P. Potocki, Jr., "The Life and Times of Poland's 'Bikini Boys,'" *The Polish Review* 39, no. 3 (1994): 263; and Maciej Chłopek, *Bikiniarze: Pierwsza polska subkultura* (Warsaw: Wydawnictwo Akademickie "Żak," 2005), 84–94.
98. Kuroń and Żakowski, *PRL dla początkujących*, 63.
99. Marek Haltof, *Historical Dictionary of Polish Cinema* (Lanham, MD: Scarecrow Press, 2007), 39.
100. Potocki, "Life and Times," 265–67.
101. Radio Kraków, "Bez patosu."
102. Siemieńska, *Nowe życie w nowym mieście*, 106–7; and Chmieliński, "Tu chciałem żyć i pracować," 448, 450. See also Radio Kraków, "Relacja Anny Siatkowskiej."
103. AAN ZMP 451/VI-40, k. 245.
104. APKr KD PZPR 60/IV/14, kk. 275–76.
105. AAN ZMP 451/VI-40, k. 246.
106. Letter by Marek Hłasko to *Trybuna Ludu*, cited in http://pl.wikipedia.org/wiki/Marek_H%C5%82asko.
107. Agnieszka Osiecka, *Szpetni czterdziestoletni* (Warsaw: Iskry, 1987), 35–37, quoted in Potocki, "Life and Times," 262–63.
108. Potocki, "Life and Times," 288.
109. APKr ORZZWK p. 594 t. 6453, n.p.
110. Flora Lewis, *The Polish Volcano: A Case History of Hope* (London: Secker & Warburg, 1959), 72.
111. Adam Ważyk, "Losy poematu," *Polityka*, 1 (1981), 10–11.
112. See also Bikont and Szczęsna, "O Nowej to Hucie poemat," 23–25; Michał Głowiński, "Wokół 'Poematu dla dorosłych'" in *Rytuał i demagogia. Trzynaście szkiców o sztuce zdegradowanej* (Warsaw: OPEN, 1992), 133–56; Dariusz Jarosz, "Jak słowo stawało się ciałem, czyli o niespodziewanych skutkach 'Poematu dla dorosłych,'" *Mówią wieki* 38, no. 10 (1996): 19–23; Marci Shore, "Some Words for Grown-Up Marxists: 'A Poem for Adults' and the Revolt from Within," *The Polish Review* 42, no. 2 (1997): 131–54; and Ważyk, "Losy poematu."
113. Author's translation.
114. Bikont and Szczęsna, "O Nowej to Hucie poemat," 23.
115. Artur Domosławski, *Kapuściński Non-Fiction* (Warsaw: Świat Książki, 2010), 68–79.
116. Ibid., 107–19.
117. Ibid., 120; cf. Jarosz, "Jak słowo," 22.
118. Ryszard Kapuściński, "To też jest prawda o Nowej Hucie," *Sztandar Młodych*, September 30, 1955, 60–61; and Bikont and Szczęsna, "O Nowej to Hucie poemat," 24.
119. See Brandys, *Nowa Huta* (Warsaw: ZG ZMP, 1950) and *Początek opowieści*; Kapuściński, "To też jest prawda"; Konwicki, *Przy budowie* (Warsaw: Czytelnik, 1950); Mrożek, "Młode Miasto," *Przekrój* (Jul. 22, 1950); and Szymborska, "Na powitanie budowy socjalistycznego miasta" and "Młodzieży budującej nową hutę" in *Dlatego żyjemy* (Warsaw: Czytelnik, 1952).

120. Quoted in Brzostek, *Robotnicy Warszawy*, 152.

121. Kaspar Maase, "Establishing Cultural Democracy: Youth, 'Americanization,' and the Irresistible Rise of Popular Culture," in *The Miracle Years: A Cultural History of West Germany, 1949–1968*, ed. Hanna Schissler (Princeton: Princeton University Press, 2001), 430, 443–46.

122. Quoted in Jan T. Gross, *Fear: Anti-Semitism in Poland after Auschwitz. An Essay in Historical Interpretation* (New York: Random House, 2006), 187–88.

123. Maase, "Establishing Cultural Democracy," 439, 443.

124. Radio Kraków, "Bez patosu."

125. Małgorzata Fidelis, "Are You a Modern Girl?: Consumer Culture and Young Women in 1960s Poland," in *Gender Politics and Everyday Life in State Socialist East and Central Europe*, ed. Shana Penn and Jill Massino (Palgrave Macmillan, 2009), 177.

126. Susan Ruddick, "Modernism and Resistance: How 'Homeless' Youth Subcultures Make a Difference," in *Cool Places: Geographies of Youth Cultures*, ed. Tracy Skelton and Gill Valentine (London: Routledge, 1998), 343–44.

127. Hebdige, *Hiding in the Light*, 35.

6. Spaces of Solidarity, 1956–89

1. Seidler, "Nowa Huta: Fakty," 1.

2. Seidler, "Tamten czas, który minął," 5.

3. Władysław Kwaśniewicz, *Czytelnictwo prasy w Nowej Hucie: Jego podłoża i funkcje społeczno-kulturowe* (Kraków: Ośrodek Badań Prasoznawczych RSW "Prasa," 1964), 67.

4. Katherine A. Lebow, "Revising the Politicized Landscape: Nowa Huta, 1949–1957," *City & Society* 11, nos. 1–2 (1999): 165–87.

5. Lebow, "Revising the Politicized Landscape," 176. On the changing appearance of Rose Avenue and its social reception as a public space, see Stanek, "The Production of Urban Space," 19–21.

6. "Ty masz konia / Jesteś wódz / A ten w Hucie / To jest buc"; "Masz rower i buty, spieprzaj z Nowej Huty." Gut, "Nowa Huta w świetle publikacji, 78.

7. Agnieszka Cygan and Agnieszka Krawczyk, eds. *U progu wolności: Nowa Huta w latach 1980–1989* (Kraków: Muzeum Historyczne Miasta Krakowa, 2005), 18.

8. E.g., Kurtyka, "Wstęp."

9. Lewis, *Polish Volcano*, 91–114.

10. Machcewicz, *Polski rok 1956*.

11. KD PZPR 60/IV/18, 322.

12. Ibid., 528–29.

13. Ibid., 546.

14. Ryszard Terlecki, "Przed pierwszym kryzysem: Nowa Huta od stycznia do września 1956 roku," in Terlecki, Lasota, and Szarek, *Nowa Huta*, 48.

15. KD PZPR 60/IV/18, 546.

16. KD PZPR 60/IV/20, 744–45.

17. Machcewicz, *Polski rok 1956*, 140, 237.

18. Author interview with Bogumił Korombel, March 20, 1998, Kraków; Lewis, *Polish Volcano*, 247; Machcewicz, *Polski rok 1956*, 237; and Zbysław Rykowski and Wiesław Władyka, *Polska próba: Październik '56* (Kraków: Wydawnictwo Literackie, 1989), 260.

19. Terlecki, "Przed pierwszym kryzysem," 50; and IPN Kr 021/2, t. 1, k. 28.

20. IPN Kr 021/2, t. 1, 23, 32.

21. Ibid. 27–35.

22. Stefan Bratkowski, ed., *Październik 1956: Pierwszy wyłom w systemie: Bunt, młodość, i rozsądek* (Warsaw: Prószynski i S-ka, 1996), 76–77.

23. Unfortunately, I was not able to find documentation of the mass meetings supposedly held in Nowa Huta on October 19–21—possibly because UB reports for the fourth quarter of 1956 are missing. See Rykowski and Władyka, *Polska proba*, 260; and Terlecki, "Przed pierwszym kryzysem," 51.

24. Machcewicz, *Polski rok 1956*, 240.

25. IPN Kr 021/2, t. 1, 34.

26. Ibid., t. 1, 36.

27. Fidelis, "Are You a Modern Girl?," 174.

28. Seidler, "Nowa Huta—Fakty po dwoch latach," 1, 4–5.

29. Matejko, "Warstość użytkowa nowych mieszkań," 71–75.

30. Radio Kraków, "Relacja Leopolda Sułkowskiego."

31. For comparable urban legends about the occupants of new housing developments in Britain and France, see Robert Lacville, "Red Devils Give a Lesson in Hygiene," *Guardian Weekly*, November 9–15, 2000, 25; and Françoise Gaspard, *A Small City in France* (Cambridge: Harvard University Press, 1995), 48.

32. Matejko, "Warstość użytkowa," 77.

33. KP PZPR 60/IV/5, k. 396.

34. Matejko, "Warstość użytkowa," 90; and Seidler, "Nowa Huta: Fakty," 1–2.

35. Radio Kraków, "Relacja Leopolda Sułkowskiego."

36. Polska Akademia Nauk, Kraków, "Sekcja Nowohucka: Posiedzenie z dnia 26 maja 1961," 167.

37. In the early sixties, the Polish Academy of Sciences (Kraków) had an entire sociological section on Nowa Huta; see Polska Akademia Nauk, Kraków, "Sekcja Nowohucka: Posiedzenie z dnia 20 grudnia," 464–91.

38. Ibid., 482–83.

39. "Rozmowa Piotra Wołkowskiego z Rozalią i Eugeniuszem Skomorowskimi," in Piekarska-Duraj, *Nowa_Huta*, 18.

40. Kwaśniewicz, *Czytelnictwo prasy*, 70–72.

41. Cf. Bogusław Blachnicki, "Równość ekonomiczna w świadomości pracowników przemysłu," *Studia socjologizne* 4, no. 67 (1977): 135–53.

42. "Elżbieta Borysławska," *Moja Nowa Huta*, 128–30.

43. "Rozmowa Basi Rostek z Marianną Zając," in Piekarska-Duraj, *Nowa_Huta*, 48–49.

44. Sulimski, *Kraków w procesie przemian*, 255–56.

45. "Rozmowa Aleksandry Ziemby z Waldemarem Cichym," in Piekarska-Duraj, *Nowa_Huta*, 78–80, 89–90.

46. Józef Gorzelany, *Gdy nadszedł czas budowy Arki: Dzieje budowy kościoła w Nowej Hucie* (Paris: Éditions du Dialogue, 1988), 24.

47. ZMP Zarząd Główny 451/VI-40, kk. 121–22; and IPNKr 021/2, t. 2, k. 14.

48. Chmieliński, "Tu chciałem żyć i pracować," 459.

49. AAN ZMP Zarząd Główny 451/VI-40, k. 122; IPN Kr 08/217, k. 13; APKr KD PZPR 60/IV/16, k. 969; and Terlecki, "Przed pierwszym kryzysem," 43. See also Jan L. Franczyk, *Na fundamencie krzyża: Kościół katolicki w Nowej Hucie w latach 1949–1989* (Kraków: Dom Wydawniczy "Rafael," 2004), 79.

50. APKr KD PZPR 60/IV/16, k. 969.

51. KD PZPR 60/IV/16, kk. 868, 922.
52. APKr KP PZPR 60/IV/4, k. 223.
53. S.L. Shneiderman, *The Warsaw Heresy* (New York: Horizon Press, 1959), 214.
54. Seidler, "Nowa Huta: Fakty," 2.
55. Antoni Dudek and Ryszard Gryz, *Komuniści i Kościół w Polsce (1945–1989)* (Kraków: Znak, 2003), 163–64.
56. Gorzelany, *Gdy nadszedł czas*, 41; and IPN Kr 08/217, kk. 11–12.
57. Shneiderman, *Warsaw Heresy*, 218.
58. Antoni Dudek and Tomasz Marszałkowski, *Walki uliczne w PRL, 1956–1989* (Kraków: Wydawnictwo Geo-Kraków, 1999), 96–97.
59. Dudek, *Komuniści i Kościół*, 164–68.
60. Teodor Gąsiorowski, "Walki o nowohucki krzyż w kwietniu 1960 r. w dokumentach Urzędu Bezpieczeństwa Publicznego przechowywanych w archiwum Instytutu Pamięci Narodowej w Krakowie," in Terlecki, Lasota, and Szarek, *Nowa Huta*, 19.
61. Dudek and Marszałkowski, *Walki uliczne*, 97–98.
62. Ewa Szkurłat, "W obronie krzyża. Nowa Huta 1960," *Tygodnik Powszechny* 45, no. 45 (1998): 5.
63. Szkurłat, "W obronie krzyża"; Gąsiorowski, "Walki o nowohucki kryż," 19; and Dudek and Marszałkowski, *Walki uliczne*, 98.
64. Dudek and Marszałkowski, *Walki uliczne*, 98–99, and Szkurłat, "W obronie krzyża."
65. Gąsiorowski, "Walki o nowohucki krzyż," 20.
66. Ibid.
67. Szkurłat, "W obronie krzyża" and Dudek and Marszałkowski, *Walki uliczne*, 102–3.
68. Almost 500 people were arrested; 87 were sentenced to between six months and five years in prison, while 123 received lesser punishments. Many lost their jobs. The number of casualties is unknown. Gąsiorowski, "Walki o nowohucki krzyż," 20–21.
69. Ibid., 20.
70. Franczyk, *Na fundamencie krzyża*, 122.
71. Marek Lasota, "Metropolita krakowski Karol Wojtyła wobec problemów Kościoła nowohuckiego," in Terlecki, Lasota, and Szarek, *Nowa Huta*, 12.
72. IPN Kr 08/217, k. 67.
73. Lasota, "Metropolita krakowski," 11, 17.
74. IPN Kr 08/217, k. 67.
75. Maryjane Osa, *Solidarity and Contention: Networks of Polish Opposition* (Minneapolis: Minnesota University Press, 2003), 91, 77.
76. Jarosław Szarek, "Chrześcijańska Wspólnota Ludzi Pracy (1979–1980) i jej założyciele w dokumentach Służby Bezpieczeństwa," in Terlecki, Lasota, and Szarek, *Nowa Huta*, 81.
77. Gut, "Nowa Huta w świetle publikacji," 82.
78. Franczyk, "Pod presją ateizacji," 28.
79. The other was Krasnik Fabryczny (Lublin province), where on April 26, 1959, a crowd of more than a thousand demolished the offices of the presidium of the municipal council and attacked militia headquarters after authorities ordered the destruction of a provisional chapel built by inhabitants. Dudek, *Komuniści i Kościół*, 163–68.
80. Lasota, "Metropolita krakowski," 13.
81. Ewa Zając, "Hutnicza 'Solidarność': Sierpień 1980-kwiecień 1989," in Terlecki, Lasota, and Szarek, *Nowa Huta*, 86.
82. Magda Zalewska, Henryk Gawinski, and John Taylor, *Solidarity Underground: Free Trade Unionism in Poland Today* (London: Polish Solidarity Campaign, 1983), 16.

83. Zając, "Hutnicza 'Solidarność,'" 95, and "Relacja Macieja Macha," in *Stan wojenny w Małopolsce w relacjach świadków*, ed. Zbigniew Solak and Jarosław Szarek (Kraków: Instytut Pamięci Narodowej, 2001), 73.

84. Jarosław Szarek, "Solidarna Nowa Huta 1980–1989," in Cygan and Krawczyk, eds., *U progu wolności*, 17.

85. Filip Musiał and Zdzisław Zblewski, "Marzec '68 i grudzień '70 w Nowej Hucie," in Terlecki, Lasota, and Szarek, *Nowa Huta*, 52.

86. Zbigniew Solak and Jarosław Szarek, eds. *Stan wojenny w Małopolsce: Relacje i dokumenty* (Kraków: Instytut Pamięci Narodowej, 2005), 79; and Zając, "Hutnicza 'Solidarność,'" 83.

87. Andrzej Brzeziecki, "Którzy jeszcze wczoraj stali daleko," *Tygodnik Powszechny* (Sept. 4, 2005).

88. Musiał and Zblewski, "Marzec '68," 54.

89. Ibid., 66, 72.

90. On sub-strike-level bargaining, see Burawoy, "Piece Rates, Hungarian Style," *Socialist Review*, 65–66; and Ost, "Polish Labor Before and After Solidarity," 36.

91. Roman Laba, "Worker Roots of Solidarity," *Problems of Communism* (July 1986): 49.

92. Ibid., 55.

93. Musiał and Zblewski, "Marzec '68," 69–72.

94. On debates over the role of intellectuals in Solidarity, see Tymowski, "Workers vs. Intellectuals in Solidarność," 157–74.

95. Cf. Jason Campbell Sharman, *Repression and Resistance in Communist Europe* (London: Routledge Curzon, 2003), 110, 113.

96. Michał Radgowski, "Burza wokół eksperymentu," *Polityka* 1, no. 6 (1957): 6.

97. Hannah Arendt, *Between Past and Future: Eight Exercises in Political Thought* (New York: Penguin Books, 2006), 3–6.

98. "Relacja Stanisława Dudka," in Solak and Szarek, *Stan wojenny w Małopolsce w relacjach świadków*, 32.

99. "Relacja Macieja Macha," ibid., 72.

100. "Relacja Wojciecha Marchewczyka," ibid., 97.

101. "Relacja Macieja Macha," 73.

102. "Relacja Wojciecha Marchewczyka," 97.

103. "Relacja Józefa Mroczka," in Solak and Szarek, *Stan wojenny w Małopolsce w relacjach świadków*, 16.

104. Maciej Lopinski, Marcin Moskit, and Mariusz Wilk, *Konspira: Solidarity Underground* (Berkeley: University of California Press, 1990), 168–69.

105. Dudek and Marszałkowski, *Walki uliczne*, 300.

106. Gut, "Nowa Huta w świetle publikacji," 84.

107. "A jednak to prawda, oni 'kochali' młodzież: Dokumenty z archiwum SFPP," in *Był taki czas*, ed. Władysław Palmowski (Kraków: Wydawnictwo Instytut Teologiczny Księży Misjonarzy, 2001), 101–2.

108. Jan Kubik, *The Power of Symbols Against the Symbols of Power: The Rise of Solidarity and the Fall of State Socialism in Poland* (University Park: Pennsylvania State University Press, 1994), and Lebow, "Revising the Politicized Landscape."

109. Gut, "Nowa Huta w świetle publikacji," 77–78.

110. "Janina Drąg," *Moja Nowa Huta*, 90–91; "Ks. Jan Bielański," *Moja Nowa Huta*, 167.

111. Quote from M. Dębicki in *Gazeta Wyborcza* (July 2, 1991) in Gut, "Nowa Huta w świetle publikacji," 101.

112. Gut, "Nowa Huta w świetle publikacji," 75, 86.

113. "Towarzysze Lenin płacze, bo idee wypaczacie, a partia temu winna, bo idea była inna." In Musiał and Zblewski, "Marzec '68," 67–70.

Conclusion

1. See http://www.laznianowa.pl/teatr/content/view/254/1/lang,polish/ (viewed September 14, 2010).
2. Radio Kraków, "Jubileusz o Marii Rokoszowej," no. aud. 2890.
3. Ryszard Kozik, "Nowohuckie Świętowanie," *Gazeta Wyborcza (Magazyn Krakowski)*, June 5, 2009, 3.
4. Sylwia Winiarek for ArcelorMittal Poland, e-mail to author, September 17, 2010; and Stenning, "Placing (Post-)Socialism," 108–12.
5. Cf. Otto, "Representing Communism," 4.
6. Sharon Zukin, *Naked City: The Death and Life of Authentic Urban Places* (Oxford: Oxford University Press, 2010), 14.
7. "Rozmowa Ewy Dębskiej z Bogumiłem Godfrejów," in Piekarska-Duraj, *Nowa_ Huta*, 29–31.
8. "Jakub Bładek," in *Moja Nowa Huta*, 176–80.
9. Otto, "Representing Communism," 238–39.
10. Joanna Weryńska, "WU-HAE: muzyk-pracoholik," *Gazeta Krakowska*, October 1, 2010, http://www.gazetakrakowska.pl/magazyn/314275,wu-hae-muzyk-pracoholik,id,t.html?cookie=1 (viewed October 12, 2010).
11. Alison Stenning, "Where is the Post-Socialist Working Class?: Working-Class Lives in the Spaces of (Post-)Socialism," *Sociology* 39, no. 5 (2005): 990.
12. Piekarska-Duraj, *Nowa_Huta*, 73, 90, 101, 115, 127, 130, 164, 177. 18,000 signatures were collected on a petition against the change. Monika Golonka-Czajkowska, "Złoty kołczyk i Jesień Narodów. Nowohucka przeszłość–historie alternatywne," *Obóz* 48 (2007), 167.
13. Magdalena Kursa, "Plac Centralny placem Reagana—To już postanowione" (October 9, 2004), http://krakow.gazeta.pl/krakow/1,44425,2275208.html (viewed September 13, 2010).
14. "Rozmowa Ewy Dębskiej z Bogumiłem Godfrejów," in Piekarska-Duraj, *Nowa_ Huta*, 33.
15. Zygmunt Bauman, *Socialism, The Active Utopia* (New York: Holmes & Meier, 1976), 17.
16. Donald Filtzer, "Standard of Living Versus Quality of Life: Struggling With the Urban Environment in Russia During the Early Years of Post-War Reconstruction," in *Late Stalinist Russia: Society Between Reconstruction and Reinvention*, ed. Juliane Fürst (London: Routledge, 2006), 96.
17. Lane and Kolankiewicz, *Social Groups in Polish Society*, 18–24; and Jarosz, "'Pastuchy,' 'okrąglaki,' 'wieśniacy,'" 115.
18. E. P. Thompson, *The Making of the English Working Class* (New York: Random House, 1963), 12.

Select Bibliography

Archives

Archiwum Akt Nowych, Warsaw (AAN)–New Documents Archive

Instytut Budownictwa Mieszkaniowa (IBM)–Housing Institute

Komenda Główna Powszechna Organizacja "Służba Polsce" (KGPO "SP")–Head Command of Universal Organization "Service for Poland"

Komitet Centralny Polskiej Zjednoczonej Partii Robotniczej (KC PZPR)–Central Committee of the Polish United Workers' Party

Najwyższa Izba Kontroli (NIK)–Supreme Oversight Office

Państwowa Komisja Planowania Gospodarczego (PKPG)–National Commission for Economic Planning

Związek Młodzieży Polskiej (ZMP)–League of Polish Youth

Archiwum Państwowe w Krakowie, Kraków (APKr)–National Archive in Kraków

Archiwum Budowy Miejskiej Nowa Huta (ABM)–Archive of City Construction, Nowa Huta

Dzielnicowa Rada Narodowa Nowa Huta (DRN)–District National Council of Nowa Huta

Komisja Specjalna do Walki z Nadużyciami i Szkodnictwem Gospodarczym przy Radzie Państwa, Delegatura w Krakowie (DKS)–Special Commission for the Struggle Against Economic Abuse and Sabotage of the Council of State, Kraków Delegation

Komitet Dzielnicowy Polskiej Zjednoczonej Partii Robotniczej—Nowa Huta (KD PZPR)–District Committee of the Polish United Workers' Party in Nowa Huta

Komitet Powiatowy Polskiej Zjednoczonej Partii Robotniczej—Nowa Huta (KP PZPR)– *Powiat* [administrative district] Committee of the Polish United Workers' Party in Nowa Huta

Komitet Wojewódzki Polskiej Zjednoczonej Partii Robotniczej—Kraków (KW PZPR)– Provincial Committee of the Polish United Workers' Party in Kraków

Miejska Rada Narodowa w Krakowie (MRN)–City National Council in Kraków

Okręgowa Rada Związków Zawodowych Województwa Krakowa (ORZZWK)–
Regional Trades Union Council of Kraków Province
Powszechna Organizacja "Służba Polsce" (SPKr)–Universal Organization "Service for
Poland"
Radio Kraków—audio archives of Polish Radio/Radio Kraków

Archiwum Urzędu Miasta Krakowa, Kraków (AUMK)–Archive of the City Administration of Kraków

Prezydium Dzielnicowej Rady Narodowej Nowa Huta w Krakowie (PDRN)–Presidium
of the District National Council of Nowa Huta in Kraków

Instytut Pamięci Narodowej—Komisja Ściągania Zbrodni przeciwko Narodowi Polskiemu, Oddziałowe Biuro Udostępniania i Archiwizacji Dokumentów w Krakowie, Wieliczka (IPN Kr)—Institute of National Remembrance—Commission for the Prosecution of Crimes against the Polish Nation, Branch Office for the Preservation and Dissemination of Archival Records in Kraków, Wieliczka

Private collection of Bogumił Korombel

Unpublished Primary Sources

Konkurs na wspomnienia i pamiętniki budowniczych Nowej Huty: Wybór na prawach rękopisu.
Kraków: 1984.
Konkurs "Wspomnienie o Nowej Hucie." Private collection of Barbara Krupa.
Stenning, Alison. Interview transcripts, "Living in the Spaces of (Post-)Socialism: The
Case of Nowa Huta." Economic and Social Research Council, July 2001.

Published Primary Sources

Albrecht, Andrzej, and Krzysztof Strzelecki. Kilofem, piórem i sercem: Nowa Huta w
wspomnieniach, kronice, i reportażu. Warsaw: Iskry, 1959.
[Anonymous.] "Z podgórskiej wsi do Nowej Huty." In *Młode pokolenie wsi Polski Ludowej.*
Pamiętniki i studia, Vol. 8 (Drogi awansu w mieście. Pamiętniki), edited by Józef
Chałasiński. Warsaw: Ludowa Spółdzielnia Wydawnicza, 1972.
Binek, Tadeusz. *Śląsk—Wojna—Kresy—Wrocław—Nowa Huta: Wspomnienia, 1930–1960.*
Kraków: Oficyna Cracovia, 1997.
Brandys, Marian. *Nowa Huta.* Warsaw: Wyddział Propagandy i Agitacji Zarządu Głów-
nego Związku Młodzieży Polskiej, 1950.
———. *Początek opowieści.* Kraków: Państwowy Instytut Wydawniczy, 1951.
Brzeziński, Szczepan. "Polubiłem ten fach." *Polityka* 14, no. 27 (1970): 1, 6–10.
Chmieliński, Edmund. "Junak." In *Moja praca, moje życie,* edited by Anna Pawłowska.
Warsaw: Książka i Wiedza, 1977.

——. "Tu chciałem żyć i pracować." In *Robotnicze losy: Życiorysy własne robotników*, edited by Aurelia Szafran-Bartoszek et al., 1:443–96. Poznań: Wydawnictwo Naukowe UAM, 1996.

Czubała, Tadeusz. *Nowa Huta, przewodnik informator.* Kraków: Komitet organizacyjny obchodu X-lecia Nowej Huty, 1959.

Drozdowski, Bohdan. *Tylko pamięć: Reportaże, 1955–1963.* Kraków: Wydawnictwo Literackie, 1964.

"Elf" (pseudonym). "Najgorszy był jednak początek." In Kozicki and Stolarek, *Krajobraz ogni,* 47–74.

Filipowicz, Kornel, et al. *Młodość miasta: Opowiadania o Nowej Hucie.* Warsaw: Czytelnik, 1954.

Gołaszewski, Tadeusz. *Kronika Nowej Huty od utworzenia działu projektowania Nowej Huty do pierwszego spustu surówki wielkopiecowej: Na podstawie materiałów archiwalnych Huty im. Lenina.* Kraków: Wydawnictwo Literackie, 1955.

Harasimiuk, Stanisław. *Warianty: Reportaże.* Kraków: Wydawnictwo Literackie, 1971.

Instytut Budownictwa Mieszkaniowego. "Wyniki wstępnego badania warunków bytu ludności w Nowej Hucie." *Materiały i dokumentacja* Seria B.4/26/1954 (1954).

Jędrzejczak, Aleksander. *Mój miliard: Reportaże o Nowej Hucie.* Kraków: Wydawnictwo Literackie, 1971.

Kozicki, Stefan, and Zbigniew Stolarek, eds. *Krajobraz ogni: Antologia reportaży o Nowej Hucie.* Warsaw: Iskry, 1971.

Krasicki, Maciej. "Rozmowa z laureatem I nagrody." *Polityka* 14, no. 27 (1970): 1.

Kuroń, Jacek. *Wiara i wina: Do i od komunizmu.* London: Aneks, 1989.

Lewis, Flora. *The Polish Volcano: A Case History of Hope.* London: Secker & Warburg, 1959.

Matejko, Aleksander. "Warstość użytkowa nowych mieszkań w świetle doświadczeń ich mieszkańców." *Zaludnienie i użytkowanie mieszkań w nowych osiedlach. Prace Instytutu Budownictwa Mieszkaniowego* 8, no. 23 (1959): 61–125.

Mianowska, Aleksandra. *Teatr "Nurt," Nowa Huta: Kartki ze wspomnień.* Kraków: Towarzystwo Przyjaciół Książki, n.d.

Minc, Hilary. "Sześcioletni plan rozwoju gospodarczego i budowy podstaw socjalizmu w Polsce." *Nowe Drogi* 5 no. 4 (1950): 46–49.

Niezabitkowski, Michał. *Moja Nowa Huta, 1949–2009: Wystawa jubileuszowa.* Kraków: Muzeum Historyczne Miasta Krakowa, 2009.

Olszewski, Zdzisław. *Dwa lata w Nowej Hucie.* Kraków: Wydawnictwo Literackie, 1970.

Osmańczyk, Edmund. *Sprawy Polaków.* Katowice: Wydawnictwo "Śląsk," 1982.

Palmowski, Władysław. *Był taki czas.* Kraków: Wydawnictwo Instytut Teologiczny Księży Misjonarzy, 2001.

Pawłowska, A., and J. Feliksiak, eds. *Młodzi stąd: Reportaże, 1950–1965.* Warsaw: Iskry, 1966.

Persky, Stan, and Henry Flam, eds. *The Solidarity Sourcebook.* Vancouver: New Star Books, 1982.

Piekarska-Duraj, Łucja, ed. *Nowa_Huta: Księga uwolnionych tekstów.* Kraków: Małopolski Instytut Kultury, 2005.

Radgowski, Michał. "Burza wokół eksperymentu." *Polityka* 1, no. 6 (1957): 6.

Rokoszowa, Maria. *O Nowej Hucie pieśń: Widowiskowy montaż literacko-muzyczny do użytku zespołów świetlicowych.* Kraków: Komitet Wojewódzki Obchodu Dziesięciolecia Polski Ludowej, 1954.

Roszko, Janusz. *Po ziemi krakowskiej szlakiem sześciolatki: Reportaże.* Kraków: Wojewódzki Komitet Frontu Narodowego, 1954.

Seidler, Barbara. "Nowa Huta: Fakty." *Nowa Kultura* (Jul. 21, 1957): 1–2.

——. "Nowa Huta—fakty po dwoch latach." *Nowa Kultura* (Jun. 14, 1959): 1, 4–5.

——. "Tamten czas, który minał." *Życie Literackie* (Jun. 24, 1979): 5.

Solak, Zbigniew, and Jarosław Szarek, eds. *Stan wojenny w Małopolsce w relacjach swiadków.* Kraków: Instytut Pamieci Narodowej, 2001.

——. *Stan wojenny w Małopolsce: Relacje i dokumenty.* Kraków: Instytut Pamięci Narodowej, 2005.

Suder, Stanisław. *Czyżyny: Wieś moich wspomnień.* Kraków: Wydawnictwo OPAL PG, 1993.

Tejchma, Józef. *Pożegnanie z władza.* Warsaw: Projekt, 1996.

——. *Z notatnika aktywisty ZMP.* Warsaw: Iskry, 1955.

Secondary Sources

Abrams, Bradley F. "The Second World War and the East European Revolution." *East European Politics and Societies* 16, no. 3 (2003): 623–64.

Adamski, Franciszek. "Nowa Huta na tle procesów urbanizacyjnych Polski powojennej." *Roczniki nauk społecznych* 3 (1975): 223–37.

Åman, Anders. *Architecture and Ideology in Eastern Europe During the Stalin Era: An Aspect of Cold War History.* New York: Architectural History Foundation, 1992.

Apolinarski, Ingrid, and Christoph Bernhardt. "Entwicklungslogiken sozialistischer Planstädte am Beispiel von Eisenhüttenstadt und Nova Huta [sic]" In *Grammatik sozialistischer Architekturen: Lesarten historischer Städtebauforschung zur DDR,* edited by Holger Barth, 51-65. Berlin: Dietrich Reimer Verlag, 2001.

Bartosz, Adam. *Nie bój się Cygana.* Sejny: Pogranicze, 1994.

Bauman, Zygmunt. *Socialism, The Active Utopia.* New York: Holmes & Meier, 1976.

Bensussan, Agnès, Dorota Dakowska, and Nicolas Beaupré, eds. *Die Überlieferung der Diktaturen: Beiträge zum Umgang mit Archiven der Geheimpolizeien in Polen und Deutschland nach 1989.* Essen: Klartext, 2004.

Bessel, Richard, and Dirk Schumann, eds. *Life After Death: Approaches to a Cultural and Social History of Europe During the 1940s and 1950s.* Cambridge: Cambridge University Press, 2003.

Betts, Paul. *Within Walls: Private Life in the German Democratic Republic.* Oxford: Oxford University Press, 2010.

Biedrzycka, Anna, ed. *Nowa Huta—Architektura i twórcy miasta idealnego: Niezrealizowane projekty.* Kraków: Muzeum Historyczne Miasta Krakowa, 2006.

Biess, Frank, and Robert G. Moeller, eds. *Histories of the Aftermath: The Legacies of the Second World War in Europe.* New York: Berghahn Books, 2010.

Bikont, Anna, and Joanna Szczęsna. *Lawina i kamienie: Pisarze wobec komunizmu.* Warsaw: Prószyński i S-ka, 2006.

Blejwas, Stanislaus A. *Realism in Polish Politics: Warsaw Positivism and National Survival in Nineteenth-Century Poland.* New Haven: Yale Council on International and Area Studies, 1984.

Bocheński, Aleksander. *Wędrówki po dziejach przemysłu polskiego, 1945–1970*. Kraków: PHILED, 1997.

Bohn, Thomas M., ed. *Von der "europäischen Stadt" zur "sozialistischen Stadt" und zurück?: Urbane Transformationen im östlichen Europa des 20. Jahrhunderts*. Munich: R. Oldenbourg, 2009.

Bren, Paulina. "Looking West: Popular Culture and the Generation Gap in Communist Czechoslovakia, 1969–1989." In *Across the Atlantic: Cultural Exchanges Between Europe and the United States*, edited by Bo Stråth, 295–322. Brussels: P.I.E.-Peter Lang, 2000.

Brenner, Christiane, and Peter Heumos, eds. *Sozialgeschichtliche Komunismusforschung: Tschechoslowakei, Polen, Ungarn, DDR, 1945–1968*. Munich: Oldenbourg, 2005.

Brunnbauer, Ulf. "'The Town of the Youth': Dimitrovgrad and Bulgarian Socialism." *Ethnologia Balkanica* 9 (2005): 91–114.

Brzostek, Błażej. *Robotnicy Warszawy: Konflikty codzienne (1950–1954)*. Warsaw: Wydawnictwo TRIO, 2002.

Buchli, Victor. *An Archaeology of Socialism*. Oxford: Berg, 1999.

Burawoy, Michael. *The Politics of Production: Factory Regimes Under Capitalism and Socialism*. London: Verso, 1985.

——. "Piece Rates, Hungarian Style." *Socialist Review* 15, no. 1 (1985): 43–69.

——. "Reflections on the Class Consciousness of Hungarian Steelworkers." *Politics and Society* 17, no. 1 (1990): 1–34.

Chłopek, Maciej. *Bikiniarze: Pierwsza polska subkultura*. Warsaw: Wydawnictwo Akademickie "Żak," 2005.

Christian, Maria. "Urząd Bezpieczeństwa w Nowej Hucie w latach 1951–1952." *Zeszyty Historyczne* 127 (1999): 48–62.

Chumiński, Jędrzej. *Ruch zawodowy w Polsce w warunkach kształtującego się systemu totalitarnego, 1944–1956*. Wrocław: Wydawnictwo Akademii Ekonomicznej im. Oskara Langego, 1999.

Clark, Katerina. *The Soviet Novel: History as Ritual*. Chicago: University of Chicago Press, 1981.

Connelly, John. *Captive University: The Sovietization of East German, Czech, and Polish Higher Education, 1945–1956*. Chapel Hill: University of North Carolina Press, 2000.

Crowley, David. *Warsaw*. London: Reaktion Books, 2003.

Crowley, David, and Susan E. Reid, eds. *Pleasures in Socialism: Leisure and Luxury in the Eastern Bloc*. Evanston: Northwestern University Press, 2010.

——. *Socialist Spaces: Sites of Everyday Life in the Eastern Bloc*. Oxford: Berg, 2002.

Depczyńska, Jadwiga. "Cyganie w środowisku pracy (na przykładzie zbiorowości Cyganów w Nowej Hucie)." *Annales Universitatis Mariae Curie-Sklodowska*, sectio H, 4, no. 11 (1970): 241–56.

Deutscher, Isaac. *Heretics and Renegades and Other Essays*. London: Hamish Hamilton, 1955.

Dobson, Miriam, and Benjamin Ziemann, ed.s. *Reading Primary Sources: The Interpretation of Texts from Nineteenth- and Twentieth-Century History*. London: Routledge, 2009.

Domosławski, Artur. *Kapuściński Non-Fiction*. Warsaw: Świat Książki, 2010.

Donert, Celia. "'The Struggle for the Soul of the Gypsy': Marginality and Mass Mobilization in Stalinist Czechoslovakia." *Social History* 33, no. 2 (2008): 123–44.

Drozdowski, Marian Marek. "Eugeniusz Kwiatkowski a Centralny Okręg Przemysłowy." *Kwartalnik Historyczny* 94, no. 3 (1987): 77–93.

Dudek, Antoni, and Ryszard Gryz. *Komuniści i Kościół w Polsce (1945–1989)*. Kraków: Znak, 2003.

Dudek, Antoni, and Tomasz Marszałkowski. *Walki uliczne w PRL, 1956–1989*. Kraków: Wydawnictwo Geo-Kraków, 1999.

Dzieszyński, Ryszard, and Jan L. Franczyk, eds. *Encyklopedia Nowej Huty*. Kraków: Wydawnictwo Towarzystwa Słowaków w Polsce, 2006.

Einhorn, Barbara. *Cinderella Goes to Market: Citizenship, Gender, and Women's Movements in East Central Europe*. London: Verso, 1993.

Eisler, Jerzy. *Polski rok 1968*. Warsaw: Instytut Pamięci Narodowej, 2006.

Elias, Norbert. *The Civilizing Process: The History of Manners*. New York: Urizen Books, 1978.

Fenemore, Mark. *Sex, Thugs, and Rock 'n' Roll: Teenage Rebels in Cold-War East Germany*. New York: Berghahn Books, 2007.

Ficowski, Jerzy. *Cyganie Polscy*. Warsaw: PIW, 1953.

——. *Cyganie na polskich drogach*. Kraków: Wydawnictwo Literackie, 1985.

Fidelis, Małgorzata. *Women, Communism, and Industrialization in Postwar Poland*. Cambridge: Cambridge University Press, 2010.

Filtzer, Donald. *The Hazards of Urban Life in Late Stalinist Russia: Health, Hygiene, and Living Standards, 1943–1953*. Cambridge: Cambridge University Press, 2010.

——. *Soviet Workers and Late Stalinism*. Cambridge: Cambridge University Press, 2002.

Fishman, Robert. *Urban Utopias in the Twentieth Century: Ebenezer Howard, Frank Lloyd Wright, and Le Corbusier*. Cambridge: MIT Press, 1994.

Fitzpatrick, Sheila. *The Cultural Front: Power and Culture in Revolutionary Russia*. Ithaca: Cornell University Press, 1992.

Franczyk, Jan L. *Na fundamencie krzyża: Kościół katolicki w Nowej Hucie w latach 1949–1989*. Kraków: Dom Wydawniczy "Rafael," 2004.

Fürst, Juliane, ed. *Late Stalinist Russia: Society Between Reconstruction and Reinvention*. London: Routledge, 2006.

Garland, David. "On the Concept of Moral Panic." *Crime, Media, Culture* 4, no. 1 (2008): 9–30.

Gleason, Abbott. *Totalitarianism: The Inner History of the Cold War*. New York: Oxford University Press, 1995.

Goldyn, Bartholomew. "Cities for a New Poland: State Planning and Urban Control in the Building of Gdynia and Nowa Huta." PhD diss., Georgetown University, 2003.

——. "Letters of Complaint as a Source for the History of Poland: The Case of Nowa Huta." *The Polish Review* 45, no. 3 (2000): 355–66.

Gołębiowski, Jerzy. *COP: Dzieje industrializacji w rejonie bezpieczeństwa, 1922–1939*. Kraków: Wydawnictwo Naukowe Akademii Pedagogicznej, 2000.

Golonka-Czajkowska, Monika. "Złoty kołczyk i Jesień Narodów: Nowohucka przeszłość—historie alternatywne." *Obóz* 48 (2007): 153–71.

Goodwyn, Lawrence. *Breaking the Barrier: The Rise of Solidarity in Poland*. New York: Oxford University Press, 1991.

Gorsuch, Anne E. *Youth in Revolutionary Russia: Enthusiasts, Bohemians, Delinquents*. Bloomington: Indiana University Press, 2000.

Gorzelany, Józef. *Gdy nadszedł czas budowy Arki: Dzieje budowy kościoła w Nowej Hucie*. Paris: Éditions du Dialogue, 1988.

Goven, Joanna. "Gender and Modernism in a Stalinist State." *Social Politics* (Spring 2002): 3–28.

Gross, Jan T. "Social Consequences of War: Preliminaries to the Study of Imposition of Communist Regimes in East Central Europe." *East European Politics and Societies* 3, no. 2 (1989): 198–214.

Gryczyński, Adam, ed. *Czas zatrzymany: Fotografie z lat 1883–1963 z terenów Nowej Huty i okolic oraz wybór tekstów.* Kraków: Nowohuckie Centrum Kultury, 2006.

Gut, Dorota. "Nowa Huta w świetle publikacji z lat 50-tych i w świadomości jej mieszkańców." MA thesis, Jagiellonian University, 1991.

Harsch, Donna. *Revenge of the Domestic: Women, the Family, and Communism in the German Democratic Republic.* Princeton: Princeton University Press, 2008.

Hebdige, Dick. *Hiding in the Light: On Images and Things.* London: Routledge, 1988.

Hellbeck, Jochen. *Revolution on My Mind: Writing a Diary Under Stalin.* Cambridge: Harvard University Press, 2006.

———. "Speaking Out: Languages of Affirmation and Dissent in Stalinist Russia." *Kritika: Explorations in Russian and Eurasian History* 1, no. 1 (2000): 71–96.

Hellwig, Jan. *Powszechna Organizacja Służba Polsce.* Warsaw: Iskry, 1977.

Hillebrandt, Bogdan. *Związek Młodzieży Polskiej.* Warsaw: Młodzieżowa Agencja Wydawnicza, 1980.

Holston, James. *The Modernist City: An Anthropological Critique of Brasília.* Chicago: University of Chicago Press, 1989.

Horváth, Sándor. "Patchwork Identities and Folk Devils: Youth Subcultures and Gangs in Socialist Hungary." *Social History* 34, no. 2 (2009): 163–83.

Irion, Ilse, and Thomas Sieverts. *Neue Städte: Experimentierfelder der Moderne.* Stuttgart: Deutsche Verlags-Anstalt, 1991.

Jajeśniak-Quast, Dagmara. "Soziale und politische Konflikte der Stahlarbeiter von Nowa Huta wahrend der sozialistischen Transformation." *Bohemia* 42, no. 2 (2001): 244–68.

———. *Stahlgiganten in der sozialistischen Transformation: Nowa Huta in Krakau, EKO in Eisenhüttenstadt, und Kunčice in Ostrava.* Wiesbaden: Harassowitz, 2010.

Janus, Boleslaw. "Labor's Paradise: Family, Work, and Home in Nowa Huta, Poland, 1950–1960." *East European Quarterly* 33, no. 4 (2000): 453–74.

Jarausch, Konrad H., ed. *Dictatorship as Experience: Towards a Socio-Cultural History of the GDR.* New York: Berghahn Books, 1999.

Jarosz, Dariusz. "Everyday Life in Poland in the Light of Letters to the Central Committee of the Polish United Workers' Party, 1950–1956." *Acta Poloniae Historica* 85 (2002): 285–311.

———. "Jak słowo stawało sie ciałem, czyli o niespodziewanych skutkach 'Poematu dla dorosłych.'" *Mówią wieki* 38, no. 10 (1996): 19–23.

———. "'Notatka o sytuacji w Nowej Hucie' z października 1955 roku." *Polska 1944/45–1989: Studia i Materiały* 2 (1996): 309–30.

———. "'Pastuchy,' 'okrąglaki,' 'wieśnacy': Miasto peerelowskie i jego chłopscy mieszkańcy." *Więź* 5, no. 583 (2007): 106–15.

———. *Polacy a stalinizm, 1948–1956.* Warsaw: Instytut Historii PAN, 2000.

———. "Wybrane problemy kultury życia codziennego kobiet pracujących w Nowej Hucie w latach 50-tych XX wieku." In *Kobieta i kultura życia codziennego wiek XIX i XX,* edited by Anna Żarnowska and Andrzej Szwarc, 405–19. Warsaw: Wydawnictwo DiG, 1997.

Jedlicki, Jerzy. *A Suburb of Europe: Nineteenth-Century Polish Approaches to Western Civilization.* Budapest: Central European University Press, 1999.

Kaliński, Janusz, and Zbigniew Landau, eds. *Gospodarka Polski Ludowej, 1944–1955.* Warsaw: Książka i Wiedza, 1978.

Kaltwasser, Martin, Ewa Majewska, and Kuba Szreder, eds. *Futuryzm miast przemysłowych: 100 lat Wolfsburga i Nowej Huty.* Kraków: Korporacja Ha!art, 2007.

Kamiński, Łukasz. *Polacy wobec nowej rzeczywistości, 1944–1948: Formy pozainstytucjonalnego, żywiołowego oporu społecznego.* Toruń: Wydawnictwo Adam Marszałek, 2000.

———. *Strajki robotnicze w Polsce w latach 1945–1948.* Wroclaw: GAJT Wydawnictwo, 1999.

Kemp-Welch, A., ed. *Stalinism in Poland, 1944–1956: Selected Papers from the Fifth World Congress of Central and East European Studies, Warsaw, 1995.* London: Macmillan, 1999.

Kenney, Padraic. "The Gender of Resistance in Communist Poland." *American Historical Review* 104, no. 2 (1999): 399–425.

———. "Polish Workers and the Stalinist Transformation." In Naimark and Gibianskii, *Establishment of Communist Regimes*, 139–66.

———. *Rebuilding Poland: Workers and Communists, 1945–1950.* Ithaca: Cornell University Press, 1997.

Kersten, Krystyna. *The Establishment of Communist Rule in Poland, 1943–1948.* Translated by John Micgiel. Berkeley: University of California Press, 1991.

Kersten, Krystyna, and Jerzy Eisler. "Dyskusa nad historią PRL." *Polska 1944/45–1989: Studia i Materiały* 1 (1995): 7–27.

Klich-Kluczewska, Barbara. *Przez dziurkę od klucza: Życie prywatne w Krakowie (1945–1989).* Warsaw: Wydawnictwo TRIO, 2005.

Klotzer, Maria. *Na peryferiach dwóch miast: 50 lat Teatru Ludowego w Krakowie-Nowej Hucie, 1955–2005.* Kraków: Teatr Ludowy, 2005.

Kochanowicz, Joanna. *ZMP w terenie: Stalinowska próba modernizacji opornej rzeczywistości.* Warsaw: Wydawnictwo TRIO, 2000.

Kolektyw Fotografów Visavis.pl, ed. *802 procent normy: Pierwsze lata Nowej Huty* [*802 Percent Above the Norm: The Early Years of Nowa Huta*] (Kraków: Fundacja Imago Mundi, 2007).

Kosiński, Krzysztof. "Pamiętnikarstwo konkursowe jako źródło historyczne." *Polska 1944/45–1989: Studia i Materiały* 6 (2003): 133–35.

Kotkin, Stephen. *Magnetic Mountain: Stalinism as a Civilization.* Berkeley: University of California Press, 1995.

Kott, Sandrine, Marcin Kula, and Thomas Lindenberger, eds. *Socjalizm w życiu powszednim: Dyktatura a społeczeństwo w NRD i PRL.* Warsaw: Wydawnictwo TRIO, 2006.

Kozubek, Monika. "Asymilacja uchodźców politycznych z Grecji (badania nad zbiorowością grecką mieszkającą w Krakowie)." MA thesis, Jagiellonian University, 1979.

Krakowskie Forum Rozwoju, *Dziedzictwo kulturowe Nowej Huty w rozwoju obszaru strategicznego Kraków-Wschód: Materiały konferencyjne.* Kraków: Krakowskie Forum Rozwoju, 1997.

Krawczyk, Agnieszka, and Agnieszka Cygan, eds. *U progu wolności: Nowa Huta w latach 1980–1989*. Kraków: Muzeum Historyczne Miasta Krakowa, 2005.

Król, Marcin. "Długie trwanie a PRL." *Nowa Res Publica* 7, no. 3 (1993): 39.

Kubik, Jan. *The Power of Symbols Against the Symbols of Power: The Rise of Solidarity and the Fall of State Socialism in Poland*. University Park: The Pennsylvania State University Press, 1994.

Kula, Marcin, ed. *Supliki do najwyższej władzy*. Warsaw: Instytut Studiów Politycznych PAN, 1996.

Kuroń, Jacek, and Jacek Żakowski. *PRL dla początkujacych*. Wrocław: Wydawnictwo Dolnośląskie, 1997.

Kwaśniewicz, Władysław. *Czytelnictwo prasy w Nowej Hucie. Jego podłoża i funkcje społeczno-kulturowe*. Kraków: Ośrodek Badań Prasoznawczych RSW "Prasa," 1964.

Kwiecień, Władysław. "Stan i dynamika stosunków demograficznych miasta Krakowa ze szczególnym uwzględnieniem Nowej Huty w latach 1955–1960." *Zeszyty Naukowe Wyższej Szkoły Ekonomicznej w Krakowie* 19 (1962): 3–54.

Laba, Roman. *The Roots of Solidarity: A Political Sociology of Poland's Working-Class Democratization*. Princeton: Princeton University Press, 1991.

Labor in Postwar Central and Eastern Europe (Special Issue). *International Labor and Working-Class History* 68 (2005).

Lampland, Martha. "Biographies of Liberation: Testimonials to Labor in Socialist Hungary." In *Promissory Notes: Women in the Transition to Socialism*, edited by Sonia Kruks, Rayna Rapp, and Marilyn B. Young, 306–22. New York: Monthly Review Press, 1989.

Landau, Zbigniew, and Wojciech Roszkowski. *Polityka gospodarcza II RP i PRL*. Warsaw: Wydawnictwo Naukowe PWN, 1995.

Landau, Zbigniew, and Jerzy Tomaszewski. *The Polish Economy in the Twentieth Century*. London: Croom Helm, 1985.

Lane, David, and George Kolankiewicz, eds. *Social Groups in Polish Society*. London: Macmillan, 1973.

Lebow, Katherine. "Nowa Huta, 1949–1957: Stalinism and the Transformation of Everyday Life in Poland's 'First Socialist City.'" PhD diss., Columbia University, 2002.

——. "Revising the Politicized Landscape: Nowa Huta, 1949-1957." *City & Society* XI, no. 1–2 (1999): 165–87.

Lefebvre, Henri. "Notes on the New Town (April 1960)." In *Introduction to Modernity: Twelve Preludes: September 1959–May 1961*, 116–26. Verso, 1995.

Lewin, Moshe. *The Making of the Soviet System: Essays in the Social History of Interwar Russia*. London: Methuen, 1985.

Lüdtke, Alf, ed. *The History of Everyday Life: Reconstructing Historical Experiences and Ways of Life*. Princeton: Princeton University Press, 1995.

Maase, Kaspar. "Establishing Cultural Democracy: Youth, 'Americanization,' and the Irresistible Rise of Popular Culture." In *The Miracle Years: A Cultural History of West Germany, 1949–1968*, edited by Hanna Schissler, 428–501. Princeton: Princeton University Press, 2001.

Machcewicz, Pawel. *Rebellious Satellite: Poland 1956*. Stanford: Stanford University Press, 2009.

Maynes, Mary Jo, Jennifer L. Pierce, and Barbara Laslett. *Telling Stories: The Use of Personal Narratives in the Social Sciences and History*. Ithaca: Cornell University Press, 2008.

Mazower, Mark. *Dark Continent: Europe's Twentieth Century.* New York: Alfred A. Knopf, 1999.

Mazurek, Małgorzata. *Socjalistyczny zakład pracy: Porównanie fabrycznej codzienności w PRL i NRD u progu lat 60.* Warsaw: Wydawnictwo TRIO, 2005.

Merlin, Pierre. *New Towns: Regional Planning and Development.* London: Methuen, 1971.

Miernik, Grzegorz, ed. *Polacy wobec PRL: Strategie przystosowawcze.* Kielce: Kieleckie Towarzystwo Naukowe, 2003.

Miezian, Maciej. *Nowa Huta: Socjalistyczna w formie, fascynująca w treści.* Kraków: Wydawnictwo Bezdroża, 2004.

Mirga, Andrzej. "Romowie w historii najnowszej Polski." In *Mniejszości narodowe w Polsce,* edited by Zbigniew Kurcz, 153–79. Wrocław: Wydawnictwo Uniwersytetu Wrocławskiego, 1997.

Mońko, Michał. "Birkut na emeryturze." *Polityka* 29, no. 17 (1985): 3.

Mosher, Anne E. *Capital's Utopia: Vandergrift, Pennsylvania, 1855–1916.* Baltimore: Johns Hopkins University Press, 2004.

Naimark, Norman. "Revolution and Counterrevolution in Eastern Europe." In *The Crisis of Socialism in Europe,* edited by Christiane Lemke and Gary Marks, 61–83. Durham: Duke University Press, 1992.

Naimark, Norman, and Leonid Gibianskii, eds. *The Establishment of Communist Regimes in Eastern Europe, 1944–1949.* Boulder, CO: Westview Press, 1997.

Neja, Jarosław, ed. *Dla władzy, obok władzy, przeciw władzy: Postawy robotników wielkich ośrodków przemysłowych w PRL.* Warsaw: Instytut Pamięci Narodowej, 2005.

Nowak, Barbara A. "Serving Women and the State: The League of Women in Communist Poland." PhD diss., The Ohio State University, 2004.

Nowohuckie Centrum Kultury. *Wiktor Pental: Nowa Huta lata pięćdziesiąte.* Kraków: Nowohuckie Centrum Kultury.

Osa, Maryjane. *Solidarity and Contention: Networks of Polish Opposition.* Minneapolis: Minnesota University Press, 2003.

Osęka, Piotr. *Rytuały stalinizmu: Oficjalne święta i uroczystości rocznicowe w Polsce, 1944–1956.* Warsaw: Wydawnictwo TRIO, 2006.

Ost, David. "Polish Labor Before and After Solidarity." *International Labor and Working-Class History* 50 (1996): 29–43.

Otto, Judith Emily. "Representing Communism: Discourses of Heritage Tourism and Economic Regeneration in Nowa Huta, Poland." PhD diss., University of Minnesota, 2008.

Otwinowska, Barbara, and Jan Żaryn, eds. *Polacy wobec przemocy, 1944–1956.* Warsaw: Editions Spotkania, 1996.

Paczkowski, Andrzej. "Communist Poland, 1944–1989: Some Controversies and a Single Conclusion." *Intermarium [electronic journal]* 3:2 (1999), http://www.columbia.edu/cu/ece/research/intermarium/vol3no2/pacz.pdf.

——. *Strajki, bunty, manifestacje jako "polska droga" przez socjalizm.* Poznań: Poznańskie Towarzystwo Przyjaciół Nauk, 2003.

Paperny, Vladimir. *Architecture in the Age of Stalin: Culture Two.* Cambridge: Cambridge University Press, 2002.

Penn, Shana, and Jill Massino, eds. *Gender Politics and Everyday Life in State Socialist East and Central Europe.* Palgrave Macmillan, 2009.

Pietsch, Ewa, Antoni Stojak, and Jerzy Sulimski. "Budowa i rozwój Huty im. Lenina oraz kształtowanie się społeczeństwa Nowej Huty." In *Huta im. Lenina i jej załoga*, edited by Antoni Stojak, 9–18. Kraków: Uniwersytet Jagielloński, 1976.

Pittaway, Mark. "Creating and Domesticating Hungary's Socialist Industrial Landscape: From Dunapentele to Sztálinváros, 1950–1958." *Historical Archaeology* 39, no. 3 (2005): 75–93.

——. *Eastern Europe, 1939–2000*. London: Arnold, 2004.

——. "Legitimacy and the Making of the Post-War Order." In *The War for Legitimacy in Politics and Culture, 1936–1946*, edited by Martin Conway and Peter Romijn, 177–209. Oxford: Berg, 2008.

——. "The Social Limits of State Control: Time, the Industrial Wage Relation, and Social Identity in Stalinist Hungary, 1948–1953." *Journal of Historical Sociology* 12, no. 3 (1999): 271–301.

——. *The Workers' State: Industrial Labor and the Making of Socialist Hungary, 1944–1958*. Pittsburgh: Pittsburgh University Press, 2012.

Poiger, Uta G. *Jazz, Rock, and Rebels: Cold War Politics and American Popular Culture in a Divided Germany*. Berkeley: University of California Press, 2000.

Polska Akademia Nauk, Kraków. "Sekcia Nowohucka: Posiedzenie z dnia 20 grudnia pod przewodnictwem czł. K. Dobrowolskiego." *Sprawozdania z posiedzeń komisji* (1963): 464–91.

——. "Sekcia Nowohucka: Posiedzenie z dnia 26 maja 1961 pod przewodnictwem prof. K. Dobrowolskiego." *Sprawozdania z posiedzeń komisji* (1961): 157–69.

——. "Sekcja Nowohucka: Posiedzenie z dnia 28 lutego 1964 pod przewodnictwem czł. K. Dobrowolskiego." *Sprawozdania z posiedzeń komisji* (1964): 154–70.

Pomorski, Jerzy Mikułowski. *Kraków w naszej pamięci*. Kraków: Secesja, 1991.

Popper, Karl R. *Conjectures and Refutations: The Growth of Scientific Knowledge*. New York: Basic Books, 1965.

Potocki, Rodger P., Jr. "The Life and Times of Poland's 'Bikini Boys.'" *The Polish Review* 39, no. 3 (1994): 259–90.

Powers, Anne. *Hovels to High-rise: State Housing in Europe Since 1850*. London: Routledge, 1993.

Prezydium Rada Narodowej, Wydział Statystyki. *Rocznik statystyczny miasta Krakowa, 1945–1960*. Kraków: Wydział Statystyki Prezydium Rady Narodowej w mieście Krakowie, 1961.

Przybysz, Kazimierz, ed. *Wizje Polski: Programy polityczne lat wojny i okupacji, 1939–1944*. Warsaw: Dom Wydawniczy i Handlowy "ELIPSA," 1992.

Purchla, Jacek. *Kraków: Prowincja czy metropolia?* Kraków: Universitas, 1996.

Radłowska, Renata. *Nowohucka telenowela*. Wołowiec: Wydawnictwo Czarne, 2008.

Reid, Susan E., and David Crowley, eds. *Style and Socialism: Modernity and Material Culture in Post-War Eastern Europe*. Oxford: Berg, 2000.

Ridan, Jerzy. "Róg Marksa i Obrońców Krzyża." *Karta*, no. 21 (1997): 119–42.

Rocznik Statystyczny, 1950. Warsaw: Główny Urząd Statystyczny Rzeczypospolitej Polski, 1951.

Rybka, Adam. *Centralny Okręg Przemysłowy a polska awangardowa urbanistyka międzywojenna*. Rzeszów: Oficyna Wydawnicza Politechniki Rzeszowskiej, 1995.

Sadecki, Jerzy. *Nowa Huta: Ziarna gniewu, ziarna nadziei*. Warsaw: Most, 1989.

Salwiński, Jacek, and Leszek Sibila, eds. *Nowa Huta, przeszłość i wizja: Studium muzeum rozproszonego.* Kraków: Muzeum Historyczne Miasta Krakowa, 2005.

Scott, James C. *Seeing Like a State: How Certain Schemes to Improve the Human Condition Have Failed.* New Haven: Yale University Press, 1998.

Shore, Marci. "Some Words for Grown-Up Marxists: 'A Poem for Adults' and the Revolt from Within." *Polish Review* 42, no. 2 (1997): 131–54.

Sibila, Leszek. *Nowohucki design: Historia wnętrz i ich twórcy w latach 1949–1959.* Kraków: Muzeum Historyczne Miasta Krakowa, 2007.

Siegelbaum, Lewis H. *Stakhanovism and The Politics of Productivity in The USSR, 1935–1941.* Cambridge: Cambridge University Press, 1988.

Siegelbaum, Lewis H., and Ronald Grigor Suny, eds. *Making Workers Soviet: Power, Class, and Identity.* Ithaca: Cornell University Press, 1994.

Siemieńska, Renata. *Nowe życie w nowym mieście.* Warsaw: Wiedza Powszechna, 1969.

Skrzybalski, Bolesław, Zygmunt Pajdak, and Elżbieta Skrzybalska. *Studium demograficzne dzielnicy Nowa Huta: Stan na 1.8.1954 r.* (Kraków: Miastoprojekt–Kraków, 1955).

Słabek, Henryk. *Obraz robotników polskich w świetle ich świadectw własnych i statystyki, 1945–1989.* Warsaw: Kutno, 2004.

——. *O społecznej historii Polski, 1945–1989.* Warsaw: Wydawnictwo "Książka i Wiedza," 2009.

——. "Socio-Political Aspects of the Polish Peasants (1944–1948)." *Acta Poloniae Historica* 57 (1988): 137–66.

Smith, S. A. *Revolution and the People in Russia and China: A Comparative History.* Cambridge: Cambridge University Press, 2008.

Stanek, Łukasz. "Simulation or Hospitality?: Beyond the Crisis of Representation in Nowa Huta." In *Encountering Urban Places: Visual and Material Performances in the City,* edited by Lars Frers and Lars Meier, 135–54. Aldershot: Ashgate, 2007.

Stauter-Halsted, Keely. *The Nation in the Village: The Genesis of Peasant National Identity in Austrian Poland, 1848–1914.* Ithaca: Cornell University Press, 2001.

Stenning, Alison. "Placing (Post-)Socialism: The Making and Remaking of Nowa Huta, Poland." *European Urban and Regional Studies* 7, no. 2 (2000): 99–118.

——. "Re-placing Work: Economic Transformations and the Shape of a Community in Post-Socialist Poland." *Work, Employment, and Society* 19, no. 2 (2005): 235–59.

Stojak, Antoni, ed. *Huta im. Lenina i jej załoga.* Kraków: Uniwersytet Jagiellonski, 1976.

Sulimski, Jerzy. *Kraków w procesie przemian: Współczesne przeobrażenia zbiorowości wielkomiejskiej.* Kraków: Wydawnictwo Literackie, 1976.

Świda-Ziemba, Hanna. *Człowiek wewnętrznie zniewolony: Mechanizmy i konsekewencje minionej formacji—Analiza psychosocjologiczna.* Warsaw: Uniwersytet Warszawski, 1997.

——. *Mechanizmy zniewalania społeczeństwa—Refleksje u schyłku formacji.* Warsaw: Uniwersytet Warszawski—Instytut Stosowanych Nauk Społecznych, 1990.

Szarota, Tomasz. "Baza źródłowa, wiedza pozaźródłowa, i literatura przedmiotu w warsztacie historyka współczesności." *Polska 1944/45–1989: Studia i Materiały* 6 (2003): 7–22.

——., ed. *Komunizm: Ideologia, system, ludzie.* Warsaw: Wydawnictwo NERITON and Instytut Historii PAN, 2001.

Szkurłat, Ewa. "W obronie krzyża: Nowa Huta, 1960." *Tygodnik Powszechny* 45, no. 45 (1998): 5.

Szuba, Ludwik Stanisław. *Powszechna Organizacja "Służba Polsce" w latach 1948–1955.* Lublin: Towarszystwo Naukowe KUL, 2006.

Terlecki, Ryszard, Marek Lasota, and Jarosław Szarek, eds. *Nowa Huta—Miasto walki i pracy.* Kraków: Instytut Pamięci Narodowej, 2002.

Thompson, E.P., *The Making of the English Working Class.* New York: Random House, 1963.

Timoszewicz, Jerzy, and Andrzej Władysław Kral. *Teatr Ludowy Nowa Huta, 1955–1960.* Kraków: Wydawnictwo Literackie, 1962.

Torańska, Teresa. *"Them": Stalin's Polish Puppets.* New York: Harper & Row, 1987.

Towarzystwo Miłośników Historii i Zabytków Krakowa. *Narodziny Nowej Huty: Materiały sesji naukowej odbytej 25 kwietnia 1998 roku.* Kraków: Towarzystwo Miłośników Historii i Zabytków Krakowa, 1999.

Tymiński, Maciej. *PZPR i przedsiębiorstwo: Nadzór partyjny nad zakładami przemysłowymi, 1956–1970.* Warsaw: Wydawnictwo TRIO, 2001.

Tymowski, Andrzej W. "Workers vs. Intellectuals in Solidarność." *Telos* 24, no. 4 (1991/92): 157–74.

Verdery, Katherine. *What Was Socialism, and What Comes Next?* Princeton: Princeton University Press, 1996.

Viola, Lynne, ed. *Contending with Stalinism: Soviet Power and Popular Resistance in the 1930s.* Ithaca: Cornell University Press, 2002.

Wedel, Janine. *The Private Poland.* New York: Facts on File Publications, 1986.

White, Anne. *De-Stalinization and the House of Culture: Declining State Control over Leisure in the USSR, Poland, and Hungary, 1953–1989.* London: Routledge, 1990.

Wierzbicki, Marek. *Związek Młodzieży Polskiej i jego członkowie.* Warsaw: Wydawnictwo TRIO, 2006.

Wilk, Hubert. *Kto wyrąbie więcej ode mnie?: Współzawodnictwo pracy robotników w Polsce w latach 1947–1955.* Warsaw: Wydawnictwo TRIO, 2011.

———. "Piotr Ożański—prawda o 'Człowieku z marmuru': Przyczynek do refleksji nad losami przodowników pracy." *Polska 1944/45–1989: Studia i Materiały* 9 (2010): 31–45.

———. "Realia współzawodnictwa pracy w Nowej Hucie (1949–1956)." *Dzieje Najnowsze* 39, no. 2 (2007): 97–116.

Wódz, Jacek. *Przeobrażenia społeczne wsi Pleszów włączonej do Nowej Huty, 1949–1969 (studium z socjologii prawa): Prace Komisji Socjologicznej Nr 22.* Wrocław: Polska Akademia Nauk—Oddział w Krakowie, 1971.

Wood, Elizabeth A. *The Baba and the Comrade: Gender and Politics in Revolutionary Russia.* Bloomington: Indiana University Press, 1997.

Woźniak, Joanna. *Trzydzieści lat Teatru Ludowego w Krakowie - Nowej Hucie.* Kraków: Krajowa Agencja Wydawnicza, 1988.

Zarecor, Kimberly Elman. *Manufacturing a Socialist Modernity: Housing in Czechoslovakia, 1945–1960.* Pittsburgh: University of Pittsburgh Press, 2011.

Zaremba, Marcin. *Komunizm, legitymizacja, nacjonalizm: Nacjonalistyczna legitymizacja władzy komunistycznej w Polsce.* Warsaw: Wydawnictwo TRIO, 2001.

———. "Społeczeństwo polskie lat sześćdziesiątych—Między 'mała stabilizacją' a 'mała destabilizacją.'" In *Oblicza marca 1968 r.*, edited by Konrad Rokicki and Sławomir Stępień, 24–51. Warsaw: Instytut Pamięci Narodowej, 2004.

Żarnowska, Anna and Andrzej Szwarc, eds. *Równe prawa i nierówne szanse. Kobiety w polsce międzywojennej.* Warsaw: Instytut Historyczny Uniwersytetu Warszawskiego/ Wydawnictwo DiG, 2000.

Zechenter, Katarzyna. "Evolving Narratives in Post-War Polish Literature: The Case of Nowa Huta." *The Slavonic and East European Review* 85, no. 4 (2007): 658–83.

Zukin, Sharon. *Naked City: The Death and Life of Authentic Urban Places.* Oxford: Oxford University Press, 2010.

Index

www.ingramcontent.com/pod-product-compliance
Ingram Content Group UK Ltd.
Pitfield, Milton Keynes, MK11 3LW, UK
UKHW042117180325
456433UK00003B/253